FDR and the Soviet Union

FDR and the Soviet Union

The President's Battles over
Foreign Policy

Mary E. Glantz

 University Press of Kansas

Published by the University Press of Kansas (Lawrence, Kansas 66049), which was organized by the Kansas Board of Regents and is operated and funded by Emporia State University, Fort Hays State University, Kansas State University, Pittsburg State University, the University of Kansas, and Wichita State University

Library of Congress Cataloging-in-Publication Data

Glantz, Mary E.
  FDR and the Soviet Union : the President's battles over foreign policy / Mary E. Glantz.
    p. cm.—(Modern war studies)
  Includes bibliographical references and index.
  ISBN 0-7006-1365-X (cloth : alk. paper)
1. United States—Foreign relations—Soviet Union. 2. Soviet Union—Foreign relations—United States. 3. United States—Foreign relations—1933–1945. 4. United States—Foreign relations—1929–1933. 5. Roosevelt, Franklin D. (Franklin Delano), 1882–1945. 6. World War, 1939–1945—Diplomatic history. 7. Soviet Union—Politics and government—1917–1936. 8. Soviet Union—Politics and government—1936–1953. I. Title. II. Series.
  E183.8.S65G57 2005
  940.53′2273—dc22   2004023690

British Library Cataloguing-in-Publication Data is available.

Printed in the United States of America

10 9 8 7 6 5 4 3 2 1

The paper used in this publication meets the minimum requirements of the American National Standard for Permanence of Paper for Printed Library Materials Z39.48-1984.

CONTENTS

ACKNOWLEDGMENTS

The publication of this book would not have been possible without the support of numerous individuals and organizations. Several people took the time to read through the book in manuscript and suggest corrections and changes. Richard Immerman, David Glantz, Denis Showalter, and Warren Kimball were especially generous with their time and advice, and I have made an effort to incorporate their valuable suggestions in the final manuscript. I also appreciate the input I have received from Russell Weigley, James Hilty, and Vladislav Zubok. Their advice was thought provoking and continues to shape my ongoing research on this subject. Russell Weigley in particular was an inspiration as a teacher, writer, and historian. Thomas A. Julian was kind enough to speak with me about my work. He has spent many years researching Philip Faymonville, and provided valuable insight and background information. Many of my fellow graduate students at Temple University were helpful in sharing ideas and developing new avenues for research. Of particular note was John Oram, who was always happy to share with me any article or book he thought might be useful.

I am also very grateful to the organizations that enabled me to conduct most of my research. One of the most difficult things about researching this topic was finding the money to support my research. The Franklin and Eleanor Roosevelt Institute provided me a generous grant that enabled me to spend time at the Roosevelt Library in Hyde Park combing through the archives. Temple University and the history department at Temple University were also extremely generous in their financial support of my research.

Numerous librarians and archivists aided my research. The staffs at the Library of Congress, the Franklin D. Roosevelt Library, the National Archives (in Washington, D.C., and in College Park), the United States Army Military History Institute, the Hoover Institution at Stanford University, and the United Kingdom Public Record Office were all very helpful and kind to a researcher who, at times, seemed very lost.

Finally, I would like to thank my friends and family, who not only helped me write the manuscript, but who also put up with me as I wrote it. Michelle Schohn was especially patient as I raced with the clock to complete it before starting my new job. My mother, Mary Ann Glantz, carefully read through each chapter with a diligence that would amaze the people who wrote the

Chicago Manual of Style. She cannot, of course, be held responsible for my thoroughness in incorporating her changes. And my father, David Glantz, not only made the suggestions I noted above, but also inspired me to become a historian in the first place. It is to my parents that I dedicate this book.

The views expressed in this work are mine alone, and do not necessarily represent those of the U.S. State Department or the U.S. government.

INTRODUCTION

In fall 1943 U.S. President Franklin Delano Roosevelt ordered a reorganization of several of the agencies and departments responsible for formulating and implementing America's policy toward the Soviet Union. The immediate catalyst for this shake-up was an acrimonious and all too public conflict among U.S. personnel in the Soviet Union. The origins of this conflict and reorganization, however, stretched to the beginning of Roosevelt's administration, and its consequences reached into the administrations that would follow.

As significant as this conflict was, there is scant attention paid to it in the historical literature of World War II. Most historians who have examined United States–Soviet relations during World War II have done so by focusing on the presidential level or "summit" diplomacy.[1] As a result, many ensuing historiographic disputes have emphasized Franklin D. Roosevelt personally. Diplomats such as Ambassador William C. Bullitt, General John Russell Deane, and others authored the initial personal accounts of United States–Soviet wartime diplomacy.[2] Most were critical of "mistakes" Roosevelt made by trusting the Soviets and naively seeking postwar cooperation with the Soviet Union. Historians of the so-called realist school, ranging from Herbert Feis to Gaddis Smith, have echoed these criticisms by charging Roosevelt with naïveté, albeit from within a historical framework that posited naïveté as a basic characteristic of American foreign policy.[3]

Subsequently, some World War II diplomatic historians have highlighted the economic underpinnings of U.S. foreign policy. They contend that Roosevelt's foreign policy represented a purposeful attempt to expand America's postwar economic influence. Historians such as William Appleman Williams, Lloyd C. Gardner, and Gabriel Kolko believe that Roosevelt's policies, plans, and actions prompted the deterioration of United States–Soviet relations.[4] Other historians of this generation contend that Roosevelt was actually realistic and was using "idealistic" Wilsonian statements simply to fool the American public.[5] Still others, such as Gar Alperovitz and Diane Shaver Clemens, have argued that Roosevelt's Soviet policy was both cooperative and realistic but was reversed by Harry S. Truman. It was this reversal that caused a dramatic deterioration in United States–Soviet relations.[6]

Despite the clear disparity in views, these interpretive schools share in common the belief that Roosevelt's concepts and wishes and U.S. foreign policy were one and the same. In so doing, they have overlooked or ignored the actual machinery and personnel of foreign policy formulation and implementation.

In an effort to overcome these limitations, some historians have shifted the focus of the study of United States–Soviet relations in World War II to a different level.[7] Studying specific and narrower aspects of the relationship, these historians have analyzed in detail much of the bureaucratic maneuvering that shaped the development of U.S. policy toward the Soviet Union.[8] In the process, they have revealed a promising approach to understanding both the development of United States–Soviet relations and the development of Roosevelt's policy toward the Kremlin. This approach offers greater understanding of the complexity of foreign policy formulation. At the same time, it promises to provide more fodder for the historiographic debate on Roosevelt's policy toward the Soviet Union. The enigma of Roosevelt's intentions will likely never be solved by a search through his written legacy; how the president dealt with his foreign policy bureaucracy is a necessary clue to unraveling that mystery.

Some historians have ventured into this territory in the history of Soviet-American relations by examining in detail the activities of Roosevelt's ambassadors to the Soviet Union.[9] Others have studied individual diplomats and the Foreign Service as a whole.[10] Despite these efforts to illuminate many important elements that contributed to the formulation and implementation of foreign policy, there are striking gaps in the work. Studies of Roosevelt's ambassadors focus almost exclusively on his colorful prewar ambassadors. There are no published biographies of World War II ambassadors, Laurence Steinhardt and William H. Standley, and there is only one of W. Averell Harriman.[11]

Another significant gap in the literature is the failure to examine the role of the military in foreign policy formulation. There is only one significant study of the role of military attachés in diplomacy, and that is a general study that only touches on the specific role of U.S. military attachés.[12] David Glantz has briefly assessed the effectiveness of U.S. military attachés in gathering intelligence on the Soviet military, but his study covers only the prewar period and does not attempt to assess the role that those attachés played in the overall foreign policy system.[13]

One military officer in the diplomatic process who has not escaped historical scrutiny is Brigadier General Philip R. Faymonville. Faymonville served as U.S. military attaché to the Soviet Union in the 1930s and returned to Moscow in 1941 as the U.S. lend-lease representative. His outspoken support of U.S. cooperation with the Soviet government has garnered him a reasonable amount of attention from memoirists and historians. Nevertheless, few historians have carefully examined the history of his role in United States–Soviet relations, and most have generally accepted without question the interpretation of his colleagues in the Moscow embassy. Those who have studied this case more critically have emerged with a more nuanced interpretation of the general's role, although they still do not place Faymonville in the context of the broader formulation and implementation of a policy toward the Soviet Union.[14]

This tendency to neglect the military role in the development of foreign policy in World War II is indicative of a more far-reaching divorce between military and diplomatic historians. Indeed, historians who examine battlefield developments alongside diplomatic ones are rare. This trend led one diplomatic historian to call for his colleagues to "consider that battles rather than politics or ideology frequently determined the parameters within which leaders could act."[15] Mark A. Stoler has already made significant inroads into this field in United States–Soviet relations in World War II. Building on his military-diplomatic history of the second front debate, he has published a groundbreaking study of the Joint Chiefs of Staff in international relations in World War II.[16] Stoler's work substantiates the argument that lower-level policy makers play a significant role in policy formulation, and that the military's role in foreign policy was increasingly important.

Notable exceptions notwithstanding, the frequent failure to consider the synergy between military actions and diplomatic developments is a significant weakness in our understanding of U.S. policy toward the Soviet Union during World War II. Far more disturbing is an inclination to treat U.S. policy formulation as if it occurred in a global vacuum. Rare indeed are the histories that examine the development of Roosevelt's policy alongside that of Stalin. Primary responsibility for this failure undoubtedly lies with Russian and earlier Soviet authorities who jealously guarded their archives and carefully restricted access to important collections. But this situation is insufficient justification for the near absence of the subject in U.S. diplomatic historical literature. Not enough U.S. diplomatic historians make use of published primary and secondary Soviet sources; those who do have made important contributions to an understanding of United States–Soviet relations.[17]

Historians of the Soviet Union in general and Soviet foreign policy in particular have produced a growing body of literature that challenges the "totalitarian" conception of the state under Stalin. Their work suggests that the development and implementation of Soviet foreign policy shared many of the complexities found in U.S. policy making.[18] It demands that historians of U.S. foreign policy consider how U.S. foreign policy shaped, and was shaped, by Soviet foreign policy. The relationship was clearly a dynamic and important one.

Looming over all these historiographical issues is the question of the cold war. In chronological terms, the cold war comprised the greatest part of the history of United States relations with the Soviet Union. This simple fact has shaped much of the study of the history of United States–Soviet relations. As a result, most historians of Soviet-American relations during World War II tend to consider that relationship as the origins of the cold war, rather than as part of the history of World War II.[19] Within this paradigm, teleological fallacies abound. For example, the Yalta conference is assessed not as an attempt to bring the war with Germany and Japan to a close, but as an agreement that contributed to the development of cold war hostilities. More strikingly, Roosevelt and his officials (when they are studied) are judged on the basis of how they handled the future conflict with the Soviet Union. All too often, historians consider the cold war inevitable and grade the performance of politicians, diplomats, and the military on the basis of how they reacted to the emerging Soviet "threat."

Thus, many historians shape current understanding of United States–Soviet relations during World War II through this paradigm and with these weaknesses. If we try to divorce ourselves from this perspective and fill in the glaring gaps in our study, it becomes clear that the history of Soviet-American relations during World War II is significant in its own right. The conflict among U.S. personnel in the Soviet Union in 1943 provides a robust opportunity to establish that.

From almost the moment that he was inaugurated, lower-level policy makers, both military and diplomatic, challenged President Roosevelt's authority and ability to carry out a policy toward the Soviet Union. At first they privately resisted his efforts to provide aid to the Soviet Union on a no-questions-asked basis. When their private resistance proved unable to modify the president's position, they made their dispute public. On several occasions, Roosevelt took extraordinary steps to achieve his foreign policy aims. All such efforts were in vain. Reorganizing institutions and replacing personnel failed to eliminate resistance to White House policy. Despite his unprecedented four terms as president of the United States, Roosevelt was unable to outlast his bureaucratic opponents. When he died in April 1945, the struggle over the formulation of American policy toward the Soviet Union ended. The lower-level officials who spent their careers battling against Roosevelt's chosen course toward the Soviet Union rushed into the information vacuum created by his death. They were the advisers whom Truman trusted to interpret Roosevelt's ambiguous legacy. Consequently, they shaped the development of Truman's policy toward the Soviet Union.

The purpose of this book is to redress the limitations in the extant literature and, in doing so, to add a new dimension to our understanding of the complex Soviet-American relationship. By examining overlooked variables in the World War II relations between Washington and Moscow, and by exploiting Soviet and Russian-language sources, this study asks such key questions as what role U.S. personnel in the Soviet Union played in formulating and implementing U.S. policy toward the Soviet Union, and what influence the attitudes of lower-level military and diplomatic personnel had in shaping the developing American-Soviet relationship.

Addressing these questions gives rise to several conclusions with manifest implications for the subsequent collapse of the Grand Alliance. Studying the role and attitudes of lower-level U.S. officials creates a more nuanced understanding of U.S. foreign policy. By distinguishing between Roosevelt's attitude and those of the military and diplomatic personnel who served him, it is apparent that there was a persistent struggle over the direction of U.S. policy toward the Soviet Union. Roosevelt was committed to a policy of cooperation with the Soviet Union. Throughout his presidency, and especially during the war, the president struggled against a foreign policy bureaucracy determined to adopt a "firmer" policy toward the Kremlin. When Roosevelt died and the new president, Harry Truman, turned toward the ambassadors and subordinate personnel for advice, the United States embarked on a new, more confrontational approach toward the Soviet Union.

At the same time, this examination of the role of U.S. personnel in United States–Soviet relations reveals the heterogeneity of U.S. foreign policy. Despite an unprecedented period in office and a well-known penchant for working around government bureaucracy, Roosevelt's power to formulate and implement foreign policy remained limited. Roosevelt could appoint ambassadors and high-ranking State Department officials who shared his worldview; he could reorganize his departments to remove entrenched resistance to his policies; he could even work around embassies that disagreed with his policies. In the end, however, the attitudes of Foreign Service and military officers mattered. Presidents came and went relatively frequently. Career government officials, however, remained in their jobs for decades. Through long and close contact, career officials developed a shared perspective and attitude that persisted regardless of the ideology in the White House. As was strikingly obvious when Truman became president, new and inexperienced chief executives relied on the government bureaucracy for advice and information. The foreign policy bureaucracy that advised Truman derived its attitudes and perspectives from the foreign policy bureaucracy that in the 1920s had been the guardian of the policy of "nonrecognition." Unlike Roosevelt, they believed the way to deal with Stalin was through a firm policy of reciprocity and retaliation.

Truman's change of course and the advice on which it was predicated were erroneous. Roosevelt was committed, despite the resistance of the foreign policy bureaucracy, to postwar cooperation with the Soviet Union. This did not mean, however, that Roosevelt was naive. On the contrary, Roosevelt was worldlier than the advisers who resisted him. He knew Stalin was cynical and manipulative. He understood that the Soviet Union and the United States did not share the same values. He also understood, however, that they did share important postwar goals. Most importantly, both the Soviet Union and the United States were committed to peace in the foreseeable future. Roosevelt believed the best—indeed, the only—way to guarantee that peace was through great power cooperation. To that end, he took the realistic step of abandoning principled, yet futile, causes. The Soviet Union would have its way in Poland and the Baltic states, and Roosevelt's demands for anything more than paeans to global public opinion would be futile and counterproductive. Far from being naive, Roosevelt accepted the inevitable and clung to his priorities and what was attainable.

Few of these conclusions are obvious if the U.S. foreign policy bureaucracy is treated as a monolith. Examining the role and attitudes of the diverse groups of personnel who made up the foreign policy bureaucracy reveals the complexity of United States–Soviet relations during World War II.

The United States and the Bolshevik State, 1917–1932: Revolution and Intervention

Nineteen seventeen was a crucial year for the formulation of American, and particularly State Department, attitudes toward the emerging Soviet government. The Russian Revolution of February 1917, the fall of the autocracy, and the establishment of the provisional government were welcomed in the United States, and by American diplomats in Russia, as a move toward the type of democratic regime alongside which the United States would be willing to fight in the Great War raging in Europe.[1]

The Woodrow Wilson administration provided the provisional government with military and economic aid and loans to continue the war effort against Germany. As 1917 progressed, the chaos and turmoil that had characterized Russia in the final years of Tsarist rule nevertheless continued unabated. As conditions worsened, the American diplomats became increasingly pessimistic about Russia's future. When in October of that same year the provisional government was overthrown and the Bolshevik Party and its leader, Vladimir Lenin, established a socialist government, the United States' hopes for an American-style government in Russia faded. Almost without exception, U.S. diplomatic and consular officials in Russia greeted the new regime with loathing and despair.[2]

Two aspects of the new regime particularly offended American diplomats. First, the Bolshevik government announced that it had no intention of repaying money loaned to the Tsarist and the provisional governments. To the Americans, this refusal was symptomatic of a profound lack of respect for both traditional diplomacy and generally accepted principles designed to support the international economic order.[3] Second, communist revolutionaries who espoused and supported world revolution ran the Bolshevik government. A government with that goal was something unheard of since the collapse of revolutionary France, and the diplomats in the U.S. Department of State who took seriously the threat of a world revolution aimed at overthrowing capitalism perceived it as particularly menacing.[4] The Bolshevik break with the traditional practices of repaying debts and not interfering in the domestic affairs of other states (by advocating violent revolution) was a firm foundation for the development of distrust and antipathy toward the Soviet Union among U.S. Foreign Service officers.[5]

Distaste for the Bolsheviks and their threat of world revolution, accompanied by a desire to convince Russia to continue the war against Germany, prompted a joint British, French, Japanese, and American military intervention in Russia.[6] The Wilson administration sent token forces to northern Russia and Siberia to show support for the United States' allies, to get Russia back into the war, and, at least in part, to cause the overthrow of the Bolshevik regime in the process. By 1919, however, the war with Germany had ended, and Russia was descending into a bloody and confusing civil war. Policy makers in Washington determined that the United States should extricate itself from Russia and refocus its attention on issues such as the negotiations at Versailles and domestic U.S. concerns. Thus ended the period of active American attempts to overthrow the Bolshevik government.

By 1920 the United States had withdrawn from the Russian quagmire, but it did not emerge unscathed by its experience. The American public soon forgot intervention. The Soviets did not, and the memory of the experience colored their subsequent views of the United States.[7] The diplomats who served in the U.S. Foreign Service, and some military officers who served in the American Expeditionary Force in Siberia during the period of intervention, were similarly marked by the experience, developing strong attitudes about the character of the new Russian regime and the correct posture the United States should assume toward it. Meanwhile, the U.S. government as a whole initiated a new course to replace the failed policy of intervention. In a note to the Italian ambassador, U.S. Secretary of State Bainbridge Colby outlined the basic principles of the U.S. policy of nonrecognition: "We cannot recognize, hold official relations with, or give friendly reception to the agents of a government which is determined and bound to conspire against our institutions; whose diplomats will be the agitators of dangerous revolt; whose spokesmen say that they sign agreements with no intention of keeping them."[8] Essentially, the U.S. government perceived the ideology and practice of the new Russian regime as so antithetical to American principles that official recognition of it was inconceivable. This perception would persist even once U.S.-Russian economic relations improved as American businessmen increasingly sought Russian markets for their goods.[9]

Throughout the decade of nonrecognition, the Foreign Service assumed the mantle of defenders of that policy, compiling evidence to support the contention that the Russian (later Soviet) government could not be trusted. In the process, many career diplomats became intractable foes of Bolshevism.[10] The belief that any sort of "normal" relations with the self-avowedly revolutionary regime in Moscow were impossible would continue to color U.S. diplomatic interpretations of Soviet intentions and capabilities.[11]

In contrast, some military officers, most notably American Expeditionary Force commander Major General William S. Graves, criticized the U.S. intervention policy and the American diplomats who advocated that policy.[12] Although not a widespread reaction, suspicion of America's professional diplomats and belief that the United States was primarily responsible for chilly United States–Soviet relations would eventually reemerge as an area of conflict in the U.S. embassy in Moscow.

Shaping Bolshevik Foreign Policy

When the Bolshevik forces emerged victorious in 1921 from their long and bloody civil war and the war with Poland, the Bolshevik Party confronted the challenging transition from revolutionary movement to ruling party. The civil war had left Russia an internal legacy of economic and political turmoil. Under Vladimir Lenin's leadership, the policy of "war communism" gave way to a "New Economic Policy" (NEP), designed to reinvigorate the economy and renew support for the Soviet regime. The NEP could not, however, resolve all of the fledgling government's problems so long as Soviet Russia remained internationally ostracized and surrounded by hostile powers. Thus, an integral part of the NEP was a policy of "peaceful coexistence" with the capitalist world—a tactical maneuver designed to ensure Russia the breathing space it needed to rebuild.[13]

Soviet foreign policy had been based on Leon Trotsky's theory of "permanent revolution"—Trotsky was the first people's commissar for foreign affairs.

Essentially, according to Trotsky, the socialist "revolution begins on the national level, develops on the international level, and is completed on the world level."[14] The survival of the revolution in Russia was predicated on the spread of revolution throughout the capitalist world. Thus, the Bolshevik regime initially eschewed traditional diplomacy, relying instead on agitation among, and support of, socialist revolutionary movements throughout Europe.[15] In the heady days after November 1917, Bolshevik leaders hoped that the revolution in Russia would spark global revolution.

For the most part, those hopes faded after the outbreak of civil war in Russia and the intervention of the allied powers in that civil war. The successful conclusion in 1922 of the Treaty of Rapallo between the Soviet Union and the other international pariah, Germany, along with the failures of a number of revolutions in central and eastern Europe before 1924, convinced the Soviet leadership to continue internationally the "temporary" breathing space tactics embodied domestically in NEP.[16] Commitment to the revolution and revolutionary proselytizing, however, did not disappear. "Peaceful coexistence," as defined by Lenin, simply meant that confrontation between the socialist and capitalist worlds would take place not in the military sphere, but in the economic and ideological spheres. Essentially, and unofficially, the Kremlin conducted a dual foreign policy through traditional diplomatic channels on the one hand and the revolutionary Comintern on the other. The relative weight of each in Soviet calculations depended on the changing needs of the Soviet state.

That balance shifted toward the traditional in the mid-1920s. Lenin's death in January 1924, the subsequent succession struggle, and the ultimate victory of Joseph Stalin and his policy of "Socialism in One Country" in winter 1927–1928 ensured continued Soviet adherence to a policy of peaceful coexistence. Stalin's first five-year plan, launched in 1928, demanded this course for two reasons: first, Stalin believed that the economic transformation of Russia required that the USSR avoid involvement in military conflict; and second, the USSR needed imports of machinery and other goods from the capitalist countries in order to industrialize according to plan.

Although not eschewing revolution abroad, the immediate responsibility of the Soviet government would be to ensure the security of the revolution in Russia. In that way, a strong and secure state could serve as the inspiration, or seed, for later revolutionary movements wherever they might emerge. Fundamental to that security was a buildup of Soviet industrial and military strength, and, most important from the perspective of U.S.-Soviet relations, a foreign policy that would provide the Soviet Union with the breathing space it needed to become strong.[17]

The Era of Nonrecognition

While the government in Moscow was struggling to determine what course it should take with regard to the rest of the world, policy makers in the United States were busy discussing the appropriate attitude of the United States toward Soviet Russia. The development of a U.S. policy toward the emerging Soviet state coincided with developments within the State Department and the Foreign Service of the United States.

The early twentieth-century expansion of active American interest abroad prompted a reorganization and reform of the Foreign Service.[18] Among the changes was an increased specialization of the diplomatic and consular corps. As a result, the State Department's Division of Eastern European Affairs and its new generation of Russian experts played an increasing role in the formulation of U.S. policy toward the Soviet Union.

The Department's Russian experts were molded from entry-level Foreign Service officers who underwent extensive regional studies training. According to regulations established in 1927, these officers first served an eighteen-month probation, during which they were posted to the region they were studying. At the end of this period, they were assessed and, if found acceptable, allowed to continue to the academic part of the training. This was a program designed by the head of the Division of Eastern European Affairs from 1926 to 1937, Robert F. Kelley.[19] He was the young officers' mentor, the man who selected the academic programs they were to attend and who directed their on-the-job training. He was also ardently opposed to Bolshevism and assigned his regional-trainee officers to locations he hoped would create officers as skeptical of the Soviet Union as he was.[20] As the head of the division, Kelley wielded considerable influence in both the shaping of the Russian/Soviet experts and in the formulation of U.S. Soviet policy. His hostility to the Bolsheviks would thus influence the State Department's attitude toward the Soviets. In fact, his influence could be seen in the numerous advisory memoranda on the Soviet Union that he submitted to the secretary of state and the president.

Kelley's influence was also evident in the developing attitudes of his subordinates in the Division of Eastern European Affairs. Loy W. Henderson was one of the subordinates who played an increasingly significant role in the division. Born in the Ozark Mountains of Arkansas, the son of a Methodist minister and a schoolteacher, Henderson followed an indirect path to the Foreign Service and the Division of Eastern European Affairs. His introduction to the region came by way of service in the American Red Cross in 1918–1921, during which time he assisted the repatriation of Russian prisoners of war. On one repatriation mission, Henderson and his companions unexpectedly discovered the Republic of Lithuania.[21] The discovery was followed shortly thereafter by an exploratory mission to the capital of Latvia, Riga. Henderson's initial forays into the Baltic states marked a turning point in his life: "I had become interested in the Baltic and in the fate of the people in that area who were displaying admirable courage in the face of almost unendurable hardship and suffering."[22] This interest and admiration would lead Henderson to accept a position in the American Red Cross Commission in the Baltic States, and eventually to seek a career in the State Department.[23] Thus, Henderson entered the field of Soviet studies via the Baltic. That perspective, combined with the influence of working under Kelley, profoundly affected the way he perceived the Soviet Union.

Henderson's State Department work also shaped the way he viewed the Soviets. Throughout the 1920s one of the main jobs of the Division of Eastern European Affairs was to keep the State Department apprised of any suspicious Soviet activity. Henderson's contribution was to study the treaties and international agreements to which the Soviets were a party. As a result of his work, Henderson became convinced that the Soviet Union was actively working against the United States in the international arena. He saw the purpose of Soviet foreign policy to be "to keep the countries of Western Europe at loggerheads."[24] By the mid-1920s, when the Soviets affirmed their commitment to a policy of peaceful coexistence with the capitalist states, Henderson had concluded, "As a result of my studies and experiences in the Eastern European Affairs Division I became convinced that the rulers in Moscow, although perhaps differing at times among themselves regarding the methods to be employed, were united in their determination to promote chaos and revolution in the noncommunist world until they could achieve their ultimate objective of a communist world with headquarters in Moscow."[25]

In Henderson's opinion, the Soviet government was illegitimate and dangerous, and it was the job of the Division of Eastern European Affairs and the U.S. legation in Riga to convince the State Department and the wider U.S. government of "the true picture of the situation in the Soviet Union."[26] This was a task that would keep Henderson occupied for much of the remainder of his thirty-nine-year career, and it was a task that fit well with the foreign policies of the Republican administrations in power during the 1920s and early 1930s.[27] The Herbert Hoover administration, for example, strongly supported the policy of nonrecognition. Secretary of State Henry L. Stimson summed up the president's Soviet policy with the following words: "no political connections with all the trade we could get."[28]

With the change in administrations in 1933, their role as critical observers of the Soviet Union would often leave Henderson and his Foreign Service colleagues disappointed and bitter over the course U.S. elected officials chose to take.[29] The same specialization that created experts capable of understanding the nuances of Soviet development created a generation of Foreign Service analysts limited in their ability and willingness to place the Soviet situation in the broader international setting. Their obsession with the threat of communist expansion would all but blind them to the increasing threat of German and Japanese militarism. This lack of global perspective produced increasing conflicts between the Soviet specialists and the presidential administrations in Washington. As time passed, the frustration felt by the members of the Division of Eastern European Affairs for seemingly being overlooked would turn into hostility over the perceived naïveté of politicians, and eventually near-rebellion against the policies Washington instructed them to implement.

Henderson and his colleagues in the Eastern European Affairs Division, like Kelley and the young graduates of his specialist program, George Kennan and Charles Bohlen, did not have a monopoly on U.S. views of the Soviet Union. As the years after the October revolution passed, many influential Americans began to soften their opposition to relations with the Soviet government. Some desired U.S. recognition of the Soviet Union because of the belief that diplomatic relations would lead to increased commercial ties; others simply found it abnormal and unrealistic to ignore the government of such a large and significant country.[30] With the deepening of the Great Depression during 1930–1932, the voices calling for recognition became louder, and the opponents of diplomatic relations became increasingly aware of the futility of their positions. By the early 1930s, key critics of the Soviet Union began to prepare for the inevitable resumption of diplomatic ties. On the eve of negotiations for recognition, Robert Kelley, on behalf of the Division of Eastern European Affairs, staked out a new position, arguing, "Formal diplomatic relations may be established, but the substance of a useful relationship will be lacking, as much for the Russians as for ourselves, unless and until we have cleared up the existing difficulties through mutual agreement and worked out a *modus vivendi* for the future."[31] Throughout this lengthy memorandum, Kelley continued to enumerate the areas of existing difficulty, which included the world revolutionary aims of the Soviet government, the Soviet repudiation of bonds and confiscation of property, and the question of the protection of the life and property of U.S. citizens in Russia. He argued that if these issues were not resolved before recognition, there was little likelihood that negotiations would be successful afterward.[32]

Thus, resigned to the fact that the new president would recognize the Soviet Union despite their best arguments, Kelley and his colleagues in the State Department determined to shape the course of the negotiations and the foundations it would lay in the U.S.-Soviet relationship.

Roosevelt's Détente, 1932–1938

The Election of 1932

By 1932 the United States was in the third year of the worst economic depression it had ever suffered. Over 10 million people, nearly 20 percent of the workforce, were unemployed. Many that were working faced dwindling incomes and the ever-present threat that their jobs would disappear. Worse yet, in the face of this surge in public need, the traditional relief apparatuses at the state and the local level were collapsing. The American people increasingly began to demand action from the federal government—action that President Herbert Hoover only reluctantly provided.[1]

This economic suffering and turmoil formed the context for the presidential campaign and election of 1932. The major issue was Hoover's unwillingness to provide direct relief to the unemployed—and New York Governor Franklin Delano Roosevelt's publicly stated commitment to doing so.[2] Campaigning on the platform of "a new deal for the American people," Roosevelt focused his speeches on the need for new solutions to the economic crises and new conceptions of the federal government's role in public life.[3] Yet he never defined precisely what measures he intended to take. Roosevelt's New Deal, both in its conception and in its applications, was never a well-laid-out plan of action. Rather, it was a number of varied, often contradictory experiments. To pull the nation through the domestic crisis, Roosevelt was willing to break with tradition and enact a more active role for the federal government. In that way, he rejected the policies that had defined the previous decade and set the country on a new course for the 1930s.

The election focused on these domestic issues, and they propelled Roosevelt toward one of the most lopsided victories in history. On 8 November 1932, Roosevelt won forty-two states, every state south and west of Pennsylvania. He won 57 percent of the popular vote, and 472 of the 531 members of the Electoral College.

Although this landslide victory can be attributed to Roosevelt's campaign on domestic issues, it would be erroneous to assume that foreign policy was far from his mind. Roosevelt possessed a strong interest in international affairs, dating to the early years of his career in public service.[4] As assistant secretary of the navy in the Wilson administration, Roosevelt absorbed many of the internationalist ideas of the president. This became evident in his unsuccessful bid for the vice presidency in 1920, when a central point of his campaign was an advocacy for U.S. membership in the League of Nations.

Consequently, although the press of domestic issues demanded most of Roosevelt's energy in 1932 and early 1933, ominous events overseas combined with Roosevelt's abiding interest in international affairs to ensure that foreign policy did not disappear from the new president's agenda. By the time of his inauguration on 4 March 1933, Germany had installed the extremely nationalist and belligerent Adolf Hitler as chancellor and Japan had quit the League of Nations in order to pursue a policy of aggression less hindered by international condemnation. Roosevelt entered the White House with a nation in crisis and a world threatened by the increasing bellicosity of two major powers.

Roosevelt's approach to these looming threats, and to foreign affairs in general, was little different from his New Deal proposals in the domestic sphere. Indeed, his policy in the international arena often resembled almost haphazard experimentation as he veered from nationalist to internationalist perspectives.[5] Nonetheless, Roosevelt's actions were driven by his underlying belief that the United States must play a role in the world, and that role necessitated some breaks from the foreign policy of the preceding administrations just as dramatic as the changes in economic policy.

In creating and implementing his New Deal both within the United States and abroad, Roosevelt encountered tremendous obstacles and resistance. His foreign policy demanded a change in the relationship between the United States and the Soviet Union, and, in so doing, ran headlong into the entrenched anti-Soviet attitudes of the State Department bureaucracy. The struggle for influence in the shaping of the United States' Soviet policy began with the recognition of the Soviet Union and persisted throughout the remainder of Roosevelt's administration. In the course of its development, it diffused laterally to include both civilian and military officials and horizontally to reach from the lowest bureaucrat to the president's closest advisers. Building on the foundation of the 1920s, the first years of Roosevelt's administration marked the emergence in this struggle of two camps: one that felt the Soviet Union could not and should not be trusted, and another that considered cooperation with the Kremlin vital to the interests of the United States. As the 1930s unfolded, these two contending stances jockeyed for position and influence within the president's foreign policy–making structure.[6]

Recognition

It is almost certain that even before his inauguration, Roosevelt had decided to establish diplomatic relations with the Soviet Union. The atmosphere of the early 1930s was undoubtedly conducive to that development. With the United States gripped by a worldwide depression, many Americans were intrigued by (some even infatuated with) a system that did not seem troubled by the economic malaise. In fact, the Soviet economy seemed to be flourishing as a result of Stalin's five-year plans. These Americans saw the Soviet Union less as something to fear and more as something to emulate.[7] Other Americans, not as enamored with the Soviet system itself, were still eager to establish diplomatic relations in the hope that it would improve trade. Although the volume of U.S. exports to the Soviet Union had actually declined in the early 1930s, some businessmen retained the hope that the healthy Soviet economy would provide an even greater market for American goods after recognition.[8] Whatever the individual rationales, the clear trend at the beginning of the decade was toward recognition. Even the stalwart defenders of nonrecognition in the State Department's Division of Eastern European Affairs had begun to prepare for what they considered the inevitability of recognizing the Soviet Union.

Preparing for the presidency, Roosevelt was well aware of this climate and the opportunities it presented. In a January 1933 meeting with outgoing Secretary of State Henry Stimson, Roosevelt brought up the subject of Soviet recognition. In response to Roosevelt's questions, Stimson explained the reasons for the nonrecognition policy and, more significantly, the criteria he believed the Soviet Union should meet before recognition. Stimson felt that all that was necessary for recognition was that the Soviet regime provide assurances that it would "behave according to the fundamental principle of the family of nations."[9] The question of recognition was not "whether," but "how."

Roosevelt revealed more of his own thoughts on the matter in an interview with *New York Times* correspondent Walter Duranty in July 1932. Duranty left the luncheon meeting impressed by Roosevelt's knowledge of Soviet affairs, which he took as a sign of Roosevelt's thoughtful consideration of recognition. Roosevelt also apparently indicated to the reporter that he considered "sentimental prejudice against the USSR" nonsense.[10]

Thus, by Inauguration Day 1933, it was becoming evident that Roosevelt was less hostile to the Soviet Union than were his professional Foreign Service officers. He perceived a need to establish a working relationship with the Kremlin for a variety of reasons: Recognition of the Soviet regime was simply acknowledgment that the powers in the Kremlin were stable and in control of their country (one of the two criteria put forth by Stimson); the United States' policy of nonrecognition was rapidly becoming moribund as all major countries, including the United Kingdom, had already established diplomatic relations with Moscow; recognizing the Soviet Union offered Roosevelt some political windfall as numbers of Americans were calling for it to help ease the United States' economic difficulties; and finally, and most importantly, Roosevelt wanted to recognize the Soviet Union in the hope that it would provide a balance against the increasing potential hostility of Germany and, more imperatively, Japan in the Far East.[11]

Roosevelt took the first tentative step toward establishing diplomatic relations with the Soviet Union on 16 May 1933. He included Soviet President Mikhail Kalinin in an appeal for military disarmament that he sent to fifty-four heads of state. Although he minimized the gesture and informed the White House press corps that Kalinin's inclusion did not constitute recognition on the part of the United States, the communication signified a crack in the United States' nonrecognition policy.

Roosevelt's initial steps toward recognition were not limited to political gestures, however. He hammered away at the foundation of that policy from other angles, most notably from the economic perspective. Almost as soon as he took office, he began to stress the importance of trade with the Soviet Union to the United States' businesses. In April 1933 Roosevelt invited the president of the American-Russian Chamber of Commerce to the White House. By stressing the development of trade, Roosevelt hoped to garner support for recognizing the Soviet Union.[12]

These small steps enabled Roosevelt to ease the country toward acceptance of diplomatic relations with the Soviet Union. At the same time, they allowed the president to move cautiously, ensuring that he had appropriate political support in the United States and could elicit an acceptable response from the Soviet Union. Regardless of the temerity of his approach, Roosevelt still had to contend with the proponents of nonrecognition in the State Department.

Roosevelt's Unconventional Diplomacy

The Division of Eastern European Affairs was happy with neither Roosevelt nor his decision to begin negotiations with Soviet Foreign Minister Maksim Litvinov. Henderson believed that even before Roosevelt took the oath of office, the president-elect offended members of the State Department by refusing to meet with Hoover, and by meeting with outgoing Secretary of State Henry Stimson without sharing the substance of those conversations with other State Department officials.[13] The appointment of assistant secretaries apparently to suit the president rather than the new secretary of state, Cordell Hull, also offended the Foreign Service professionals. They perceived it as an effort to bypass the secretary and to undercut the State Department's Foreign Service officers.[14] Henderson concluded (correctly) that Roosevelt had an attitude of indifference to or contempt for the State Department, an attitude that was manifested in the way Roosevelt chose to explore opening relations with the Soviet Union. Instead of using the State Department, Roosevelt went to Secretary of the Treasury Henry A. Morgenthau Jr. and asked him to investigate the possibilities for recognition.[15]

It was not simply a matter of protocol that created strained relations between the president and his career Foreign Service officers. Given the Division of Eastern European Affairs' self-appointed role as the guardian of the policy of nonrecognition throughout the preceding decade, it is not difficult to understand why the president would choose to work outside traditional channels. Indeed, Kelley and his colleagues in the State Department stepped up their efforts to prove that the Soviet Union was not a respectable member of the global community of nations in the weeks and months after Roosevelt's inauguration.[16] Not surprisingly, Roosevelt considered the Department of State "unfriendly to the idea of opening negotiations with the Russians." Hence, he turned to Morgenthau and Special Assistant to the Secretary of State William C. Bullitt to approach the Soviets. When the Roosevelt-Litvinov talks on the terms of recognition began, Bullitt headed the U.S. team.[17]

Bullitt was a longtime advocate of U.S. relations with the Bolshevik government, dating back to his service as Woodrow Wilson's special emissary to Lenin. His support of recognition stemmed from his commitment to the principle of "liberalism" in U.S. foreign policy. He believed that the United States needed open markets—both economic and political—around the globe; and he believed that violent revolution often threatened this. In the period after the Bolshevik revolution in Russia, Bullitt argued that global political actors could be divided into three groups: imperialists, liberals, and revolutionary socialists. The United States needed liberal support in order to struggle against imperialists and revolutionaries, but the Bolshevik revolution and the Allied intervention had split world liberal opinion. In Bullitt's opinion, the United States should make peace with the Bolsheviks to ensure liberal support of the United States and to prevent Russia from joining forces with imperialist Germany.[18]

Despite his support for recognition, Bullitt initially shared many of the reservations of the Eastern European Affairs Division of the State Department. In October 1933, Hull asked Assistant Secretary of State Judge Walton Moore and Bullitt to submit memoranda outlining their views of recognition. Bullitt's memorandum echoed many of Kelley's earlier considerations: "Whatever method may be used to enter into negotiations with the Soviet Government, it seems essential that formal recognition should not be accorded except as the final act of an agreement covering a number of questions in dispute. Before recognition and before loans, we shall find the Soviet Government relatively amenable. After recognition or loans, we should find the Soviet Government adamant."[19] Bullitt was particularly concerned with the prohibition of Comintern and Soviet communist propaganda in the United States; the protection of the civil and religious rights of Americans in the Soviet Union; the repayment of U.S. loans to the provisional government; and the settlement of private American claims for assets seized by the Soviet government.[20] Despite these reservations, Bullitt remained optimistic about the future of U.S.-Soviet relations and shared Roosevelt's conviction that the details of some of the agreements could be worked out in postrecognition negotiations.

On 16 November 1933, Roosevelt and Litvinov exchanged a series of notes establishing diplomatic relations between the United States and the Soviet Union and outlining the agreements reached during the negotiations. One of these notes expressed the Soviet government's commitment to prohibit from its territory any organization or group "which has [as] an aim the overthrow or the preparation for the overthrow of, or the bringing about by force of a change in, the political or social order of the whole or any part of the United States, its territories or possessions."[21] Roosevelt, Bullitt, and the State Department believed that the note, although not explicitly naming the Comintern, included that organ of international communism. They expected the Soviet government to uphold its commitment to prevent its meeting on Soviet territory.

The Roosevelt-Litvinov Agreements also addressed the issue of Soviet debts to the United States. This issue was resolved by means of a "gentleman's agreement" that specified that "the Soviet Government will pay to the government of the United States on account of the [Alexander I.] Kerinsky [provisional government] debt or otherwise a sum to be not less than $75,000,000 in the form of a percentage above the ordinary rate of interest on a loan to be granted to it by the Government of the United States or its nationals."[22] Despite Kelley's warning and Bullitt's own reservations about the success of postrecognition talks, the exact sum of the Soviet payment was left for future negotiations between the American ambassador and Soviet foreign minister in Moscow.

Recognition dramatically altered the nature of the United States–Soviet relationship. The establishment of diplomatic relations meant the expansion of contacts between the two states. Not only career Foreign Service officers but also military attachés and ambassadors would populate the American embassy in Moscow. In the increasingly turbulent years of the 1930s, the United States would rely ever more heavily on information from all three of these sources to determine the intentions and capabilities of the Soviet Union.

Collective Security

The establishment of diplomatic relations between the United States and the Soviet Union came at a time of unprecedented possibility for cooperation between the two states. It was fortuitous that both Roosevelt and Litvinov (and his boss in Moscow, Stalin) had a common goal for their foreign policy: to preserve peace in the face of a rising German and Japanese threat. Indeed, the contacts that led to U.S. recognition stemmed from a common conception of how to attain that goal. For while Roosevelt clung to his memories of what might have been with the League of Nations, changes in the international environment in the early 1930s prompted the Soviet leadership to reconsider its policy of "peaceful coexistence."

Predicated on economically and ideologically exploiting the contradictions among *all* capitalist powers, that policy had in fundamental ways masked the Kremlin's need to discern between more and less aggressive or threatening states. The Japanese attack on Manchuria in September 1931 brought into sharp focus the danger of isolation this policy posed to the Soviet Union. Moscow could not risk simultaneous pressure in both the Far East and Europe. As a result, the Soviet Union took some tentative steps toward rapprochement with some of the capitalist powers in Europe. Moscow signed a series of nonaggression pacts with Poland (July 1932), Finland (January 1932), Latvia (February 1932), Estonia (May 1932), Lithuania (May 1931), and France (November 1932). In addition, the Soviet Union took part in the Geneva World Disarmament Talks in 1932.[23]

The real impetus for change in Soviet foreign policy, however, occurred in 1933, shortly after the National Socialist victory in Germany and Adolf Hitler's emergence as German chancellor. After that election, the Soviet leadership—hesitant to abandon the policy it had pursued toward Germany since the signing of the Rapallo treaty in 1922—reached out to the new German government. Hitler, however, rejected the Soviet overtures. As a result of these rebuffs, by December 1933 the Kremlin turned toward a policy of "collective security" against German aggression, although at no point did the leadership abandon entirely the efforts to maintain some form of cooperation with Germany.[24] The Soviet Union feared German expansionism, especially expansion aimed specifically at the Soviet Union, but it still did not trust the other capitalist powers not to form an anti-Soviet bloc with Germany. Consequently, the Kremlin pursued a dual course. Collective security against German aggression was their primary aim, but until they could be assured of British and French support, the Soviets would also seek peaceful relations with Germany.[25]

The difficult task of implementing the new Soviet foreign policy fell to the people's commissar for foreign affairs, Maksim Litvinov, whose tenure as commissar was characterized by increasing Soviet commitment to the principle of collective security. The Roosevelt-Litvinov talks that led to the establishment of diplomatic relations between the Soviet Union and the United States late in 1933 can be seen in this light. Litvinov, as realistic in his assessment of the international balance of power as Roosevelt, understood that normal relations with the United States (and the other major capitalist powers) served the best interests of the Soviet government.[26]

The influence of this new foreign policy line was evident in many areas. For example, reversing its long-standing role as an opponent of the Versailles settlement, in 1934 the Soviet Union joined the League of Nations and actively cooperated with or urged the western powers to adopt measures designed to contain aggression. In a concrete sign of this commitment, Moscow concluded mutual assistance pacts with France and Czechoslovakia in May 1935. Litvinov undoubtedly hoped for similar results in Anglo-Soviet relations. Since 1932 he had been urging the Soviet ambassador to London, Ivan Maisky, to improve relations between the United Kingdom and the Soviet Union.[27]

Litvinov's dedication to the concept of collective security notwithstanding, key U.S. diplomats remained skeptical of Soviet intentions. Aware of the revolutionary nature and origins of the Soviet regime, these diplomats correctly assumed that the Soviet Union had not abandoned its desire for revolutionary (and Soviet) expansion. What they apparently failed to comprehend was that, at least for the moment, United States and Soviet international goals coincided and that cooperation was not only possible but desirable.

The Obstacle of Institutional Bias:
The State Department and the Soviet Union

Despite the skepticism of the United States' career Foreign Service officers and Roosevelt's resultant hesitancy to trust them, the establishment of relations with the Soviet Union required the creation in Moscow of an American embassy that would necessarily be staffed by the State Department. The president did have significantly more leeway in his selection of an ambassador. Roosevelt chose Bullitt. As the first U.S. ambassador to the Soviet Union, Bullitt's attitude toward the USSR seemed to be a perfect balance to the skeptical or hostile position of the State Department. This was particularly relevant because joining Bullitt in the creation of the new embassy in Moscow were the counselor, John Wiley; the chief of the Economic Section, Loy Henderson; and Third Secretaries Charles "Chip" Bohlen, George Kennan, and Bertel Kuniholm. The latter three were all products of Kelley's tutelage, and Henderson, although not directly a pupil of Kelley's, was shaped by his working relationship with him.[28]

Despite his integral role in the establishment of relations between the United States and the Soviet Union, Bullitt proved to be a poor choice for ambassador. His personality was unsuitable for diplomacy. Described as "mercurial" by his biographer, Bullitt was given to emotional extremes and an arrogant belief that he was always right.[29] This combination was volatile. Once he formed an opinion, he became emotionally committed to it and would see only what he expected to see. If events did not develop the way he believed they should, Bullitt responded with passionate anger. President Wilson and his advisers learned this in 1919 when an infuriated Bullitt revealed all he knew about the Versailles negotiations and U.S. relations with the Bolsheviks to the Senate Foreign Relations Committee. Bullitt's anger stemmed from a brief (one week) period in 1919 he spent in Moscow on a fact-finding mission for Wilson. He arrived in Moscow convinced he would like what he saw, and he was not disappointed. What he did not like, he simply ignored. Wilson, the French, and the British refused to share Bullitt's opinion and did nothing about the proposals he brought from Lenin. Despite the rejection of his report, nothing that occurred in the period between 1919 and 1933 forced Bullitt to revise his judgment. He thus departed for the Soviet Union still wearing rose-colored glasses from a decade earlier.[30]

Bullitt took great pride in his personal role in the establishment and continuation of friendly relations between the two countries. The Soviet leadership was not unaware of Bullitt's weakness and took great advantage of it by showering the American ambassador with lavish praise and even an unexpected audience with the otherwise unapproachable premier, Joseph Stalin. In a telegram to the State Department reporting on his initial period in Moscow, Bullitt described his impressive reception:

> [T]he Soviet Union is so anxious to have peace that it is obvious that even our moral influence is valued very highly by the Soviet Government. It is difficult to exaggerate the cordiality with which I was received by all members of the Government including [M. I.] Kalinin, [V. M.] Molotov, [K. Y.] Voroshilov and [J. V.] Stalin. Especially noteworthy is the fact that Stalin, who until my arrival had never received any ambassador, said to me "at any moment, day or night, if you wish to see me you have only to ask and I will see you at once."[31]

So long as the Soviets continued to stroke his ego, Bullitt remained optimistic about the state of Soviet–United States relations. And so long as the Soviet Union needed cooperation with the United States, it would continue to favor the American ambassador.

As it became increasingly clear to the Soviets that the United States was not going to work actively with them against a possible Japanese threat in the Far East, Soviet enthusiasm for the new ambassador began to wane. No longer treated as a most-honored dignitary in the Soviet Union, Bullitt found himself forced to endure the numerous slights and indignities heaped on all foreign envoys in Moscow. He explained the situation in a letter to Roosevelt: "The honeymoon atmosphere had evaporated completely before I arrived. . . . The Russians are convinced that Japan will not attack this spring or summer and, as they no longer feel that they need our immediate help, their underlying hostility to all capitalist countries now shows through the veneer of intimate friendship."[32] Compounding this loss of status was the emergence of difficulties over debts and other issues left unresolved during the recognition negotiations. Bullitt interpreted Litvinov's arguments in the renewed negotiations as personal insults and signs of disrespect. His attitude toward the Soviet Union deteriorated correspondingly.[33] On 19 July 1935 Bullitt summarized his interpretation of Soviet foreign policy in a letter to Hull:

The aim of the Soviet Government is and will remain, to produce world revolution. The leaders of the Soviet Union believe that the first step toward this revolution must be to strengthen the defensive and offensive power of the Soviet Union. They believe that within ten years the defensive position of the Soviet Union will be absolutely impregnable and that within 15 years the offensive power of the Soviet Union will be sufficient to enable it to consolidate by its assistance any communist government which may be set up in Europe. To maintain peace for the present, to keep the nations of Europe divided, to foster enmity between Japan and the United States, and to gain the blind devotion and obedience of the communists of all countries so that they will not act against their own governments at the behest of the Communist Pope in the Kremlin, is the sum of Stalin's policy.[34]

By the time the Soviet Union hosted the Seventh Congress of the Third Communist International (Comintern) in August 1935, Bullitt's perception of Soviet aims was essentially the same as that of the career Foreign Service officers Roosevelt had sent him to Moscow to balance. In Bullitt's view, the Soviet Union was a pariah among nations. The United States could neither trust nor work with the Soviet government because it was dedicated to the violent overthrow of capitalist states like the United States. An angry Bullitt dismissed the Seventh Congress' declaration of a "united front" against fascism as "an obvious tactical maneuver" designed to expedite the various communist parties' achievement of their revolutionary aims.[35] To the American ambassador, the Congress' proceedings sent an obvious message to the world: "Citations from past and present Comintern proceedings confirm convincingly and with eloquence the thesis that the capitalist world enjoys, at best, only a period of armistice with Bolshevism."[36] With the support of his State Department staff, Bullitt argued that the presence of the Seventh Congress of the Comintern in Moscow constituted a clear breach of the Roosevelt-Litvinov agreements, and he proposed a series of measures to show American anger. Yet despite his obvious anger and sense of betrayal, Bullitt concluded that the violation was not sufficient for the United States to sever relations with the Soviet Union. The embassy in Moscow had become an increasingly important observation post for the United States.[37]

A New Ambassador and New Approaches

Despite his admission that relations with the Soviet Union were important, Bullitt's position in Moscow became increasingly untenable as he became ever more vocally anti-Soviet. The ambassador went so far as to urge foreign correspondents to write articles hostile to the Soviet government.[38] His attitude, combined with that of the State Department, contributed to the growing estrangement between the Soviet Union and the United States. As global tension increased in the mid-1930s, it was an estrangement that Roosevelt saw as increasingly dangerous, although his ability to act on this was limited as a result of the imminent 1936 election and the growing strength of isolationism in the United States.[39]

Roosevelt's landslide victory in November 1936 eased this situation somewhat. Free once again to pursue his policy of attempting to find a *modus vivendi* with the Soviet government, in November 1936 he replaced Bullitt, who had resigned his post in May, with Joseph E. Davies. Unlike Bullitt, Davies had no illusions about the attitudes of the Bolsheviks. Thus, he could not become disillusioned. Yet although he constantly spoke of his "capitalist" mind, Davies was no intractable foe of Soviet Bolshevism. In fact, Davies was one of the New Deal generation who held out hope for Soviet-American friendship on the premise that the two societies were developing along convergent paths. The Soviet Union would eventually move away from the worst excesses of Bolshevism, as the United States seemed to be moving away from the worst injustices of capitalism.

In addition to this belief in convergence, Davies was a loyal servant to Roosevelt. Roosevelt told Davies that his mission was to improve relations with the Soviets, and Davies was determined to execute that mission.[40] To the horror of his embassy staff, Davies always looked for the best in Soviet actions and approached the Soviet government from that perspective. A clash between the Foreign Service officers conditioned to distrust the Soviet Union and the ambassador willing to go to extreme lengths to understand issues from the Soviet point of view was almost inevitable and not long in coming. On Davies' first night in Moscow, his embassy staff gathered together for a secret meeting to discuss what they should do with this new ambassador.[41]

The dispute between Davies and the professional Foreign Service officers did not end with the private meeting. For the remainder of his tenure in Moscow, the clash between the ambassador and his staff was obvious to all who received reports from that country. The embassy personnel and Davies differed on issues ranging from the nature of Soviet industry to the possibility of United States cooperation with the Kremlin.[42] The dispute was particularly clear on the subject of show trials; the embassy dispatched reports from Davies that were directly contradicted by those from other Foreign Service officers.

The period of show trials and purges is one of no precise chronological boundaries. The murder of Leningrad party secretary Sergei Kirov on 1 December 1934 was the event that either triggered, or was used as, a justification for much of the subsequent "terror."[43] Whatever its relationship to subsequent events, Kirov's death ushered in a period of repression shocking to most western observers. Particularly damaging to assessments of the Soviet Union's value as a potential ally was Stalin's purge of the Red Army. In the course of the purge, the officer corps was decimated, with most of the well-known, innovative military thinkers executed. To the Foreign Service officers observing the Soviet Union at that time, the reasons for the arrests and accusations were clear. Only two weeks after Kirov's murder, the American chargé to the Soviet Union, John Wiley, was already reporting to the State Department:

> The Soviet Government is a revolutionary government. Its antecedents are those of violence and direct action. . . . The regime, though, is not yet sufficiently mature to forget the violence of its origins. In Bolshevik eyes, the victory by being won might, paradoxically, be lost. The struggle must continue, and must continue on both fronts; against foreign foe and the "class enemy" at home. Bolshevik tactics do not permit of "free-wheeling."[44]

As Wiley's comments indicate, the purges, trials, arrests, and fear pervasive in the Soviet Union in the latter half of the 1930s would confirm many American diplomats' perceptions of both Soviet domestic and foreign aims.

This period of terror did not have the same impact on Ambassador Davies. Like the U.S. Foreign Service officers in Moscow, Davies had no illusions about the nature of the Soviet regime. In his diary and private correspondence, he expressed unmitigated horror at some of its actions.[45] To Davies, the Soviet government was "oriental in its cruelty and in its complete disregard for individual life."[46] But unlike the U.S. embassy personnel, Davies did not let his distaste for the Soviet regime bias his assessment of the importance of the Soviet Union in the world. The Soviet government was a "tyranny, clothed in horror," but it was a tyranny that would grow in international importance, and with which the United States would have to cooperate.[47] Davies understood that his role in this cooperation was to counter the uniformly hostile attitude of the U.S. embassy in Moscow.

This understanding is reflected in his dispatches on the show trials. Davies' reports to the secretary of state displayed almost painful contortions to understand Soviet law and thinking, and later historians have castigated Davies for naively believing the Soviet charges against the defendants.[48] Indeed, reporting on the trial of the Trotskyist Bloc on 13 March 1938, Davies concluded that the prosecution established that the defendants were guilty of crimes under Soviet law.[49] He reaffirmed this conclusion on 1 April 1938, when he wrote that the Soviet government had established "beyond a reasonable doubt" the existence of a strong group of men organizing or participating in "unlawful and treasonable activities."[50] Still, Davies' reports were not uniformly uncritical of the Soviet regime, nor did they reflect an unquestioning belief in Soviet jurisprudence. In fact, while acknowledging that the defendants were proven guilty *under Soviet law,* he couched his conclusions in a wealth of qualifications. Davies acknowledged that the "pleaded admissions and alleged statements of fact give the impression of propaganda"; the trials relied too heavily on confession evidence in "a system which affords practically no protection for the accused"; and that there was much in the trials that was untrue.[51] Davies found the Soviet justice system horrifying, but in his official correspondence, he sought to downplay his disgust in the interest of U.S.-Soviet harmony. The Soviet Union, in Davies' mind, was and would remain an important European power, with whom the United States must cooperate:

> From the viewpoint for the survival of democracy, which is going on in the world today, and in view of the fact that England and France are being imminently threatened by complete domination of Fascism in Europe, it is rather difficult to understand why the strength that is here available should not be fostered and used, at least to the extent that it is in accord with the maintenance of international morals and justice in world affairs. The man power here is tremendous. The resources here, not only actually, but potentially, are such that inevitably these people here will be of enormous and growing influence on conditions of life both in Europe and throughout the world. In my opinion, they constitute now a lesser actual menace than the Fascist states. In any event Hitler is threatened in the East unless his eastern door is closed. That is a classic accepted by German strategists as a basis for any war against the Western Powers.[52]

The ability to report objectively on the Soviet Union was becoming increasingly difficult for the State Department's Soviet experts. For these individuals, already conditioned by years of experience and education to distrust the Soviets, living in Moscow through the purges only hardened their suspicions and reinforced their hostility to the Soviet government. In a particularly telling example, Henderson reported to the State Department his assessment of the effect of the purge of various segments of the Soviet population. Studying the mood of the peasantry, inexperienced industrial workers, seasoned industrial workers, the bureaucracy, engineers, technicians, the intelligentsia, and the Red Army, Henderson correctly determined that important groups were either indifferent to or supportive of the purges. In Henderson's own assessment, the peasantry was indifferent while the industrial workers supported the arrests and took advantage of the opportunities they presented them. In contrast, the bureaucracy, engineers, technicians, intelligentsia, and the Red Army, who may have had reason to fear "remarks which might be construed as indications of disloyalty or lack of admiration for Stalin," were frightened by the arrests. Ignoring the support of significant segments of the population for Stalin's policy, Henderson contradicted his own observations and concluded that "the prestige of Stalin at present is lower than at any time since his assumption of power 13 years ago."[53]

As the decade passed, the reports of the experts increasingly reflected an antagonistic interpretation of Soviet intentions and a pessimistic assessment of the Soviet government's ability to defend itself from enemies both domestic and foreign. Henderson argued in November 1936 that the ultimate goal of Soviet foreign policy remained "the establishment of a Union of World Soviet Socialist Republics"; Soviet advocacy of a policy of "collective security" was merely a temporary measure designed to protect the Soviet Union from military attack until it could become "a great impregnable fortress."[54] In February 1938 Henderson advanced this interpretation of Soviet foreign policy in another report to the State Department. He argued that the Soviet Union was moving away from the policy of participation in international affairs it had pursued from 1933 to 1936, and returning to a policy of exploiting the differences among the capitalist states. Henderson reminded the secretary that this policy was the "governing principle of Soviet foreign policy in regard to its relations with European countries."[55] In Henderson's opinion, Soviet intentions remained hostile to the United States. Other Foreign Service officers in the Moscow embassy shared this point of view. In a dispatch transmitting two editorials on Soviet-American relations, Alexander Kirk, Stuart Grummon, and Chip Bohlen argued that Soviet gestures of friendship were purely opportunistic, and that no foreign government could trust sustained Soviet cooperation.[56]

The Foreign Service officers in Moscow were no less pessimistic when assessing the ability of the Kremlin to defend itself. On the same date that he examined Soviet foreign policy, Henderson forwarded the secretary of state a report on the impact of the purges and the establishment of political commissars on the Red Army. He reported that the generally accepted opinion of military attachés in Moscow was that the Red Army's fighting efficiency was damaged and would not become effective again "so long as the political commissars are permitted to exercise the power they now have."[57]

In contrast to Henderson's assessment, Davies remained optimistic about the Red Army's strength. He acknowledged that the army was "shaken" by the purge, but he argued that it was "first class."[58] In June 1938 Davies expressed this optimism in even stronger terms. He pointed out that the strength of the Soviet military was "impressive," and "it would be exceedingly difficult to conquer or annihilate these forces, with their ally the Russian winter."[59]

The Role and Influence of Philip Faymonville

Although his interpretation of Soviet attitudes and abilities differed from that of the Foreign Service officers in his embassy, Davies was not alone in his judgment of the Soviet Union. From the moment of his arrival in Moscow, Davies developed a close relationship with the second challenger of the otherwise unanimously anti-Soviet tenor of embassy reporting: the U.S. military attaché, Colonel Philip R. Faymonville.

Faymonville could not have been more different from his diplomatic colleagues in the embassy.[60] Whereas Henderson and most of his fellow Soviet experts approached their study of the Soviet Union from the perspective of Europe and the Baltics, Faymonville was a student of the Pacific and the Far East. Born in San Francisco and educated at Stanford, Faymonville returned to the Pacific area after graduating ninth in his class from the United States Military Academy. Although he was an ordnance officer in the army, Faymonville was drawn to intelligence work, at which he was extremely gifted. Already fluent in Japanese, as early as 1916 or 1917 he began to study Russian because he predicted a future war between the United States and Japan, and he considered Russia to be the United States' natural ally in such a conflict.[61] Thus, from the very beginning of his interest in Russia and (later) the Soviet Union, Faymonville viewed the Soviet Union and Soviet-American relations through the lens of Japanese-American or Japanese-Soviet relations.[62]

Faymonville's perspective was further developed in 1918 when he served as the chief ordnance officer and judge advocate in the American Expeditionary Force under Graves. Faymonville sympathized with Graves' criticisms of U.S. policy and shared Graves' suspicion of professional diplomats.[63] By 1920, when he left Siberia, Faymonville was convinced that the Bolsheviks would prevail in their civil war and that the United States' efforts to undermine them were dangerous folly. In addition, Faymonville's assignments in the Far East did not lessen his concern over Japanese intentions. A short tour as American military observer in the "Far Eastern Republic" preceded a tour as assistant military attaché and military attaché in Japan, where he received commendations from both the military attaché whom he replaced and Ambassador Cyrus Wood.

As the 1920s progressed, Faymonville became a sharp critic of the policy of nonrecognition. In his opinion, the United States should have been pursuing a policy of economic and political rapprochement with the Soviet Union.[64] Not only was the Soviet Union the United States' natural ally against Japan, but the Soviet Union was also a perfect target for American businesses. Lenin had seemingly replaced the worst excesses of war communism with the New Economic Policy, and the Soviet Union appeared to be developing economically along more capitalist lines. For Faymonville, this meant that the United States could trust the Soviet government and could deal with it as a normal political entity.

By 1933 Faymonville was a student at the U.S. Army War College, where he became a vocal proponent of U.S. cooperation with the Soviet government.[65] At the same time, he assumed the role of senior military aide to the White House.[66] This assignment no doubt pleased Faymonville as the happy coincidence of his views with the new president's became daily more apparent, but it is extremely unlikely that his White House duties led to any significant meetings with President Roosevelt. White House appointment logs indicate that their paths officially intersected on only two occasions, both dinner parties where Faymonville was but one of a number of guests.[67]

Thus, it was probably not as a result of his assignment as military aide, but rather a consequence of his entire military career, that Faymonville came to the attention of Ambassador Bullitt as he sought to staff his embassy in Moscow. In January 1934, Bullitt wrote the president: "If you wish, our military and naval men can play the part of an advisory military mission. If we send men who will be absolutely on the level with the Soviet Government and will refrain from spying and dirty tricks of every variety we can establish a relationship which may be useful in the future."[68] Faymonville seemed to Bullitt to be the natural choice.[69] So Faymonville traveled to Moscow, where his primary role was to establish cordial relations with the Soviet government and military.

Faymonville carried out this mission with zeal and efficiency. Fluent in Russian and eager to work with his Soviet counterparts, he soon established close and friendly relations with them. To foster these relationships, Faymonville tried to distance himself from the Foreign Service officers in the embassy and the nasty negotiations over the details of the recognition agreements continuing between the embassy staff and Soviet officials.[70] This apparent preference for Soviet over American company engendered a great deal of hostility among the other embassy personnel. Bohlen summed up the general feeling among the Foreign Service officers: "The weak link in the staff was the chief military attaché, Colonel Philip R. Faymonville, a slender, pink-faced man with a fringe of white hair who had a definite pro-Russian bias."[71]

Despite the assumptions of his Foreign Service colleagues, Faymonville's "pro-Russian bias" did not hinder his ability to report on Soviet military developments in the 1930s.[72] In contrast to the State Department experts' opinions of Soviet intentions and abilities and in conformity with the views of Ambassador Davies, Faymonville sent more optimistic reports back to the United States. He diligently reported the impressive development of the Red Army in the early 1930s as it adopted mechanized warfare and deep battle doctrine, and he noted the damage Stalin did to the Red Army during the purges. However, unlike most foreign observers, in Faymonville's opinion, the Red Army was damaged by the purges of its officers, but not irreparably. It still retained a significant *defensive* capacity. More importantly, given the global conditions at the time, the Red Army remained a valuable potential ally. Faymonville believed it would take several years to rebuild it to its earlier condition, but that the Red Army was capable of it. Consequently, Faymonville continued to believe in, and continued to advocate, cooperation with the Soviet Union to help protect world peace and the United States' interests.

Although they could not silence this dissent within the embassy, the resident diplomats—including Henderson, who was serving as chargé d'affaires for periods while Davies was out of the Soviet Union—took great care to ensure that the U.S. government knew Faymonville was almost alone in his opinion. Henderson sent a report to the Department of State directly contradicting the reports sent by Faymonville and attributing his own assessments to "the consensus of opinion of competent observers here."[73] Unlike Faymonville, the professional diplomats who did not relish the idea of cooperating with the Soviet Union before the devastation of the purges saw even less use in cooperating with Moscow now that Stalin had decimated his military.

This small dispute marked the beginning of what would become a significant clash between Faymonville and Henderson during the early years of Soviet-American wartime cooperation. Henderson and the Foreign Service officers saw Faymonville and Davies as a team that was dangerously pro-Soviet. These professional diplomats continued to view the Soviet Union as untrustworthy and incapable of functioning normally within the "family of civilized nations." Faymonville and Davies, in contrast, believed the United States must strive to work for cooperation with the Soviet Union. In their opinions, the Soviet Union was capable of playing a vital balancing role for peace in Europe and the Far East, and was not inherently opposed to playing such a role.

The Changing of the Guard and the Failure of Détente

By 1937 it appeared that Faymonville and Davies' shared vision would shape the development of the U.S. policy toward the Soviet Union. Recognizing the Soviet Union was not Roosevelt's final act in his struggle with America's career diplomats. It was merely an opening salvo in a struggle that continued throughout Roosevelt's first term and into his second. Another episode in that conflict occurred in 1937 when the State Department amalgamated the Eastern European Affairs Division and the Western European Affairs Division into a new Division of European Affairs. Kelley was transferred to Ankara, Turkey, where he no longer directed the State Department's analysis of Soviet policy. Although Roosevelt never made clear his motivation for the department's reorganization, it is reasonable to assume that the president hoped to minimize resistance to his Soviet policy. At the very least, the Soviet experts now subordinated to general European affairs certainly perceived the amalgamation as a threat to their expertise. As a result, whatever Roosevelt's intention, this episode became another chapter in the struggle between the bureaucrats and the president over U.S. policy toward the Soviet Union.[74]

As dramatic as the abolition of the Division of Eastern European Affairs and the exile of Kelley may have appeared, its practical impact was much less gratifying to Roosevelt and the proponents of friendlier relations with Moscow. The 1937 State Department reorganization left untouched the lower levels of the bureaucracy, including the staff of the embassy in Moscow. Although the reforms forced the former members of the Division of Eastern European Affairs to emerge from their "insularity," the Foreign Service officers in Moscow were becoming an even tighter-knit group. Together they endured life and work in Moscow during the worst years of Stalin's terror, and together they developed a common view of the nature of the Soviet regime. In their view, it was a regime whose fundamental precepts were diametrically opposed to those of the United States.[75] This view competed with the perceptions of Davies and Faymonville for influence with policy makers in Washington.

By the end of the decade, however, the policy analyses and recommendations emanating from Moscow were solely those of the career diplomats. Although he had taken a keen interest in the Soviet Union and had become vital to Roosevelt's ability to assess Soviet policy, Davies had never intended to remain in the Soviet Union for long. Recently married to the wealthy socialite

Marjorie Post, Davies had in fact hoped for a more prestigious (and comfortable) assignment that both he and his bride could enjoy. Although his hopes for a plum assignment in Berlin or Paris came to naught, Davies accepted the position of ambassador to Belgium and minister to Luxembourg in 1938, where he remained until November 1939.[76]

Although no longer ambassador to the Soviet Union, Davies maintained an interest in Soviet affairs and the development of relations between the United States and the Soviet Union. On the latter account, Stalin gave the departing ambassador much to think of when he surprised Davies during a farewell call on Premier Vyacheslav Molotov. In this meeting, the Soviet dictator brought up several issues of common interest to the countries, including the nagging difficulties of the Kerinsky debt.[77] Although nothing significant came of this meeting, Davies was reassured that his perceptions of the Soviet Union and Stalin were not wrong.

The importance of Davies' continued interest and goodwill was foreshadowed soon after his departure. Struggling with domestic policy and the growing force of isolationism at home, Roosevelt did not immediately replace Davies in Moscow. For the remainder of 1938 and much of 1939, the U.S. embassy in Moscow was run by a career Foreign Service officer, Alexander Kirk, as chargé d'affaires. Faymonville remained the sole voice calling for increased cooperation with the Soviet Union in the struggle to ensure peace in Europe and Asia. Faymonville, although earning the respect and friendship of his Soviet counterparts, had earned the enmity of many of his American colleagues. The War Department's Military Intelligence Division had determined that Faymonville's reports were of little use and that he had been tainted by his pro-Soviet feelings. In 1939, when his second tour of duty in Moscow expired (Davies had intervened earlier to gain Faymonville an extension as military attaché), the army decided to order him back to the United States.[78]

Davies considered Faymonville's attitudes and assessments vital for the further development of U.S.-Soviet relations, and, despite the fact that he was no longer ambassador to the Soviet Union, he requested that Faymonville be granted yet another extension. The matter made it as far as Roosevelt before it concluded. Roosevelt informed Davies that he saw no reason why Faymonville should not comply with the War Department orders returning him to the United States.[79]

Consequently, in what would prove to be the most significant time period leading up to the outbreak of World War II—the months between the capitulation of Britain and France in Munich in September 1938 and the signing of the Nazi-Soviet pact in August 1939—the White House was dependent on the interpretations of Kelley's Soviet experts for analyses of Soviet intentions and capabilities. With the removal of Davies and Faymonville from Moscow, the voices attesting to the importance of the Soviet Union and the possibility of cooperating with the Kremlin were momentarily silenced. In their absence, Roosevelt's policy in Moscow would be carried out and influenced by diplomats and officers who thought it foolhardy to trust or cooperate with the Soviet Union. The struggle between a president who tried to shape foreign policy independently of career foreign policy officials, and those officials with expertise in Soviet affairs, would continue to define the formulation of United States–Soviet relations throughout Roosevelt's presidency.

From Munich to Barbarossa

Changes in International Relations

The years 1938 and 1939 marked a sea change in the struggle for peace in the world as the balance of power and correlation of forces in European politics swung precariously between the democratic powers of France and Britain and the emerging fascist threats of Germany and Italy. Both the Soviet Union and the United States struggled to adapt to these rapidly changing circumstances. For the Kremlin, the basic aim of ensuring the security of the Soviet state remained the same, but the strategy adopted to achieve that aim changed. This alteration would have a profound impact on the relationship between the Soviet Union and the United States.

The End of Collective Security

Soviet efforts to create a collective security system faced increasing difficulties as the decade progressed. German aggression became more apparent with the remilitarization of the Rhineland in 1936, an occasion that revealed British and French unwillingness to stand firm against Germany. The outbreak of the Spanish civil war in 1936 also contributed to the unstable situation by driving a wedge between the Soviet Union and Germany and fueling mistrust between the Soviet Union, Britain, and France. Finally, the failure of the League of Nations to oppose effectively Italy's war against Abyssinia (Ethiopia) intensified Moscow's fear that the western powers were maneuvering for a pact with Germany against the Soviet Union. Although not prepared to abandon the idea of "collective security," the Soviets became more wary of British and French aims.[1]

The death knell of Soviet efforts to establish a collective security system was sounded at Munich in September 1938. For some time Hitler had been claiming the right to protect the German populations in the Austrian and Czechoslovak border areas. In March 1938 Hitler's claims led to the German annexation of Austria. Hitler then shifted his attentions to the Sudetenland, a province of Czechoslovakia bordering Germany and containing a significant German minority. After several months of progressively more speeches and propaganda about the Sudeten Germans, at the Nuremberg Rally in September 1938, Hitler announced his support for Sudeten German autonomy.

France and the Soviet Union had mutual assistance pacts with the Prague government. Thus, they were interested in the resolution of the dispute. The Soviet Union was perhaps more interested because of long-standing ties with its fellow Slavs, and because Czechoslovakia fell within an area of Soviet security interests. Regardless of the reason, however, the Soviet Union intended to uphold its obligations to Czechoslovakia, and Moscow let the United Kingdom, France, and Czechoslovakia know this, even going so far as to mobilize approximately ninety divisions.[2] After receiving the first proposal from the British and French governments (calling for Prague to surrender those Sudeten areas with a majority German population), the Soviet Union informed Czechoslovak President Eduard Benes that it would fulfill its obligations under the mutual assistance agreement and support a Czechoslovak appeal for aid in the League.[3] The British and the French were not interested, however, and re-presented their proposals to Benes in the form of an ultimatum. Although Prague accepted these stringent conditions, Hitler did not. As a result, and notwithstanding Soviet interest in the situation, on 29–30 September 1938, French Premier Eduard Daladier, Italian Prime Minister Benito Mussolini, U.K. Prime Minister Neville Chamberlain, and Hitler met in Munich—without the Soviets or the Czechs—to discuss the fate of the Sudetenland. After two days of negotiations, they had decided it: all of the Sudetenland was to be given to Germany for annexation.

Upon his return to Britain, Chamberlain made his infamous declaration of "peace in our time." The Soviets, however, believed that British and French appeasement at Munich guaranteed that Hitler could no longer be stopped by the threat of war alone. The immediate Soviet response to the Munich events was a retreat into isolationism as the Kremlin considered its foreign policy options. That retreat would end, however, with the German occupation of the Bohemian section of Czechoslovakia in March 1939. As the historian Geoffrey Roberts points out, in the spring of 1939 the Soviet Union would not abandon cooperation with Britain and France, but they would abandon their failed policy of collective security. Believing war now inevitable, Moscow chose to pursue a policy of collective *defense* toward Britain and France—that is, the creation of military-defensive alliances with the two western European powers.[4] The Kremlin had not yet decided on the appropriate policy to pursue toward Germany.

Soviet-German Rapprochement

The Soviet search for an alternative to collective security coincided with a period during which the United States did not have an ambassador in Moscow. From Davies' departure in July 1938 until August 1939, the U.S. embassy in Moscow was headed by a chargé d'affaires. Both the United States and the Soviet Union adopted a wait-and-see attitude toward one another.

For a variety of reasons, Roosevelt in 1938 felt constrained in his relations with the Soviet Union. One reason for this was that as Europe moved closer to war, isolationism became stronger in the United States and in the U.S. Congress. This was evident in a series of neutrality acts beginning in 1935. Roosevelt was concerned about war in Europe, yet he felt it necessary to move cautiously in any statements and actions he made about the war. The need for caution was made painfully clear after the president made his famous "quarantine speech" of 5 October 1937. Democratic party leaders received the speech in silence, while the opposition expressed outrage.[5] As Roosevelt purportedly observed, "It's a terrible thing to look over your shoulder when you are trying to lead—and find no one there."[6] Roosevelt was aware that the United States would have to play a role in either the prevention of war or the prosecution of it, but he was also certain that before that was possible, he had to garner the support of the American public.[7] Assuming a leading or even vocal role in Europe threatened to undercut that support. At the same time, the idea of a "partnership for peace" with the Soviet Union would alienate many potential supporters in the United States who were wary of or hostile to the Soviet Union in the light of developments in the 1930s.

Throughout the period 1938–41, U.S. policy toward the Soviet Union reflected Roosevelt's need to walk a political and diplomatic tightrope. In the first year of this period, as the Soviet Union searched for options in Europe and took a wait-and-see approach toward the United States, U.S. policy reflected a similar ambiguity. Roosevelt's failure at first to identify a new ambassador and his eventual selection of Laurence Steinhardt for the post reveal the president's unwillingness to pursue any particular course at this point.

Even without these foreign policy inhibitions, Roosevelt was constrained by broader domestic events. A variety of factors combined to threaten his New Deal agenda. The 1937 court-packing scandal weakened Roosevelt's political power and sparked a break with the progressive isolationists, who had been important to his 1936 reelection. Autumn 1937 also marked the beginning of a new economic recession in the United States. The economy failed to improve, taking a sharp downturn in March 1938.[8] This contributed to the growing opposition to the New Deal from both the left and the right. That opposition was strengthened by a poor Democratic showing in the congressional elections of 1938. It was apparent to Roosevelt that if he continued to push his New Deal program, the Democrats risked losing the White House in 1940. Roosevelt responded to these developments by forging closer ties with the urban business and financial community and with conservative southern Democrats, the proponents of internationalism in the Democratic party. At the same time, he shifted his focus from his embattled domestic agenda to foreign affairs.[9] Roosevelt began incrementally to break free from the constraints of isolationism.[10]

Meanwhile, the Soviet Union actively explored other international avenues to safeguard its security. One of the more promising roads, at least early in 1939, involved cooperation with the United Kingdom and France. A 31 March British guarantee of Polish sovereignty was soon followed by Germany's denunciation of the German-Polish nonaggression pact at the end of April. Apparently the next German move would be toward the east, closer to the Soviet frontier. Thus, German aggression posed a threat not only to the western democracies, but also to Soviet communism.

At the same time, the Soviet Union was threatened in the Far East. Japanese expansion into China following the outbreak of a Sino-Japanese war in 1937 brought them into closer contact with the Soviet border. That contact exploded into combat at Lake Khasan in mid-1938 and Khalkin Gol in spring and summer 1939. Soviet successes in these encounters did not significantly reduce the menace to the Soviet Far East.[11] This threat had been particularly pressing since 17 November 1936, when Japan joined Germany and Italy in the anti-Comintern pact. As a result of this agreement, the Soviet Union faced the danger of a two-front war. As 1939 progressed, therefore, the prevention of a situation in which the USSR would be pressed from both east and west became a high priority for the Kremlin.

Domestic events heightened the danger of the two-front war. Years of collectivization, forced industrialization, and purges had taken their toll on Soviet society and the organs charged with securing the regime. In a massive purge of his military, Stalin decimated the Red Army, laying waste to most of its leaders and their innovations, which had made the Red Army a powerful military and valuable potential ally.[12] Even the most optimistic estimates from foreign observers stressed that the Red Army would require time to rebuild before it would again be an effective military force. Most foreign observers, however, felt that the Soviet Union would be unable to reconstruct its damaged armed forces in time to be a factor in any current or near-future calculations of the balance of forces in Europe. Events from 1941–1945 would prove the more optimistic assessments correct, but, unfortunately for Stalin, perceptions mattered more than reality in the world of the 1930s. Perceived Soviet weakness and entrenched anticommunist prejudices led the western democracies to devalue the possibility of cooperation with the Soviet Union.[13]

Consequently, Soviet negotiations with the United Kingdom and France dragged on for months with little result. The United Kingdom and France underestimated potential Soviet contributions to a military alliance, and the Soviet Union, still reeling from the Munich agreement, regarded any British or French promises with skepticism. The Soviets wanted a concrete military treaty guaranteeing their security, but it seemed (at least from the Soviet perspective) that the British and French were not serious about such a treaty. The British and French military delegations literally traveled by slow boat to the Soviet Union. They were made up of members low in rank and status, who lacked the power to sign an agreement with the Soviets. Britain and France had no operational or strategic plans for a joint war against Germany, and in any case provided only relatively small forces for mobilization. In addition, the two countries were reluctant to press Romania and Poland to grant the USSR a right of passage across their territories.[14] Finally, the Soviets were receiving other indications that the western allies were hesitant to sign an agreement with them. On 14 July British parliamentarian Lloyd George told Maisky that Chamberlain was continuing his efforts to appease Hitler and was delaying any agreement with the Soviets.[15] It was unknown to British and French negotiators, however, that Moscow was looking to places other than the western democracies for its security guarantees.

In spring 1939 Germany approached the Soviet Union about the possibility of improving relations between the two countries.[16] Stalin's primary aims were to prevent a two-front war and to secure the breathing space he needed to rebuild the strength of his state. If the British and French governments were unwilling to provide that, an agreement with Germany would suit these exclusively defensive aims just as well. An agreement with the United Kingdom and France would have left the Soviet Union in much the same position as Russia in 1914. In contrast, an agreement with Germany meant that in the event of war, Germany would turn west and face off against Britain and France, while the Soviet Union gained valuable time to rebuild its military forces.[17] In addition, a good relationship with Germany might offer the opportunity to persuade Japan to stop pressing on the Soviet Far Eastern frontier. Stalin also perceived definite advantages accruing to his military-industrial complex through increased trade with Germany.[18] Recently released documents from the Stalin Archive indicate that Stalin was interested in the possibility of increasing trade with Germany to strengthen Soviet defensive capabilities. In January 1939 the Politburo of the Central Committee of the Communist Party of the Soviet Union ordered several officials to produce a list of "absolutely necessary machine-tools and other types of equipment which could be ordered on German credits."[19]

The replacement of Litvinov by Vyacheslav Molotov on 3 May 1939 signaled a new development in German-Soviet relations. Recognizing Litvinov as the author and chief advocate of Moscow's collective security policy, historians have traditionally considered his dismissal a sign of a change in Kremlin policy.[20] Other historians have challenged this assessment, however, arguing that Litvinov's removal was the result of domestic political developments.[21] In contrast to the traditional interpretation, some have even contended that Molotov's replacement of Litvinov represented a renewed Soviet commitment to agreement with France and Britain.[22] Whatever the reason for Litvinov's replacement, he was viewed as the chief Soviet proponent of collective security. In addition, he was Jewish, and his replacement by Molotov was perceived in Germany as a signal of increasing Soviet openness to German approaches.[23] German-Soviet negotiations continued throughout the spring and summer of 1939, resulting in late August in the announcement of the German-Soviet nonaggression pact. In addition to the published terms of the agreement, the pact included secret terms under which the Soviet Union acquired a significant sphere of influence in eastern Europe (including eastern Poland, Latvia, Lithuania, Estonia, Finland, and Bessarabia). While enforcing this sphere of influence constituted de facto territorial expansion, the primary (perhaps exclusive) focus of Stalin's foreign policy at this point was on increasing Soviet security.[24]

On 1 September 1939, a few days after the announcement of the pact, Germany invaded Poland, initiating World War II. Less than a month later, on 17 September, the Soviet Union invaded and occupied the eastern half of Poland. Stalin had gained his valuable space. All that remained was to see if he had gained enough time.

Observing and Assessing the Soviets

UNITED STATES STATE DEPARTMENT AND EMBASSY IN MOSCOW

These developments coincided with the arrival in Moscow of the United States' new ambassador, Laurence Steinhardt. Like Bullitt and Davies, Steinhardt was not a career diplomat. A lawyer by vocation, Steinhardt acquired his first diplomatic post, minister to Sweden, as a reward for his hard work in Roosevelt's presidential campaign. He enjoyed the work in Sweden so much that he decided to make a career in the Foreign Service, and he was pleased when in 1937 Roosevelt named him ambassador to Peru. It was his excellent work in Sweden and Peru that led Steinhardt to the ambassadorship in Moscow.[25]

By the time he arrived in Moscow on 8 August 1939, Steinhardt was well acquainted with the issues surrounding United States–Soviet relations. Before assuming his post, he prepared himself by conscientiously reading the voluminous correspondence between the State Department and its diplomats in Moscow.[26] These communications vividly illustrated the injustices, slights, and indignities meted out by the Kremlin to the diplomatic community, and they often contrasted with the situation enjoyed by Soviet diplomats in the United States. This situation caught Steinhardt's attention. Even before he departed for the Soviet Union, he resolved to place United States–Soviet interactions on a reciprocal basis.[27]

The need for reciprocity in Soviet-American relations was not the only conclusion Steinhardt reached before assuming his post. In June he received several letters from the Soviet Union that had obviously been opened and read, presumably by officials of the Soviet government. Steinhardt was clearly displeased by this action, seeing it as further evidence of the need to begin treating Soviet officials as the Soviets were treating Americans.[28]

Thus, unlike his two predecessors, Steinhardt did not arrive in Moscow giddy with the possibility of cordial, even friendly, United States–Soviet relations. Nevertheless, he did not share the vehemently anti-Soviet attitude that Bullitt had developed by the end of his tour in Moscow. In fact, Steinhardt became so bogged down in the day-to-day details of United States–Soviet interaction (he was described as "the best consul who ever came to Moscow") that he often did not consider the nature of the broader U.S.-Soviet relationship at all.[29]

Dealing with the daily issues of living and working in the Soviet Union was certainly enough to keep one occupied. The Soviet government had not become any more sensitive to the position of foreign diplomats in Moscow than it had been during Bullitt's tenure as ambassador. Consequently, the U.S.

embassy and Ambassador Steinhardt were plagued with constant difficulties that prejudiced the ambassador's view of the Soviet Union.[30] Some difficulties, like the weather, housing shortages, office space, food availability, Soviet currency exchange rates, and isolation from Soviet citizens, were common to all diplomats in Moscow. But Steinhardt also dealt with some issues of particular concern to the United States.

Of continual concern to Steinhardt were frequent Soviet violations of the Litvinov-Roosevelt agreement on U.S. citizens arrested in the Soviet Union. Steinhardt was also upset by unreasonable Soviet customs practices. The U.S. government was extending customs courtesies to Soviet officials in the United States that were clearly not being granted to American diplomats and officials in the Soviet Union. When the embassy surgeon, Dr. Walter Nelson, planned to leave the Soviet Union, the embassy requested that a Soviet customs official visit the doctor's apartment (because his baggage included sterilized surgical supplies and equipment). Soviet officials refused, despite the fact that similar courtesies were regularly granted in the United States.

Steinhardt saw the perfect opportunity to implement his policy of reciprocity when the Soviet Foreign Commissariat requested that the Soviet steamer *Kim* be allowed to pass through the Panama Canal without the required bill of health. Steinhardt sent Hull a telegram requesting that, in light of the Soviet response to Dr. Nelson's request, the *Kim* not be granted a waiver.[31] Loy Henderson, now serving at the State Department's Division of European Affairs, supported Steinhardt's position.[32] Hull agreed to detain the *Kim,* and on 2 September 1939 Steinhardt reported that the Soviets had agreed to conduct the inspection of Nelson's goods in his apartment.[33] The Nelson-*Kim* affair served as convincing evidence to Steinhardt that his principle of reciprocity was the right approach to take in United States–Soviet relations.[34]

Repeatedly throughout the next two years, Steinhardt would find ample reassurance that reciprocity was working. Just one month after the Nelson-*Kim* affair, Steinhardt assured the American minister to the Baltic states, John Wiley, that Soviet refusal to allow the U.S. embassy in Moscow to export gasoline to the U.S. Mission in Riga would result in "retaliation." Expounding on his effective tactics, Steinhardt explained to Wiley, "While on the subject of retaliation I might say to you that I have found that it works magnificently— the results thus far have been a hundred per cent and 'believe me' I am an expert retaliator."[35] This would become the leitmotif of Steinhardt's personal correspondence throughout the remainder of his service in the Soviet Union. As each incident served to convince Steinhardt of either the success of his tactics or the need for them, he became more committed to this policy. He was persuasive in his advocacy; his colleagues in the State Department came to share his conviction that the Soviet Union only responded to tit-for-tat policies. Roosevelt even found an opportunity to suggest retaliation for Soviet restrictions on the U.S. embassy's long-distance phone calls.[36] Perhaps if Soviet-American relations had been limited to these routine interactions, Steinhardt's policy would have remained U.S. policy toward the Soviet Union. The role of the Soviet Union in European and world affairs became increasingly important, however, and drew the attention of U.S. diplomats and policy makers away from the indignities and injustices that demanded so much of Steinhardt's attention.

The fact that Steinhardt based his policy of retaliation on the details of routine diplomatic interaction did not mean that the ambassador was not interested in grander diplomacy. Arriving in the Soviet Union as Soviet-German relations culminated in the Soviet-German pact, Steinhardt considered the pact a poignant example of why the Soviets could not be trusted. He believed that the Soviet Union was never negotiating with Britain in good faith and that Russia was "in full alliance with Germany in this war."[37]

These views fit in well with the dominant view among the State Department's Soviet experts. American diplomats carefully watched developments in the Soviet Union's relations with other states, and, for the most part, what they observed confirmed their long-held views of the nature of Soviet foreign policy.[38] Thanks to a well-placed source in the German embassy, the United States was aware that throughout the summer of 1939 the Kremlin was negotiating with Germany as well as with Britain and France. This no doubt reinforced the prevailing conception of Soviet duplicity held by American observers in the U.S. embassy in Moscow as they questioned whether the Soviet Union really desired an agreement with the British at all. From their perspective, Britain was willing to compromise on a key sticking point: the Baltic states. Yet the Soviet Union still quibbled. These doubts were shared by Henderson in the State Department's Division of European Affairs in Washington.[39] When the Molotov-Ribbentrop pact was announced on 23 August 1939, Henderson and the other diplomats' most pessimistic assessments of Soviet intentions seemed to be confirmed. To these observers, it appeared obvious that the "tactics of the united front," which the State Department's Soviet experts had never believed really existed, were dropped as the Soviet Union "returned to the old slogan of converting imperialist wars into class wars."[40] The conclusion of the agreement between Germany and the Soviet Union made most American diplomats more suspicious of and even more bitter toward the Soviet Union. That bitterness was especially evident in correspondence from Wiley, who speculated that the Soviet-German pact would have little impact on the international situation because the Soviets were barely capable of helping themselves, much less of providing aid to friends and allies.[41]

The perceptions of U.S. diplomats were flawed on many levels. Most fundamentally, they failed to perceive that the conclusion of the Nazi-Soviet pact was in many ways the consequence of a self-fulfilling prophecy. American diplomats shared with their French and British counterparts a distrust of and distaste for the Soviet regime. This anti-Bolshevism led them to discount the possibility of the Soviet Union as a partner. As a result, they hesitated to negotiate in completely good faith.[42] Consequently, the Soviet Union dropped the tactics of the united front because they seemed to be failing, thereby placing them in ever increasing danger of a two-front war.

American, British, and French diplomats also underestimated the worth of the Soviet Union as an ally. Rejecting the interpretations of Davies and Faymonville, the U.S. diplomatic corps and military attachés relied on the interpretation of others in the diplomatic community. The U.S. assistant military attaché, Ivan Yeaton, found the interpretations of the German military attaché particularly useful.[43] Yeaton's strong bias against the Soviets was indicated by his acceptance of the German's contention that the Soviets were not worthy allies. It does not seem to have occurred to the young American officer to inquire why, then, the Germans sought an alliance with Moscow.[44]

Questions of Soviet competence, however, took a decided second place to the issue of Soviet perfidy in the minds of American officials in Moscow in winter 1939–1940. The Soviet invasion of Poland later in September 1939 and the *City of Flint* incident, in which Soviet officials refused to allow American diplomats to visit the crew of an American ship captured by Germany and towed to a Soviet port, confirmed the diplomats' beliefs in the impossibility of trusting Stalin. Every Soviet action seemed to be drawing the Kremlin into closer collaboration with Berlin. Soviet demands for mutual assistance treaties with, and military bases in, the Baltic states of Estonia, Latvia, and Lithuania throughout September and October 1939 hinted at Soviet revanchism and a "return to Rapallo" in Soviet-German relations.[45] These developments spurred greater antipathy toward the Soviet Union in the United States Foreign Service. Observing events from Riga, Wiley wrote to Henderson, "I must say that, having been utterly convinced that the Kremlin was populated by apes and the Narkomindel [Foreign Ministry] by their lowly parasites, I have been taken aback with awestruck admiration by the brilliance of Soviet diplomatic maneuvering."[46]

Former Ambassador Bullitt was no more restrained in his criticism of Soviet foreign policy, or, as he referred to it, the policy of the "world's ultimate swine": "I still consider that the so-called Soviet Government is a conspiracy to commit murder and nothing else. The Soviet Union is the base from which the conspirators operate and nothing else. . . . I think Stalin intends to eat like a cancer into Europe so long as the war goes on. . . . A Bolshevik *Welt Macht* directed from Moscow is, I think, his aim."[47]

Another blow to those who hoped for Soviet–United States cooperation fell on 30 November 1939, when the Soviet Union attacked Finland, beginning the Winter War of December 1939 to March 1940. This naked aggression against "small Finland" outraged many in the United States. Foreign Service officers who had always been wary of the Soviet Union found reassurance in the American reaction to the war. Henderson was pleased that he saw anti-Soviet feeling in the United States "fully as strong as anti-German" feeling and observed that finally, "the American people are really commencing to understand something about the Soviet Union."[48] In fact, Henderson was surprised, or at the very least smugly self-assured, at the strength of U.S. indignation toward the Soviet Union. As he pointed out in a letter to Charles "Chip" Bohlen in Moscow, Henderson found Soviet actions since the Nazi-Soviet pact fully in accord with past Soviet "habits and mentality." To those who were familiar with the Soviets, Henderson argued, "It was . . . just the same old Soviet Union."[49]

Steinhardt was one of those outraged by Soviet action against Finland. Unlike the State Department's Soviet experts, Steinhardt had no significant experience in Moscow during the 1930s. His earlier diplomatic experience had been in Peru and in Sweden. Steinhardt's experience in Sweden, though, may have helped to shape his reaction to the Russo-Finnish war: he was very sympathetic to the plight of the Finns.[50] But sympathy for the Finns was not the only reaction Steinhardt had to the war. He also concluded that Soviet military performance against Finland indicated that Soviet military effectiveness was "lower than even the most pessimistic evaluation."[51] Further, he believed the combination of the dismal Soviet performance in Finland and the diplomatic reaction against the Soviet Union had pushed the Soviets into a greater degree of reliance on German friendship.[52] According to the ambassador, Stalin was interested in imperialist, territorial expansion and was "leaning heavily on the German alliance." Steinhardt argued that the U.S. government should expect Soviet-German cooperation to continue.[53] He would maintain this position throughout 1940 and into spring 1941, dispatching to the State Department observations that would please Henderson and lead Bullitt (observing events from the embassy in Paris) to become one of Steinhardt's "ardent admirers."[54]

Steinhardt's attitude became more jaded as a result of the constant tension and hostility felt by U.S. diplomats living and working in the Soviet capital. As the global situation, Soviet policy, and U.S. policy evolved throughout 1940 and 1941, Steinhardt found himself increasingly unable to adapt. He remained deeply committed to his belief that the Soviets "need us a great deal more than we need them and as the only language they understand is the language of force I think it high time we invoked the only doctrine they respect [Steinhardt's doctrine of reciprocity]."[55]

Henderson and others in the State Department continued to share Steinhardt's opinions. As a result, they continued to emphasize that the Soviet regime could not be trusted. In an October 1940 survey of Soviet-American relations, the State Department's Division of European Affairs enumerated the instances when the Soviet Union had broken its word in dealings with the United States and other powers. Stressing that the leaders of the Soviet Union have "never departed from their ultimate aim to enlarge their domain and to include under the Soviet system additional people and territories," the author of the report concluded that "it becomes apparent that no action or policy should be based upon the word of the Kremlin, however solemnly pledged."[56]

Until the very eve of the Soviet-German war, officials in the State Department proclaimed the futility of attempting to cooperate with the Soviet Union. When they were not arguing that the Soviets could not be trusted, they were arguing that the regime would not survive a German invasion.[57] The conclusion to be drawn from their advice was inescapable: regardless of the course of Soviet-German relations, the United States should not pursue a partnership with the Kremlin.

MILITARY ASSESSMENTS AND OBSERVATIONS

The U.S. government's military observers shared their State Department colleagues' views of the Soviet Union. The War Department and the Military Intelligence Division of G-2's assessments of Soviet capabilities and intentions were provided by the military attachés in Moscow. After Faymonville's departure from military attaché duty in Moscow in 1939, this responsibility fell primarily to the new military attaché, Major Frank Hayne, and his successors, Major Ivan Yeaton and Captain Joseph Michela. Unfortunately for U.S. military intelligence, for a variety of reasons, Faymonville's successors would prove to be less than capable of the exceptional analyses he had provided.

The quality of military attachés in general was not outstanding in the interwar period. The position of attaché was often viewed as a career dead end, and most ambitious officers chose to pursue commands that would lead to their promotion.[58] The financial situations of military attachés also restricted the number of officers who could consider accepting the assignment. Attachés frequently served in areas with very high costs of living, and they did not receive any cost-of-living adjustment in their salary. In practice, this meant that many officers were selected on the basis of income rather than ability.[59] The position of attaché to the Soviet Union in the late 1930s was complicated by the relatively recent development of a program to train U.S. Army officers in the Russian language. Only when it became apparent to military officials that they would need a military attaché in the Soviet Union did they establish a training program.[60]

It is unclear why Yeaton and his classmates were selected for training. Perhaps it was because Yeaton, like Faymonville, had served in the American Expeditionary Force in Siberia from 1919 to 1920. Whereas Faymonville left Siberia convinced of the legitimacy of the Bolshevik regime, Yeaton returned to the United States impressed by the communists' disregard for human life.[61] In July 1936 the U.S. Army ordered Yeaton to report to the University of California, Berkeley, for a quick course in the Russian language. His classmates included Michela and Hayne. The three developed similar interpretations of the Soviet Union, its policies, and its capabilities.[62]

Even before departing for his new post, Yeaton was vigilant against spying and other Soviet trickery. A 1939 meeting in New York City with Faymonville convinced Yeaton that his predecessor was a dangerous tool of the Soviets; Yeaton believed that he would have to guard against falling into the same trap, or allowing other Americans to do so.[63] It was thus clear from the beginning of his tenure as attaché that Yeaton saw himself in an adversarial position to the Soviet Union.

In a 1940 report analyzing the impact on discipline in the Red Army of the Soviet abolition of the dual command system (military commander and political commissar sharing responsibility), Yeaton concluded that the reform would have little influence, given the broader social environment in which the Red Army existed:

> The question of lack of discipline in the Soviet Union is, however, a more far reaching one than just that which alone concerns the armed forces. Lack of discipline among the children seems to this observer to be the basic cause of this widespread fault. . . .
>
> Not only are the children without the proper supervision but they see in their elders thousands of examples daily of complete disregard for authority. Militia, trying to enforce the new law against jaywalking put into effect on January 1st, 1940, are, after six months, still frantically blowing their whistles and being generally ignored.[64]

In Yeaton's view, this disrespect for authority must be reflected in the nation's military. Moreover, Yeaton believed the lack of discipline that this disdain for authority reflected had causes that ran much deeper than command structure. In this same report, he outlined what those causes were and what was required to overcome them:

> For months the actions of the population of both city and villages have been closely observed and it is apparent that from a social standpoint the people of this country form one of the most backward societies on earth. . . .
>
> In conclusion, it is believed that even though the armed forces have special buying privileges, that until *living conditions* as a whole are *greatly improved* within the Soviet Union, it will be impossible to create a high state of morale and discipline in the Red Army.[65] [emphasis in the original]

Yeaton's conclusions regarding the Red Fleet were essentially identical:

> The external and internal forces adversely affecting the morale and discipline in the Red Fleet are numerous. The most important are: (a) a backward society trying to adapt itself to a modern technique; (b) the constant secret supervision by the N.K.V.D. . . . ; (c) the deplorable living conditions of the population in the cities and villages; (d) the widespread lack of discipline and supervision during adolescence; and (e) the lack of unhampered and skilled leaders.[66]

Yeaton's analyses of the combat potential of the Red Army and Fleet were absolutely vital in 1940 and 1941 as the United States weighed the value of the Soviet Union as a potential ally against Germany. In Yeaton's opinion, there was little value in a partnership with the Soviet Union. As late as April 1941 he reported that "it is believed that it [the Red Army] can hold out for three months at the most."[67]

Yeaton's views were shared by his assistant military attaché and eventual successor, Joseph Michela. In a June 1941 report entitled "Characteristics of the Population," Michela focused on a "description of the national character of the U.S.S.R." and recommended the policy that should be pursued with the Soviet government:

> A study of the national character of the Soviet Union with hope of predicting reactions under certain external influences only emphasizes the fact that the heterogeneous elements which make up this nation have produced a people which, as a whole, has conflicting impulses. However, out of this conflict emerge two characteristics which affect the entire country—their unreliability and their understanding of force. . . .

The Great Russians are primarily an East Baltic race with a mixture of Nordic and Mongolian blood. . . . They are a short-legged, squatly-built breed with flat noses but light complexion. . . .

The mixture of Nordic and Mongolian bloods has produced a people which has always been an enigma to psychologists. The Asiatic characteristics of resignation, endless patience and small evaluation of life make these people receptive to forceful and even brutal control and is in sharp contrast to the spasmodic emotional outbursts of affection, loyalty, friendliness and hospitality so often encountered by foreigners, past and present. . . .

This country is still a peasant nation. . . . They are incapable of any progressive movement of their own as a whole and wholly incapable of any sustained *voluntary* mental or physical efforts as individuals.[68] [emphasis in the original]

Having completed his assessment of the nature of "the masses" in the Soviet Union, Michela analyzed the ruler of the Soviet Union and recommended the policy that the United States should pursue in dealings with him:

The ruling hierarchy is an ignorant one. It is cunning, shrewd, cruel and unscrupulous. Its policies are based on expediency alone. It has no honor, and an agreement concluded one day will be shamelessly repudiated the next. . . .

This observer is firmly convinced that the approach to any dealings with any members of the present ruling hierarchy, either individually or collectively, including internationally, must be accompanied with a forceful, decisive, blunt and almost rude, and in appropriate cases even contemptuous personal demeanor, which will indicate that business is meant. *Any other approach will be interpreted as a weakness.*[69] [emphasis in the original]

Michela's opinions were also evident in his assessments of the Soviet military. In a report dated 16 June 1941, Michela concludes, "It is difficult to picture an efficient Red Army growing out of a country which is still practically illiterate and mechanically backward."[70]

The real danger of Michela's reports, however, lay not in the undiplomatic, even offensive, language in which they were written. Michela, after all, was not a diplomat; he was a military analyst. The attitude reflected by Michela's language, however, led him seriously to misjudge Soviet military capabilities. Although some of his observations about the readiness of the Red Army were correct, many were flawed. For example, Michela concluded that the Red Army lacked "sufficient heavy modern tanks" and that the medium tanks had "insufficient armament."[71] In fact, Red Army medium and heavy tanks were more numerous than and superior to their German counterparts.[72] Similarly, Michela's conclusion about the state of the Red Army artillery forces was that it had very little modern weaponry.[73] In fact, the Red Army's artillery pieces were modern and equal to the German arsenal.[74]

The most significant reason for the inferiority of their reports was, however, simply their prejudices against everything Soviet. This animosity was accompanied by a disdain that was evident in his official reports and in his unofficial correspondence.[75] The military attachés' unwillingness to read the Soviets' own publications, their inability to observe the military (because of Soviet restrictions), and their own preconceptions regarding Soviet backwardness led to these glaring intelligence failures.[76] The artillery and tanks scorned by Michela would play a significant role in the eventual Soviet victory over Germany. More important, these mistakes reflect the fundamental assumption—that the Soviet Union was backward—that would lead Yeaton and Michela to misjudge the value of the Red Army as a partner against Germany. Obsessed with the "backwardness" of the Soviet Union, they would fail to understand what their predecessor, Faymonville, understood clearly: the Red Army, no matter its current state, possessed a tremendous military *potential.* Given the time to mobilize that potential, the Soviet military system would grind inexorably forward toward victory.[77]

The U.S. government would not learn this from the staff at the U.S. embassy in Moscow in June 1941. As a result of the anti-Soviet bias in all quarters of the U.S. embassy in Moscow, the State and War Departments in Washington were forming a flawed picture of the situation in the Soviet Union.[78] As the war spread in Europe and Asia, the United States struggled to determine what sort of policy it should pursue vis-à-vis the Soviet Union. The military and diplomatic personnel in Moscow had their own ideas about what shape that policy should take, and they did not hesitate to share them. Their ideas were flawed. The toll that their prejudices had taken on their reporting is nowhere more evident than in a report sent by Yeaton on 7 June 1941, a mere two weeks before the German invasion of the Soviet Union: "I am still of the opinion that there is little or no prospect of a Soviet-German conflict at the present time."[79] Even as Yeaton was writing, Roosevelt was turning toward other sources for advice on his Soviet policy.

U.S. POLICY APPROACHES

In the period between August 1939 and summer 1940, the U.S. government, from the president to the diplomats in Moscow, was unhappy with the

Soviet Union and, at most, cautiously optimistic about the future. Despite this hostility, the United States maintained relations with Moscow. As Bullitt had pointed out five years earlier, the U.S. embassy in Moscow was too valuable to close. In addition, it is probable that Roosevelt, despite his anger at the Soviets' actions, understood that the war in Europe would not be resolved satisfactorily without the Soviet Union. In July 1939 Roosevelt met with Faymonville. Although there is no record of the conversation at that meeting, there is little doubt the former attaché would have assured Roosevelt of the value of the Soviet Union in any future war against Germany.[80] This view was buttressed by correspondence from the former ambassador, Joseph Davies, who now served as special assistant to Hull.[81] In the meantime, United States–Soviet relations continued much as they had before the war, with Steinhardt pursuing his reciprocity agenda.

That policy began to change in summer 1941 when, unbeknownst to Steinhardt, the administration initiated a different approach toward the Soviet Union. If in 1939 Roosevelt had suspected that the Soviet Union would be important in a war against Hitler, the events of spring 1940 convinced him of it. In April German armies turned their attention to the west and invaded Norway. In May and June German tank and infantry forces swept through the Low Countries and France. In a few short weeks, the Germans were victorious, and the British Expeditionary Force and what was left of the French Army scrambled to escape through the French port city of Dunkirk. On 18 June 1940 the French asked the Germans for armistice negotiations; on 22 June the French capitulated. The United Kingdom remained the sole western European country standing against Hitler and Germany. Within a few weeks of the French surrender, Hitler directed his attention and his Luftwaffe across the narrow English Channel and began a concentrated air campaign designed to destroy Britain's defenses and leave it vulnerable to invasion.

As bombs rained down on Britain and Americans tuned their radios each night to Edward R. Murrow's broadcasts from London, the Roosevelt administration began cautious overtures to the Soviets. In summer 1940 Roosevelt instructed Undersecretary of State Sumner Welles to start a discussion with Soviet Ambassador Constantine Oumansky on a variety of issues of interest to both countries. The talks ultimately achieved little, but it was the gesture that was significant. The Roosevelt administration was attempting a rapprochement with the Soviet Union. Despite the fact that Roosevelt used his undersecretary of state as a tool of this policy, the administration's new attitude toward the Soviet Union would lead to the final split between Roosevelt's White House and his State Department and embassy in Moscow.

This new attitude also coincided with developing Soviet policy. In July 1940 Hitler ordered his General Staff to draw up plans for an invasion of the Soviet Union. The Soviets were not aware of this decision, but they were aware of the changing tone of Soviet-German relations. The Soviet Union began a massive buildup and restructuring of its armed forces and the economic/ industrial infrastructure of the state. It also expanded its defensive perimeter, prompting the annexations in northern and southeastern Europe that so enraged the State Department's Soviet analysts. Moscow viewed the Baltic states as the primary corridor for a potential German invasion, and it considered the acquisition of territory from Finland vital for the defense of Leningrad, located less than twenty miles from the Finnish border.[82]

Soviet efforts to increase their security in southeastern Europe included both territorial annexations and diplomatic maneuvering. Negotiations in spring 1941 led to a neutrality agreement with Turkey. Efforts to court Bulgaria were less successful, and Bulgaria joined the anti-Comintern pact and allowed German troops to enter Bulgaria in February–March 1941. Similar negotiations with Yugoslavia also appeared to fail in March 1941, when Yugoslavia decided to join the Axis powers. A coup reversed that development as the military overthrew the regent, Prince Paul, replacing him with King Peter II. The Soviets were quick to support the new Yugoslav government because it did not advocate alliance with Germany and Italy. Fissures in the Soviet-German relationship became more apparent when the Soviets signed a nonaggression pact with Yugoslavia on 5 April, just before the Germans invaded that country on 6 April. After the rapid German victory in Yugoslavia, Stalin resorted to a policy of appeasement of Germany. Beginning with a very friendly public greeting of German Ambassador Schulenberg on 13 April 1941, the Soviet Union made a series of diplomatic gestures toward Germany. On 9 May the Kremlin reversed its earlier position toward Yugoslavia by withdrawing its recognition of the government in exile. At the same time, the Soviet Union continued to avoid any new breach with Berlin. Throughout the spring, trainloads of Soviet materials traveled into Germany, while German planes continued their numerous reconnaissance flights into Soviet airspace unmolested by Soviet antiaircraft defenses.[83] By this point, it was apparent to most observers that the Soviet Union and Germany would go to war; it was just unclear when.

The Eve of Barbarossa

Stalin believed—or hoped—that he had until 1942 to prepare for war with Germany. The United States and the United Kingdom tried, but failed, to disabuse him of that notion. On 1 March 1941 the State Department telegraphed Ambassador Steinhardt and instructed him to deliver to Molotov the following message:

> The government of the U.S., while endeavoring to estimate the developing world situation, have come into the possession of information which it regards as authentic clearly indicating that it is the intention of Germany to attack the Soviet Union in the not distant future. It would appear that the plan to attack the Soviet Union is contingent upon the extent to which England, supported by American endeavor, will be able to oppose not only the military strength but also the economic efforts of Germany.[84]

The State Department informed Steinhardt that he could refuse to deliver the message if he objected to it. Steinhardt exercised that option. On 3 March 1941 Steinhardt explained his objections to the communication:

> The cynical reaction of the Soviet Government to approaches of this character would lead it to regard [the] gesture as neither sincere nor independent, and my visit to Molotov might be made the subject of [a] Tass communiqué or be imparted to the German Government, notwithstanding any previous assurances to the contrary. Furthermore, should the Soviet Government have no advice of its [own?] tending to confirm our information regarding German attack, and especially should developments fail to confirm the information, our action would thereafter be regarded by the Soviets as having been merely an attempt to drive a wedge between the Soviet Union and Germany, at British instigation. On the other hand, should the Soviet Government already possess information of this character, our action would be regarded as confirmatory and might lead to one or more of the following consequences:
>
> It might hasten the conclusion of a Soviet-Japanese political agreement . . .
>
> It might cause the Soviets to consider a deal with Germany at Turkey's expense.
>
> . . . it might tempt the Soviets to consider the occupation of Finland.
>
> It probably would be availed of to justify renewed demands by the Soviet Government on the United States for further concessions and increased assistance.
>
> It might accelerate Soviet assistance to Germany in an endeavor to avoid or postpone a German attack.[85]

In Steinhardt's view, absolutely nothing positive could come of sharing this information with the Kremlin. In this case, the State Department did not share Steinhardt's outlook. In a 1 March meeting with Oumansky, Welles informed the Soviet ambassador of German plans.[86] None of the contingencies feared by Steinhardt came to pass.

Steinhardt's exchange with Washington revealed that knowledge of an imminent Soviet-German war did not change the attitudes that had already developed. Yeaton and Michela continued to dispatch reports denigrating the capabilities of the Red Army and the military value of a relationship with the Soviet Union.[87] Military intelligence assessments within the War Department reflected their reports. In a memorandum for Chief of Staff George C. Marshall dated 19 June 1941, the acting assistant chief of staff, G-2, predicted the following outcome in the event of a Soviet-German war: "A comparison of the size, equipment, training standards, and leadership of the rival armies permit no other prediction than that Germany can rapidly defeat Russia, overthrow the Stalin regime, and seize her western provinces. It is also possible that she could totally destroy the Russian Army before the end of 1941, thereby securing to herself European Russia and those parts of Siberia west of Lake Baikal."[88]

Diplomatic assessments and attitudes were also unwavering. The personnel in Moscow, particularly Ambassador Steinhardt, were convinced of their opinions of the Soviet Union.[89] Even if the Soviet state survived the impending German onslaught (a doubtful prospect, in their opinion), U.S. policy and tactics toward the Soviets should remain unchanged. The Soviets could not be trusted, and no one could work with them on anything but a strictly quid pro quo basis. The State Department in Washington reflected the embassy's attitudes. In a 14 June 1941 telegram, Hull spelled out U.S. policy toward the Soviet Union. It would include exacting a "strict *quid pro quo* for anything which we are willing to give the Soviet Union," and a day-to-day relationship based "so far as practicable on the principle of reciprocity."[90]

On 21 June 1941, Loy Henderson and Edward Page of the Division of European Affairs authored a memorandum proposing the basis on which interactions with the Soviet Union should be handled. Although softening the tone of the previous telegrams slightly (it would allow the relaxation of export restrictions to the Soviet Union), it was a far cry from unconditional aid in the event of war. Economic aid should be given "on the basis of mutual advantage," and the United States "should steadfastly adhere to the line that the fact that the Soviet Union is fighting Germany does not mean that it is defending, struggling for, or adhering to, the principles in international relations which we [the United States] are supporting."[91]

The State Department and the military and diplomatic personnel serving in the U.S. embassy in Moscow remained committed to their skepticism of the Soviet Union and their beliefs that the Soviet Union must be dealt with firmly. They continued to allow their anti-Soviet prejudices and biases to fog their perception. Aware that long-term Soviet objectives clashed with long-term U.S. objectives, the diplomats and military officers charged with attaining those ends failed to understand that in the 1930s and early 1940s, Soviet and American aims coincided. The immediate and most pressing threat to both countries was German aggression (and to a lesser extent, Japanese expansion), and it would take the cooperation of both to end that threat. Roosevelt did understand that necessity and pursued a foreign policy based on it. That would, however, bring him and his advisers into increasing conflict with the professional diplomats and military attachés in the U.S. embassy in Moscow.

Roosevelt Feeds the Bear: The Decision to Aid the Soviets

Introduction

At 3:15 AM on 22 June 1941, all along the Bug River that served as a border between German and Soviet occupied territory, German artillery began to fire. To the unfortunate Soviet internal security service border guards pounded by the shells, the German action represented a horrifying end to their hopes that war with Germany could be averted. To Winston Churchill and the beleaguered British, it meant a renewed hope that German attention would shift away from the bombardment and eventual invasion of the United Kingdom. To Roosevelt and his advisers in Washington, the meaning of the German invasion was ambiguous.

To a greater extent than at any time since he decided to recognize the Soviet government, in summer 1941 Roosevelt was pulled in a number of directions by advisers with dramatically differing interpretations of events in the Soviet Union. From his official advisers in the State and War Departments, Roosevelt received opinions based on the attitudes and assessments of American diplomats and military attachés in Moscow. The diplomats' and attachés' arguments reflected their opinions of events in the Soviet-German war, filtered through the prism of the attitudes they had developed through a decade-long study of the Soviet Union.

Roosevelt had long developed the habit of formulating policy outside official channels, however. Years of bypassing the governmental bureaucracy had produced a number of advisers to whom the president would turn for advice on numerous issues. It is likely that in 1941 the American ambassador to the Soviet Union was not one of these presidential advisers. In contrast to the relationship between the president and former ambassadors to the USSR Davies and Bullitt, there is no evidence to indicate that Roosevelt ever asked Steinhardt to correspond with him personally and directly, and there is no extant collection of correspondence to suggest that such communication ever occurred. When Steinhardt was selected as ambassador to the Soviet Union, Roosevelt showed little interest in the appointment. Constrained by domestic politics, and operating in an international environment that left him uncertain as to how to approach the Soviets, Roosevelt was content to allow Hull to use the Moscow ambassadorship as an award for a political appointee who had found his calling in the diplomatic corps. Roosevelt was simply not interested enough in the attitudes of the Moscow embassy to communicate regularly with the U.S. ambassador there. As a result, the Moscow embassy was left without a voice among the advisers Roosevelt turned to most often. Those advisers joined a loud chorus of dissonant voices clamoring for the president's attention as the Wehrmacht plunged into the Soviet Union.

As the Soviet Union fought for its survival throughout the summer of 1941, key figures in the U.S. foreign policy-making apparatus—official and unofficial—struggled to determine the future policy of the United States toward Moscow. Rehashing the debates waged in the halls of the U.S. embassy in Moscow, the new conflict assumed greater urgency as events unfolded on the battlefields of eastern Europe. The primary questions facing the American president were whether to send aid to the Soviet Union and what form such aid should take. The contending parties in this dispute pressed their cases vigorously, even after Roosevelt decided the issue.

The period from the German invasion of the Soviet Union to the American entry into World War II witnessed the genesis of a struggle that engaged the U.S. foreign policy apparatus for four years. Building on the foundations of positions staked out in the 1930s, the two emergent camps created the groundwork for a long and often bitter contest to shape the course of United States–Soviet relations.

Barbarossa

The power of the German onslaught against the Soviet Union threatened to render the debate over aid moot. As the artillery pounded Soviet forward defense positions, German bombers swooped from the sky to wreak havoc on the Soviet air force. Within a few hours, 1,200 Soviet airplanes were destroyed.[1] The German Luftwaffe roamed the skies virtually unmolested.

Soviet ground forces did not fare much better. Surprise was complete from the Bug to Moscow, and command and control of the defending forces was one of the principal victims. Before the first bomb detonated, German special operations troops secretly breached the Red Army's lines, severing telephone lines and the vital communications they enabled.[2] Unable to communicate with each other, the various Red Army commands found organizing an effective response to the invasion impossible.

The German military, utilizing its battle-tested "Blitzkrieg" methods, took full advantage of the Red Army's shock and confusion. North of the Pripiat' Marshes, along the roads that led toward Moscow and Leningrad, the initial German onslaught was horrifyingly successful. German armored forces bypassed what little resistance they met, encircling and destroying major Soviet units along the way. In this northern area, the German offensive engulfed over 417,000 Soviet soldiers before the end of June and left in its wake the shattered remnants of several Soviet armies.[3]

In comparison to the gains in the north, German forces were not so successful to the south, along the axis that led to Kiev and the rich industrial and agricultural areas of the Ukraine. More effective preparations by the Soviet commander, Colonel General M. P. Kirponos, in this region contributed to a more effective Soviet response to the German attack. As a result, Red Army forces were able to organize a counterattack that succeeded in delaying the German forces by approximately a week.[4] That delay proved vital as German forces in the north continued their push toward Moscow; worried by the resistance in the south, in October, Hitler diverted to the south much-needed armored forces from the German armies marching toward Moscow.

In the early days of Barbarossa, German commanders were unaware of any impending difficulties. Their operation seemed to be unfolding with dramatic success. By 30 June German armored forces had captured Minsk and pushed to the Dvina and the Dnepr Rivers. On 3 July General Franz Halder, the chief of the German Army General Staff, wrote in his diary that Russia was finished. He indicated that crossing the Dvina and Dnepr was a foregone conclusion. Halder believed that the bulk of the Red Army was west of those rivers, while east of the rivers there were only partial forces.[5]

Although Halder expressed great optimism in his war diary, in July 1941 Germany had not yet won the war. Serious German weaknesses were shrouded behind the veil of Barbarossa's success. First, as German armies swept through Soviet territory, the much-anticipated (at least by foreign observers) uprising of the local populace against the Stalin regime failed to materialize. Indeed, resistance to the German invaders became widespread, paralleling the incidence of brutality and murder perpetrated by German soldiers.[6] Consequently, as Soviet forces retreated, they left in their wake an organized and effective network of partisan detachments, hampering the German effort against the Red Army.[7]

In addition, the Wehrmacht had proven incapable of sealing off their encirclements of Soviet forces. Although they left their heavy equipment behind, thousands of Soviet soldiers escaped through the German lines to fight again. Hitler sought to eliminate this problem by ordering his units to stop and annihilate the encircled troops. This and all other German operations were hindered by the fierce resistance of the individual Soviet soldier, who often fought to the death. As a result, the German Blitzkrieg slowed, and the Red Army gained invaluable time to regroup.[8]

In summer 1941 the most immediately devastating German weakness, however, was its intelligence. Beyond the Dvina and Dnepr, where Halder envisioned only "partial forces," lay Marshal S. M. Budenny's Reserve Front of five field armies. German intelligence was unaware of its existence until the German army plowed into it around Smolensk in July–August 1941. Achieving a surprise of their own, the Red Army brought the German Blitzkrieg to a sudden, if transient, halt. Although it slowed the German advance by only a month, the Red Army was able to use that month to prepare for the defense of Moscow.[9]

For the German army, that month represented more than a threat to the hope of capturing Moscow in 1941. The intelligence shortcoming that led to the surprise encounter with Budenny's Reserve Front also failed to grasp Soviet mobilization potential. By June 1941 the Soviet Union, as a result of the 1938 Universal Military Service Law, had 14 million men with at least basic military training. That number, combined with a mobilization procedure adopted by the War Commissariat, meant that in 1941 the Red Army was able to create units as fast as the Germans destroyed them. The numbers mobilized by the Soviet Union were staggering: by the end of June, 5,300,000 reservists were called up. The Red Army created thirteen new field armies in July, fourteen in August, one in September, four in October, and eight in November and December. Meanwhile, it shifted other active duty forces from the Soviet Far

East. By the end of December 1941, the Soviet Union had fielded over 600 divisions. German prewar estimates had concluded the Soviets were capable of fielding only 300.[10]

The enormity of Soviet achievements in mobilization of manpower was matched by other accomplishments in national mobilization. On 29 June the government and the Communist Party issued a directive outlining the "scorched earth" policy. This directive instructed that the retreat of the Red Army was to be accompanied by a removal of everything that could be moved, and the destruction of everything that remained.[11] Between July and December 1941, the Soviet government moved and reorganized heavy industry along the Volga River, in Siberia and in Central Asia.[12] The scorched earth policy, unforeseen by German intelligence, shocked German economic planners and wreaked havoc on German Army logistics.[13]

Thus, even as seemingly unstoppable German tanks rolled across the Soviet land mass, the Barbarossa campaign slowly fell apart. In July and August Hitler changed the German objective, redirecting the main effort from Moscow to the Donets Basin and the Crimean Peninsula in the south and Leningrad in the north.[14] German successes appeared to mount as Hitler's forces destroyed more Soviet units and captured more Soviet cities. Yet the lightning-fast blow that gave "Blitzkrieg" its name was dissipating as German forces plunged deeper into the Soviet Union. Destruction of the Red Army did not occur before the Dnepr and Dvina as Halder had hoped.

U.S. Assessments of Barbarossa

THE MILITARY ATTACHÉ IN MOSCOW

U.S. observers in summer 1941 were awestruck by the German offensive against the Soviet Union. Although as summer turned to fall U.S. military planners noted unexpectedly strong Soviet resistance and hoped this would delay eventual German victory, most American military analysts remained blind to the important failures in Plan Barbarossa. In the summer of 1941 some members of the U.S. military intelligence community, still influenced by their prewar anti-Soviet biases, failed to note the impressive resistance of the Soviet soldier and the extraordinary mobilization and logistical capabilities of the Soviet military leadership. In Moscow the U.S. military attaché, Ivan Yeaton, was impervious to any suggestion that the German offensive was faltering. Abandoning his late-spring certainty that there was "little or no chance of [a] Soviet-German clash," he slipped easily into the role of prophet of

Soviet defeat.[15] His dispatches from late June until late October, when he left the Soviet Union, are an unceasing chronicle of Soviet catastrophe and impending defeat.

From the first days of the German invasion, Yeaton clung to his pessimism, even as some of his colleagues were beginning to see hope for the Soviet Union. His earliest assessments can justifiably be attributed to the chaos of the situation. In June and early July, the Soviets were indeed trying desperately to establish a defensive line and stem the German advance. Thus, Yeaton's 27 June 1941 dispatch referring to an impending disaster was not unfounded.[16] Less based in reality was his contention on 30 June that the Germans would be in Moscow in five days.[17] Even the ambitious German planners did not believe they would be marching across Red Square within two weeks of fording the Bug. In fact, by 5 July, the date when Yeaton believed German troops would be in Moscow, the Germans were on the banks of the Dnepr River, with Budenny's Reserve Front guarding Smolensk on the road to Moscow. The German Army spent most of July and August defeating this resistance.

The failure of the German Army to keep up with Yeaton's timetable did not discourage his prophesy of Soviet doom. As Soviet forces continued their bloody defensive struggle around Smolensk, Yeaton reported that the U.S. embassy was preparing to evacuate. He informed the Military Intelligence Division (MID) that the "Soviet government indicates intentions to remain in and defend Moscow which may result [in] all remaining being caught."[18] At the same time Yeaton's assessments were diverging from those of other trained observers. By midsummer 1941, British military planners had begun to acknowledge that the Soviets were performing better than expected. In a 14 July 1941 letter, the head of the British Military Mission in Moscow, Lieutenant-General Noel Mason-MacFarlane, explained that he believed the Soviet military was performing well and would exceed British expectations.[19]

Yeaton's assessments contrasted so starkly with those of Mason-MacFarlane and the British that the MID asked Yeaton to discuss the differences. Yeaton responded that the "British here [are] entirely optimistic, [they] interpret all local signs as Soviet strength and Ger[man] weakness. I have seen damage as reported[,] they deny it."[20] Yeaton similarly dismissed other reports more optimistic than his. On 9 August 1941, MID asked Yeaton to assess the validity of a report by Harry Hopkins, envoy for Roosevelt, contending that the Soviet Union was willing and able to resist the German aggression.[21] Yeaton dismissed what Hopkins learned in his meeting with Stalin: "[I] believe Stalin told Hopkins total number Soviet divisions but little other military info. . . . Believe Soviets preparing all out defense Moscow which if unsuccessful will greatly jeopardize hoped for future resistance. Cannot change picture painted by my office before war."[22] The picture Yeaton referred to was drawn in a report dated 21 April 1941. In that telegram, the military attaché informed his superiors in Washington that the Soviet Union would defend itself on all fronts, with the final western defensive line the Dnepr River. Yeaton estimated the "maximum time [of Soviet] resistance [at] *three months'*[23] (emphasis Yeaton's). Although certainly not as dire as his earlier image of German troops enjoying summer in Moscow, Yeaton's updated observations still incorrectly predicted a Soviet defeat in early autumn 1941.

Yeaton's analyses were not entirely misguided. He did correctly note the Soviet effort to move their industry, although he referred to the effort as "belated."[24] He also accurately reported Soviet deficiencies in guns, tanks, and airplanes.[25] Yeaton's worthwhile intelligence, however, was lost in a sea of dangerously inaccurate reports.

Entirely misreading reality at the front, Yeaton informed MID that most farmers and many city workers would cooperate with the Germans if only the Germans promised land to the farmers and workers.[26] This allegation attracted the immediate attention of the War Department, who wrote to Yeaton that it was very important news. MID inquired as to the reasons why Yeaton believed it, the sources he relied on for his assessment, and whether his colleagues agreed with him.[27] Yeaton's reply elaborated on his view of the situation outside Moscow:

> Believe Stalin bureaucracy loyal and [government] not threatened internally but great majority people completely disillusioned and desire change. Ger[mans] not popular here but many ready to cooperate [with] them if necessary to effect change [in] govt. Locally it appears passive resistance will only slightly hinder Ger[man] war effort if fair govt set up. . . . Ger[man] leaflets [in] villages promising return of land and churches causing much discussion and many farmers secretly hiding grain and potatoes to keep from destroying. British observ[er]s violently disagree. Others agree or disagree depending on political tendencies.[28]

Indeed, British observers did disagree. As early as 14 July, Mason-MacFarlane reported to his superiors that the popularity of peasants' collective farms was on the rise, and consequently, the army was unlikely to melt away if the Germans promised them land.[29]

As the Soviet-German war continued, more observers began to share Mason-MacFarlane's optimism and contest Yeaton's predictions. By late August 1941 both British civilian and military officials retreated from their predictions of imminent Soviet defeat. British officials gathered intelligence on the Soviet military from a variety of sources. One advantage the British held over Yeaton was their access to decrypted diplomatic traffic from Germany. Top-secret decryption aside, much of the material the British analyzed was equally available to the American military attaché. British military representatives in Moscow obtained detailed information from the attachés at other embassies, particularly the Polish and the Czech embassies. Yeaton, however, hesitated to cooperate with anyone. He distrusted the Soviet authorities (a feeling the Soviets appeared to reciprocate); and he thought cooperation with the British military mission unwise because of British overoptimism.

Yeaton's weaknesses were apparent to many as the Soviet-German war progressed. The foreign correspondents in Moscow were most forthcoming in their criticism of the hapless attaché. Alexander Werth, Reuters' special correspondent in Moscow, remarked that Yeaton was certain the Red Army would be smashed in a short time.[30] The critique of Cyrus L. Sulzberger, the *New York Times'* Moscow correspondent, was more withering:

> The United States military attaché was Ivan Yeaton, a hearty, agreeable, ill-informed professional officer of Scandinavian extraction who reminded me of the old saw: "What's dumber than a dumb Englishman? A bright Swede." From the first day he was convinced the Soviet army and air force had been destroyed, that the war was over on the Eastern Front. When we were ordered out of Moscow he assured his colleagues that the special train would never escape the Nazi's [*sic*] iron ring around the capital.[31]

Margaret Bourke-White and Erskine Caldwell, representatives of *Life* magazine in Moscow, expressed even more concern over Yeaton's attitude. In an interview with Lieutenant Colonel Frederick D. Sharp of the MID on their return to the United States from Moscow, the two stated their shared belief that Yeaton was unfit to be military attaché in the Soviet Union. They attributed the tenor of Yeaton's comments to his total reliance on German radio propaganda. In a damning condemnation, Bourke-White and Caldwell contended that "the M.A. was obviously influenced by German propaganda, so much so that the invincibility of the German military machine is taken as a foregone conclusion by the M.A. and German radio reports are accepted as correct." The two further contended that Yeaton placed no confidence in Russian claims. They ended the interview by advising Sharp that the British military attaché had a better understanding of what was going on, and that their opinion was shared by the other American correspondents in Moscow.[32]

Journalists were not the only individuals concerned with Yeaton's attitude.

Yeaton's views of the Soviet Union were especially disturbing to Roosevelt's special adviser, Harry L. Hopkins. Hopkins, after an August 1941 visit to Moscow during which Stalin had personally reassured him about the security of the Soviet-German front, felt compelled to warn Secretary of War Henry L. Stimson to accept Yeaton's analyses with "the greatest reserve."[33] Hopkins warned that Yeaton was "so biased against the Russians that if his opinions were accepted here the Department may find itself very badly advised."[34]

MILITARY INTELLIGENCE DIVISION

Unfortunately, the Military Intelligence Division did not heed the warnings about Yeaton's competence. Rather, the MID produced estimates (routed to the secretary of war, the chief of staff of the Army, the War Plans Division, and the Office of Naval Intelligence) that contained many of Yeaton's most damaging inaccuracies. Virtually all of the estimates exaggerated German capabilities and disparaged the Red Army's strength and capabilities. Intelligence Branch Estimate 85, dated 19 June 1941, correctly calculated Soviet strength, but estimated the Red Army's quickly mobilizable force at 3,250,000.[35] In fact, within 30 days of the invasion, the Soviets had a mobilized strength of 7,850,000.[36] This underestimation of Soviet mobilization potential coincided with Yeaton's reports, and contributed to the MID's prewar conclusion that "Germany can rapidly defeat Russia, overthrow the Stalin regime, and seize her western provinces. It is also possible that she could totally destroy the Russian Army before the end of 1941, thereby securing to herself European Russia and those parts of Siberia west of Lake Baikal."[37]

Events on the battlefield did not immediately change the War Department's perspective. Continuing to parallel Yeaton's assessments, the War Department, via Acting Secretary of State Sumner Welles, informed Ambassador Steinhardt on 4 July 1941 that "German troops would be able, if they desire so to do, to enter Moscow within a week."[38] Yeaton's broader observations about the inevitability of Soviet defeat were also widespread in MID. In a 17 July 1941 memorandum to the chief of the MID, General Sherman Miles, Colonel Percy G. Black refers to the imminent defeat of Russian armies in the west.[39]

The Intelligence Branch Estimates did not entirely adhere to the position Yeaton advanced from the embassy in Moscow. In fact, Estimate 108 on Soviet Guerilla Warfare proposed a view of Soviet resistance dramatically at odds with Yeaton's vision of Soviet collaboration with the Germans. The MID described an armed body of civilians cooperating with the Soviet secret police and laying waste to the country in the path of the Germans. This body was also active in the German communications zone "with considerable effectiveness."[40]

Although differing in details, some very significant, the overall tone of the MID's analyses corresponded with the assessments of their military attaché in Moscow. The shared perspective in the reports reflected the MID's respect for Yeaton's reports. An underestimation of the Red Army was widespread in the military. Lieutenant Colonel Paul M. Robinett, assistant chief of staff, G-2, observed in the week after 22 June 1941, that "there was almost unanimous agreement among all military men that Russia would be quickly and decisively destroyed. The only difference of opinion seemed to be concerning how long it would take. No one that I knew of had any other view."[41] An even greater indication of the esteem in which Yeaton was held was that on his return from Moscow, the War Department assigned Yeaton to duty in the Intelligence Branch of the Military Intelligence Division. From November 1941, Yeaton had an even more direct role in shaping the analyses sent to the chief of staff of the army and the secretary of war.

THE AMBASSADOR

Ambassador Steinhardt shared Yeaton's initial panic and pessimism regarding Soviet chances of success versus Germany. On the day the German offensive began, Steinhardt evacuated the embassy staff to a dacha outside Moscow.[42] Residence outside Moscow, however, was clearly only a stopgap measure, particularly in the face of continued German success at the front. For the next few weeks, Steinhardt was unable to hide his concern about the German occupation of Moscow.

Steinhardt first expressed his worries to his colleagues in Washington. On 26 June 1941, Steinhardt warned the State Department that he anticipated the imminent departure of the Soviet Government from Moscow. His fear of the German advance combined with a distrust of the Kremlin to lead him to state, "I suppose, although it is by no means certain, that arrangements will be made for the Diplomatic Corps to accompany or follow it."[43] Less than a week later, Steinhardt advised the State Department that he hoped to move the embassy east before it was "too late."[44]

Continued Soviet defeats, probably enhanced by the pessimism of his military attaché, prompted Steinhardt to voice his fears to a broader circle of people. In several conversations with British Ambassador Sir Stafford Cripps, Steinhardt pointed out that he felt Cripps' assessments were too optimistic. On 28 June, he responded to Cripps' assertion that the Germans would not take Moscow in under sixty days with the admonition that this might occur much earlier. Hence, it was important to prepare in advance for the contingency of the evacuation of Moscow.[45] The positions of the two men remained essentially the same in a conversation on 9 July. According to Steinhardt, he again disputed Cripps' optimism concerning the ability of the Red Army to defend Moscow. Steinhardt argued that the German General Staff was fully in control of the situation.[46]

Steinhardt did not restrict sharing his opinion of the war situation to his American and British colleagues. In several interviews with Soviet officials, he pressed the matter of the evacuation of the American embassy. On 29 June Molotov summoned Steinhardt for a discussion of U.S. offers to provide material aid to the Soviet Union. At the end of the meeting, the American ambassador raised the issue of the evacuation of Moscow: "At the conclusion of the interview I attempted to elicit from Molotov some assurance that should the Soviet Government find it necessary to abandon Moscow I would be given notification of its intention or that at least provision would be made for me to join the Government at its new place of residence."[47]

Steinhardt mentioned the issue again in an interview with Deputy Foreign Minister A. Lozovski on 7 July 1941. This time the ambassador proposed only that the United States be allowed to establish a "provisional" consulate somewhere further east and dispatch several members of the current embassy staff to it.[48] The Soviets eventually granted Steinhardt permission to evacuate some of his staff to Kazan.

Steinhardt's fears for the fate of his embassy were prompted in large part by his view of the military situation. In the initial period of war, he fully shared Yeaton's opinion of developments at the front. In addition to the views he discussed with Cripps, Steinhardt informed the State Department that Stalin's 16 July order reestablishing the commissar system stemmed from the dangerous deterioration of morale in the Red Army. In the same telegram, he added that there were also indications of difficulties in the Red Army command.[49]

In contrast to Yeaton, however, as the initial shock of Barbarossa faded, Steinhardt began to produce more balanced and prescient analyses of the military situation. In doing so, Steinhardt revealed the diplomatic professionalism that had won him recognition in Sweden and Peru. The Foreign Service officers and military attachés in Moscow had all undergone some form of specialized training to qualify them as Soviet experts. Steinhardt arrived in Moscow as a reward for a job well done as ambassador in Peru. If Steinhardt was ideologically opposed to the Soviet Union, his hatred of communism was not as deeply ingrained as that of the military attachés and the Foreign Service officers. Thus, despite the frustration and isolation of life in Moscow, when necessary, Steinhardt struggled to provide the information his government needed. His professionalism enabled him to overcome prejudices that otherwise would have distorted his observations. As a result, on 5 August he observed that the German advance toward Moscow had slowed. He acknowledged that the

Germans might use this period for reorganization, but he noted that the Soviet side would also benefit from the same opportunity. Steinhardt argued that a renewed German offensive would no doubt meet stiff Soviet resistance. The ambassador argued there were several reasons for optimism:

> If I am correct in the foregoing conclusion the significance lies in its bearing upon two factors of vital importance: (1) The ability of the Soviet armies effectively to engage the bulk of the German armies until the advent of winter; and (2) their ability eventually, if necessary, to withdraw in force with their equipment and to continue hostilities farther east. . . . the general picture as I see it at the moment warrants a conviction that both of these desirable objectives may be attained at least in part.[50]

The quality of Steinhardt's reports seemed to improve as the war continued. On 23 August he sent an excellent analysis of the current military situation to the State Department. Although certainly acknowledging potential Soviet failures, such as the probability that the Germans would either take or cut off Leningrad, Steinhardt also correctly assessed the impact that the Soviet defense of Smolensk had on German momentum toward Moscow. Steinhardt also mentioned reports of collaboration with the German invaders, but he contrasted them with his observation that the morale of the general population was "exceptionally good." Finally, Steinhardt concluded his dispatch by placing all of his observations in perspective. Noting that it was already almost the first of September, Steinhardt pointed out that not only had the German Blitzkrieg "failed to achieve victory," but also the Germans had "not yet succeeded in occupying any of the three major cities of European Russia."[51]

Steinhardt's conviction that the Soviet Union might successfully defend itself against Germany was also apparent in his reports on the civil situation. Two days after expressing optimism regarding the Red Army's capabilities, he observed that the population of Moscow was becoming more accustomed to German air raids and more capable of withstanding them.[52] Similarly, Steinhardt noted that the Soviets were moving "substantial quantities" of industrial material to the east, and although the citizenry of Moscow was becoming increasingly aware of the severity of the situation, the Soviet regime was determined to fight to the bitter end.[53] Even after the evacuation of government officials and the diplomatic community to Kuibyshev in October, Steinhardt affirmed his conviction that the regime would be able to retain its authority throughout the country and that the Soviet government was determined to fight the war to its conclusion.[54]

Thus, as the Soviet-German war progressed, there emerged and developed a divergence of opinion between the U.S. ambassador and the military attaché. In the early days of the conflict, however, when policy makers in Washington were wrestling with how to respond to the invasion, the opinion from the Moscow embassy was unanimous: there was little hope the Soviet Union would withstand the German onslaught.

AMBASSADOR DAVIES

Although U.S. representatives in Moscow were speaking with one voice in June 1941, Roosevelt was not solely dependent on that interpretation. After the German invasion of the Soviet Union, Ambassador Joseph E. Davies returned to Washington to persuade his former boss of his views on Soviet military capabilities.[55]

Embarking on a personal crusade to ensure U.S. support of the Soviet war effort, Davies approached the White House on 30 June to ask for permission to see the president and discuss the possibility of serving as an intermediary between the U.S. and Soviet governments. Stephen Early, the man in charge of Roosevelt's relations with the press, granted Davies an appointment for two weeks later.[56] Davies spent the intervening time shuttling from office to office in the capital discussing the Soviet-German war with anyone who would listen.[57]

On 8 July Davies met with Harry L. Hopkins, the president's closest adviser and "unofficial secretary of state." Obviously still influenced by his (and Faymonville's) observations of the Red Army and Soviet industrial potential in 1938, Davies followed up his meeting with Hopkins with a memorandum. In this short survey of the Russian situation, Davies argued that the Soviet Union had a great potential to hold out militarily even if Belorussia and Ukraine fell to the Germans. Stressing Soviet reserve potential, the ability of the Red Army and Soviet regime to fall back to the east, and the impact of guerrilla warfare on the German army, Davies argued that the real risk to U.S. interests was not a Soviet defeat, but a "separate peace" between Hitler and Stalin. To prevent that, Davies argued: "Word ought to be gotten to Stalin that our attitude is 'all out' to beat Hitler and that our historic policy of friendliness to Russia still exists."[58]

The underlying premise of Davies' memorandum and his accompanying approaches to both Soviet and American officials was that military issues were of secondary importance to political ones. Fundamental to that premise, however, was Davies' conviction that Germany was not going to crush the Red Army. That was a conviction shared by very few in early July 1941. Certainly at that point Roosevelt was by no means certain of the outcome of the war. He was still being advised by his secretary of war that Germany would defeat the Soviet Union within a few short months.

Policy Dilemmas

The issue of aid to the Soviet Union emerged as the central factor in the debate over U.S. policy as a result of the history of America's role in the conflict with Germany. As German forces rolled to victory in northern and western Europe, the Roosevelt administration became increasingly concerned for the survival of Britain. Britain faced Hitler virtually alone, as Roosevelt inched the United States toward involvement in the war. Beginning with a "destroyers for bases" deal in August 1940, the United States gradually began to assume the role of the "arsenal for democracy" outlined in Roosevelt's 29 December 1940 fireside chat with the American people. On 11 March 1941, Roosevelt signed into law the Lend-Lease Act, which enabled him to provide material aid to "any country whose defense the President deems vital to the defense of the United States."[59] Thus, lend-lease provided the framework within which the United States interacted with adversaries of Hitler. When the Soviet Union in June 1941 became an enemy of Germany, the immediate focus of debate became whether the Soviet Union would also receive aid.

Even before the German invasion, Roosevelt had given some thought as to how to respond when it finally occurred. On 14 June 1941, British Prime Minister Winston Churchill, who also had early warning of the German plans, sent Roosevelt a letter. Churchill informed Roosevelt, "Should this new war break out we shall of course give all encouragement and any help we can spare to the Russians, following the principle that Hitler is the foe we have to beat."[60] It was a sentiment with which Roosevelt concurred. He replied the next day via the American ambassador in London, John G. Winant. Roosevelt assured Churchill that in the event of war he would support "any announcement that the Prime Minister might make welcoming Russia as an ally."[61]

Churchill wasted no time in carrying out the plans he had mentioned to Roosevelt. When news of the Soviet invasion reached him on Sunday morning, 22 June, Churchill spent several hours preparing before he spoke to his nation. With characteristic florid prose, the prime minister declared his reasons for supporting the Soviet Union in its struggle against Hitler's Germany:

> Any man or state who fights on against Nazidom will have our aid. Any man or state who marches with Hitler is our foe. . . . That is our policy and that is our declaration. It follows, therefore, that we shall give whatever help we can to Russia and the Russian people. We shall appeal to all our friends and allies in every part of the world to take the same course and pursue it, as we shall faithfully and steadfastly to the end.[62]

True to his word, Roosevelt supported the prime minister's declaration, although not as vigorously as Churchill's recollection of Winant's message indicated he would. On 23 June Acting Secretary of State Sumner Welles announced, "Hitler's armies are today the chief dangers of the Americas."[63] The next day a newspaper quoted Roosevelt as having stated that he supported Welles' statement.[64] Despite what he may have communicated to the British prime minister, Roosevelt was caught in the center of a debate among his foreign policy team about the appropriate response to the Soviet-German war. He would have to analyze those arguments before "welcoming Russia as an ally."

THE WAR DEPARTMENT POSITION

Important officials in the U.S. War Department and the military shared Churchill's welcome of Soviet participation in the war against Germany. Secretary of War Henry L. Stimson believed that the Soviet-German war offered the United States and Britain a respite of three months, during which they could win the Battle of the Atlantic and ensure Britain's survival.[65] Stimson's views reflected the impact of the military's assessments of Soviet capabilities. He (and Secretary of the Navy Frank Knox) felt that all American resources should be directed to the North Atlantic and the naval struggle with Germany there. They accepted Soviet defeat as a foregone conclusion. Consequently, they rejected as futile any discussion of efforts to aid the Soviet military effort.

Stimson and Knox derived their views almost entirely from the analyses the Military Intelligence Division provided them.[66] Those analyses, in turn, reflected the skepticism within G-2 and the Joint Planning Committee for Soviet military capabilities. The military's analyses also reflected a prevailing pessimism regarding any single power's ability to withstand a German attack. In fact, one year earlier, these same military bodies had predicted the imminent defeat of the United Kingdom.[67]

Within this context of strategic assessment, the debate over U.S. aid policy to the belligerent powers took shape. From the early days of American aid to Britain, responsible military authorities opposed most of Roosevelt's policies. These military leaders believed that Britain, and later the Soviet Union, would be defeated. As a result, any supplies sent to them would be wasted. At the same time, the U.S. military leadership actively lobbied for a buildup of American military power. With the defeat of Britain and the Soviet Union, the United States would face the full military power of Germany (and possibly Japan) alone. Worse, the U.S. military was woefully unprepared to meet that challenge. In the minds of American military leaders, every piece of war material that U.S. industry could churn out was desperately needed by American military forces, but Britain and other foreign powers were laying claim to it.[68]

Army Chief of Staff George C. Marshall supported Roosevelt's policy of aid to Britain, the Soviet Union, and other powers fighting the Soviet Union. Yet he also feared stripping the U.S. military of material necessary to train and to fight.[69] It was this concern, more than anti-Soviet prejudice, that shaped the actions of higher ranking military and War Department officials in the early years of World War II. These were the arguments his military advisers pressed on Roosevelt as he struggled with the decision of whether, and what sort of aid, to provide the Soviet Union in summer 1941.

THE STATE DEPARTMENT POSITION

Officials in the State Department also hesitated to support unrestricted aid to the Soviet Union. Secretary of State Cordell Hull's later recollection during June and July 1941—that he "was in constant touch with the President and Welles, urging that we give Russia the most vigorous assurances of all the help we could extend"—was not indicative of the general attitude in the State Department.[70] On the contrary, most State Department officials accepted the recommendations in the European Affairs Division's 21 June memorandum. They supported limited aid for the Soviet Union and expected that the aid would be provided on a quid pro quo basis.

The rationale for State's policy was partially based on the fear that the Soviet Union was not militarily capable of withstanding the German invasion. In addition, State Department officials feared a political collapse in the Soviet Union. Many U.S. diplomats believed that even if the Soviet Army were not defeated on the battlefield, Stalin's regime could not survive the war. Consequently, they did not want to complicate relations with a successor regime by providing assistance to the current one.[71] They also feared giving the Soviet Union any material that might fall into German hands should the Kremlin make peace with Hitler.[72]

These concerns regarding Soviet military and political weakness were compounded by hostility toward and distrust of the Soviet regime. Attitudes that had developed in the U.S. diplomatic corps throughout the 1920s and 1930s were firmly entrenched in the bureaucracy by June 1941. As assistant chief of the Division of European Affairs, Loy Henderson remained just as concerned about Soviet global aspirations as he had been as a young Foreign Service officer charged with keeping tabs on Bolshevik foreign policies.[73] In July 1941, even as the U.S. military warned of the collapse of the Soviet war effort, Henderson and Assistant Secretary of State Adolf A. Berle wrote a memorandum to Acting Secretary of State Sumner Welles. They cited attempted Soviet espionage and Soviet policy aims as grounds for withholding military secrets from them and restricting the activities of Soviet engineers in the United States. In conclusion, Berle and Henderson reasserted the necessity for a policy of reciprocity. They pointed out that the unwillingness of the Soviet government to provide access to similar information to the U.S. military attachés was sufficient justification for rejecting Soviet requests.[74]

Henderson and other State Department officials' distrust of the Soviet Union not only manifested itself in concern over Soviet espionage and postwar aspirations. Despite the changed circumstances wrought by the Soviet-German war, the Division of European Affairs resumed the leitmotif of Steinhardt's tenure in Moscow and kept a record of all Soviet slights and affronts. On 30 June 1941, Acting Chief of the Division of European Affairs Ray Atherton informed Soviet Ambassador Oumansky that the United States was applying the same restriction on movements of Soviet officials in the United States as the Soviet government was applying to American officials in Moscow. Atherton clearly indicated that this was a tit-for-tat policy: "I pointed out to him, however, that these restrictions were placed on Soviet officials in this country with considerable regret but such action had been forced upon us by discrimination against American officials in Moscow."[75] Less than a month after the start of the war, Berle drafted a memorandum to Welles in which he pointed out that the Soviet Union "is thus far not showing itself to be over-cooperative in disposing of a number of relatively minor outstanding problems existing between the two Governments."[76] As a result, Berle recommended: "we should make no concessions with regard to Soviet military attachés or with regard to travel restrictions on the Soviet embassy until the Soviet Government shows a disposition to meet the reasonable requests of Mr. Steinhardt."[77]

Thus, as the early stages of the Soviet-German war unfolded, Roosevelt's diplomatic advisers warned him against providing too much aid to the Soviet Union. They also encouraged him to seek advantages and concessions for any aid or concessions the United States granted Moscow. They shared Steinhardt's prewar belief that the only way to work with the Kremlin was on a quid pro quo basis.[78]

ROOSEVELT'S DECISION

In summer 1941 Roosevelt's professional military and diplomatic advisers cautioned restraint in assisting the Soviet Union. Popular and congressional opinion shared this view. Although popular opinion polls taken in summer 1941 indicated overwhelming support for the Soviet Union in its war against Germany, most people did not support aiding Moscow as the United States had been aiding Britain.[79] The public elite (for example, educators and journalists) shared the military leadership's view that the Soviet-German war represented an opportunity to increase aid to Britain.[80]

The political climate, therefore, dictated caution. Roosevelt's less than vigorous public support of Churchill's statements on the Soviet-German war reflected this. Ever the effective politician, Roosevelt proceeded cautiously, testing the limits of what he was able to do while remaining committed to the principle that Germany was the leading threat to American security. At a press conference on 24 June Roosevelt took a tentative first step when he announced his administration's willingness to provide aid to the Soviet Union. On that same day, he thawed approximately $40 million in Soviet assets in the United States. On 25 June Roosevelt declared that the provisions of the Neutrality Act did not apply to the USSR, thus allowing the Soviet Union to purchase war materials from the United States.[81]

On 30 June 1941, Constantine Oumansky, the Soviet Ambassador to the United States, presented the administration with Moscow's first official aid request. Along with the public steps Roosevelt had taken to ease America toward cooperation with the Soviet Union, the government bureaucracy had been preparing to provide aid when the Soviet government requested it. Once the Soviet Union formally requested assistance, the administration established a committee (the Curtis Committee, named for its chairman in the Department of State) to provide aid to the USSR. The Curtis Committee was made up of representatives from the State Department, the Division of Defense Aid Reports (Lend-Lease), the Office of the Administration of Export Control, the Office of Price Administration and Civilian Supply, the Office of Production Management, the Army-Navy Munitions Board, and the Maritime Commission.[82] It did not have jurisdiction over military items. The Curtis Committee was also hampered by its own policy guidelines. The members of the committee believed that aid should be provided the Soviet Union, but in allocating resources, it gave priority to the defense needs of the United States and the other nations already receiving American aid.[83]

As a result of these limitations, the Curtis Committee was ineffective in aiding the Soviet Union. As July progressed, Soviet complaints and pleas for help became more strident.[84] Joining the incessant cries from Oumansky, Davies assumed a role as unofficial liaison between the Soviet embassy in Washington and the Roosevelt administration. Davies continued to have influence with both the president, who had appointed him ambassador to the Soviet Union five years earlier, and with Roosevelt's most trusted adviser, Hopkins.[85] At the same time as these advocates of greater aid to Russia were pressing their case on the White House, the State and War Departments were losing their influence with the president. The most significant reason for their waning influence was simply that their dire predictions of Soviet collapse had failed to materialize. As each day passed without Stalin's capitulation, Roosevelt became more wary of the advice his "experts" were providing.[86]

By early July Roosevelt was unhappy with the ineffectiveness of the Curtis Committee's aid program. He intervened to ensure that more material was sent to the Soviet Union.[87] By 11 July Roosevelt had decided to abandon the failed committee system, and he placed the Soviet aid program in the hands of Harry Hopkins and Major General James H. Burns, the head of the Division of Defense Aid Reports.[88] Burns then created a special section for Soviet aid within his division. To direct this section, he recalled to Washington Colonel Philip R. Faymonville, the controversial former military attaché to Moscow.[89]

The appointment of Faymonville to head the Soviet aid section of the Division of Defense Aid Reports reduced some of the difficulties in the aid system. Under the watchful eyes of Hopkins, Burns, and Faymonville, aid to the Soviet Union became one of the government's highest priorities. Yet this section did not eliminate all of the problems hindering assistance to the Soviets. The U.S. aid efforts were hampered by severe shortages in shipping and transportation, shortages in supplies, bureaucratic disorder, and legal technicalities. In addition, the Division of Defense Aid Reports relied on a number of other organizations to implement the aid program. Many of these organizations remained convinced that the Soviet Union would collapse, and their efforts (and scarce materials) would be wasted.[90]

To overcome these problems, Roosevelt needed more evidence that the Soviet Union would be able to withstand the German invasion. He also needed to know what exactly the Soviets' needs were, and how best the United States could meet those needs. In typical Roosevelt fashion, the president received that information not from the bureaucracy, but from his close friend Harry Hopkins.

The Hopkins Mission

Hopkins was already in Great Britain when the idea for a journey to Moscow occurred to him in July 1941. He was on a mission to work out the details of the upcoming secret meeting between Roosevelt and Churchill. As Hopkins and the British prime minister attempted to hammer out the details on a variety of strategic and supply issues, it became evident to both that their calculations depended on an accurate assessment of the massive battle between Germany and the Soviet Union. According to Hopkins' biographer, Robert Sherwood, Hopkins was well aware of the paucity of accurate information available to American and British planners in summer 1941. To remedy this situation, on 25 July 1941 Hopkins volunteered to travel to Moscow and interview Stalin, the one man capable of providing answers about the military situation in the Soviet Union.[91]

Information gathering, as necessary as it was, was not the only motive for Hopkins' trip to the Soviet Union. In pressing his case for a mission to Moscow, Hopkins provided several additional reasons for the dangerous journey. These rationales revealed concerns that would remain in the forefront of his and Roosevelt's minds throughout the war. First, Hopkins stressed "that everything possible should be done to make certain the Russians maintain a permanent front even though they [will] be defeated in this immediate battle." Emphasizing the "great stakes" involved, Hopkins contended that a visit by a personal representative of the U.S. president would mean that "Stalin would then know in an unmistakable way that we mean business on a long term supply job." To Hopkins the defeat of Germany required cooperation between the United States and the Soviet Union. Roosevelt evidently shared Hopkins' views. On 26 July he and Acting Secretary of State Welles accepted Hopkins' proposal.[92]

On 27 July 1941 Hopkins embarked on an uncomfortable and dangerous journey from Scotland to Archangel'sk in the extreme north of the Soviet Union. Tucked away in his personal baggage was a message from Roosevelt to Stalin. This message explained to the Soviet leader that the purpose of Hopkins' visit was to discuss "the vitally important question of how we can most expeditiously and effectively make available the assistance which the United States can render to your country."[93]

To American Ambassador Laurence Steinhardt, Hopkins provided a different justification for his visit. Hopkins stressed that "the main purpose of his visit was to determine whether the situation was as disastrous as it was pictured in the War Department—and particularly in the cables from the Military Attaché, Major Ivan Yeaton."[94] Hopkins was concerned with the possibility of biased interpretations from the U.S. embassy in Moscow, and the effect they might have on U.S.-Soviet cooperation.[95] His concerns were no doubt heightened by his encounters with Yeaton—encounters that undoubtedly contributed to the warning Hopkins sent to Stimson questioning the reliability of Yeaton's assessments. According to Yeaton, Hopkins stated that aid to the Soviet Union would never be used as a bargaining chip. Yeaton was horrified, but did not reply. During their next meeting, however, Yeaton told Hopkins that a quid pro quo was essential in dealing with Stalin. When Hopkins flatly rejected this assertion, Yeaton exploded. Yeaton recounted this incident years later: "Thats [*sic*] when I, unfortunately, lost my temper and what was said thereafter I can not be sure of. However, the substance was that he, Hopkins, did not know the temper of the people he was dealing with and that neither was his approach one which would ever again gain him any respect from Stalin who despised weakness."[96]

Hopkins had an opportunity to judge the temper of Stalin himself on the evening of 30 July. In his first meeting with the Soviet leader, Hopkins rejected Yeaton's recommendation that the United States seize the opportunity to bargain with the Soviet Union. Instead, he opened the meeting by informing Stalin of "the President's belief that the most important thing to be done in the world today was to defeat Hitler and Hitlerism." Hopkins then "impressed upon him the determination of the President and our Government to extend all possible aid to the Soviet Union at the earliest possible time." Hopkins did not try to bargain with Stalin. He only asked him to explain what the Soviet Union's immediate and long-term requirements were.[97]

In the 30 July and subsequent 31 July meetings, Stalin outlined in great detail Soviet requirements, both immediate and long range, and detailed the present military situation.[98] In response to Hopkins' query about the Soviet Union's immediate needs, Stalin explained that the Red Army required anti-aircraft guns and ammunition, machine guns, and rifles. It was Stalin's statement of the Soviet Union's long-term requirements, however, that most impressed Hopkins. Stalin explained that the Soviet Union required materials already requested by Soviet officials in Washington—aviation fuel, and aluminum for the manufacture of airplanes. Hopkins believed the request for aluminum a most significant indicator of Stalin's intention to continue to resist the German invasion. As Sherwood explained, "A man who feared immediate defeat would not have put aluminum so high on a list of priorities."[99]

Hopkins' hopes for successful Soviet resistance were buoyed as well by Stalin's overly optimistic assessment of the situation at the front. In outlining the current and probable future military situation, Stalin explained to Hopkins that the German offensive would probably halt for the winter on 1 October, in front of a Leningrad-Moscow-Kiev line. In reality, Stalin's optimism was not justified. The Germans would capture Kiev, nearly encircle Leningrad, and continue to threaten Moscow until the beginning of December. But accurate or not, Stalin's conversations with Hopkins were vital for the development of United States–Soviet relations in World War II. Hopkins returned to the United States convinced that the Soviet Union would continue to resist Germany. He was likewise certain that the United States should do everything possible to aid that resistance. To that end, he proposed to Stalin a British-

American-Soviet conference to formulate an aid policy and schedule, and he recommended to Roosevelt that Steinhardt be removed from his post as ambassador.[100]

Hopkins' mission to Moscow was arguably a turning point in the relationship between the United States and the Soviet Union. Warren Kimball makes the case that Roosevelt was committed to long-term aid to the Soviet Union even before Hopkins made his perilous trek. There is no "smoking gun" to support this; the president was not one to write down his plans as he was formulating them. Nonetheless, Kimball compares the nuances of what Roosevelt said to what he actually did, and argues persuasively that "the mission to Moscow, or at least a policy of long-term support for the Soviet Union, had been discussed before Hopkins left Washington."[101] In any event, after Hopkins' mission, there was no doubt that the Roosevelt administration was committed to a long-term policy of aid, with no strings attached, to the Soviet Union. Roosevelt affirmed this approach at the Atlantic conference in August by joining Churchill in authorizing a three-power conference in Moscow that would establish a more formal aid program. Churchill named William Maxwell Aitken, first Baron Beaverbrook, minister of aircraft production, as the British representative. Roosevelt appointed W. Averell Harriman, who had been coordinating U.S. lend-lease in Britain. Despite the positive meetings he had had with Stalin, Hopkins had long suffered from ill health and was too weak to undertake another journey in such a short time.[102]

The Harriman-Beaverbrook Mission

The weeks between Hopkins' visit to Moscow and the Harriman-Beaverbrook mission witnessed continued difficulties in aiding the Soviet Union. Roosevelt's personal intervention in the process in July did not eliminate every problem. Consequently, as the war progressed, Roosevelt found it necessary to become involved time and again. On 2 August 1941, he sent a memorandum to Wayne Coy (an administrator working on Russian orders) complaining about the delivery of materials to Siberia:

> Frankly if I were a Russian I would feel that I had been given the run-around in the United States.
> Please get out the list and please, with my full authority, use a heavy hand—act as a burr under the saddle and get things moving! . . .
> Step on it![103]

Less than a month later, Roosevelt reiterated his belief in the importance of aid to the Soviet Union. In a memorandum to Stimson, the president clearly explained his views on the matter: "I deem it to be of paramount importance for the safety and security of America that all reasonable munitions help be provided for Russia, not only immediately but as long as she continues to fight the Axis powers effectively. I am convinced that substantial and comprehensive commitments of such character must be made to Russia by Great Britain and the United States at the proposed conference."[104] Throughout summer 1941, Roosevelt and his top officials struggled continuously to provide the type and amount of aid to the Soviet Union the president desired. Yet delays persisted in supplying the materials Moscow requested.[105]

Full implementation of the president's desires remained a struggle for a number of reasons. One of the most significant was simply resistance from the bureaucracies charged with providing that aid. Resistance was present throughout the executive branch and compounded the existing supply and transport difficulties, but it was most pronounced in the military.[106] Throughout July, August, and into September, the military and the War Department remained opposed to munitions aid. The U.S. Army based its opinion of the likelihood of Soviet collapse on the reports of the Military Intelligence Division and the military attaché in Moscow. As a result, it did not share the White House's optimism regarding the chances of Soviet success.[107] Believing it still likely that the Soviets would be defeated, the military hesitated to waste material so vitally needed for the buildup of America's own armed forces. That is why, for example, Stimson and Army Chief of Staff General George C. Marshall were so chagrined at repeated Soviet requests for scarce American aircraft.[108]

The actions of Ambassador Umanskii did not encourage military willingness to part with scarce material. The Soviet ambassador blustered his way around Washington, greatly offending most with whom he came in contact. Marshall and other military leaders were irritated by Oumansky's inconsiderate behavior and, naturally, were ill-disposed to greet his requests (or, often, demands) favorably.[109]

Bureaucratic resistance aside, by September the wisdom of aid to the Soviet Union had become increasingly clear. By midmonth the military planners gave the highest priority to aid to Russia. The Army War Plans Division realized that a Soviet defeat would make Germany invincible. This realization was compounded by the recognition in late 1941 that Congress was not likely to approve the creation of a land army of the size deemed necessary to defeat Germany.[110] Thus, the best—perhaps only—way to ensure the defeat of Germany would be to maintain the Soviet front.

At the same time as the U.S. Army's leadership was grasping the importance of the Soviet front to the achievement of American national objectives, the Soviet position in the struggle with Germany was taking a dramatic turn for the worse. The Germans regrouped from their struggle outside Smolensk and renewed their push toward the Soviet capital. American observers began to fear a separate, negotiated peace between Hitler and Stalin.[111] The precarious situation brought home to many the importance of U.S. aid to the Soviet war effort.[112]

As the need for U.S. assistance became more apparent, the political climate in the United States became more amenable to increased aid for the Soviet Union. The renewed German push toward Moscow stimulated heroic Soviet resistance. That in turn increased American respect and admiration for the Soviet army as it fought in the face of overwhelming odds. As a result, growing numbers of Americans felt that the Soviet soldiers deserved U.S. assistance.[113] The negative aspect of this, in the administration's view, was that many people also held out hope that aid to the Soviet war effort would eliminate the need for American soldiers and sailors eventually to join the fighting. Hopkins expressed this concern in a letter to the American ambassador in London, John G. Winant: "I found public opinion here [in Washington, D.C.] a little discouraging. The Russian business seems to have convined [*sic*] everyone that Russia is going to do all the fighting. Therefore none of the rest of us have to help much. That seems to operate in almost all quarters except with the President, who feels that, of course, this is the opportune time to bring pressure on Hitler."[114] The administration's concerns about eventual U.S. military involvement in the war notwithstanding, fall 1941 was indeed an opportune time to press Hitler by providing increased aid to the Soviet Union. Roosevelt and Hopkins intended for the Harriman-Beaverbrook mission to seize that opportunity.

The primary purpose of the Anglo-American mission to Moscow was spelled out in a telegram from Hopkins to Churchill:

> [Roosevelt] considers it essential that the two Russian missions be instructed to communicate to the Russian Government the definite aid to be furnished by the American and British governments prior to July 1942. Those missions should also obtain from the Russian Government full information of Russian production capacity and Russian requirements from outside sources necessary to keep the Russian forces in the field for the purposes of defeating the Axis powers.
>
> With reference to the Victory Production Program, the understanding

of British and Russian requirements will make it possible to examine all needs with a view of integrating and relating them to the realities of production possibilities.[115]

The mission would help overcome the supply difficulties in the United States by ascertaining precise Soviet needs and integrating them into the overall U.S. production program. That would lessen the practical difficulties encountered in supplying material to the Soviet Union.

The Beaverbrook-Harriman mission also set out with the goal of reassuring the Soviets that the United States and Britain were sincere in their promises of assistance.[116] This was no doubt encouraged by Hopkins, who demanded that he be kept informed of every detail of the mission.[117] Beaverbrook and Harriman shared Hopkins' conviction that a fundamental ingredient in persuading Stalin of Anglo-American goodwill was that the Anglo-American team would give no indication that it was seeking any sort of concession from the Soviet leadership. The Beaverbrook-Harriman mission was not on a journey to bargain with Stalin.[118]

Shortly after his arrival in Moscow on 28 September 1941, Harriman met the personnel of the U.S. embassy in Moscow. Although they were friendly to the visiting dignitary, the embassy staff appeared to Harriman to view his mission as "an exercise in futility."[119] Harriman later noted that a third secretary in the embassy, Charles Thayer, pointed out to him that the diplomatic corps was still largely anti-Soviet. Moreover, the staff worried that the Soviets would be provided aid without enough strings attached.[120]

The meetings among the British, American, and Soviet negotiating teams lasted three days, during which time Beaverbrook and Harriman held three separate meetings with Stalin. While the lower-ranking delegations ferreted out the details of Soviet supply requirements, Harriman and Beaverbrook apparently accomplished their mission of reassuring Stalin of Anglo-American sincerity. Although their second meeting at the Kremlin was notable for Stalin's hostility toward the two visitors, the third and final meeting was equally distinctive for its cordiality. At this meeting Beaverbrook presented Stalin with a long list of supplies that Britain and the United States would send Moscow, and Stalin seemed visibly pleased.[121]

Harriman concluded that the mission had accomplished much in the way of reassuring Stalin, and he established further guidelines for guaranteeing future Soviet trust. In the memorandum of the conversation, Harriman summed up two fundamental principles which the Roosevelt administration would later adopt and attempt to adhere to throughout the war:

I left feeling that [Stalin] had been frank with us and if we came through as had been promised and if personal relations were retained with Stalin, the suspicion that has existed between the Soviet Government and our two governments might well be eradicated. . . .

The British representation in Moscow, particularly the Military Mission, have been quite petty and have fanned the mutual suspicion by their clumsy attempts to get military information. Beaverbrook's point of view concurred with mine that we should ask for information only when it was necessary to determine the supply problem.[122]

Thus, it was vitally important that the United States and Britain follow through on the promises made at these conferences. In addition, contrary to the expressed wishes of the American embassy staff, not only should there be no strings attached to Anglo-American aid, there should be no action that the Soviet leadership could conceive of as attaching conditionality to the assistance. This directly contravened the advice of everyone in the U.S. embassy, from the ambassador to the third secretary to the military attaché. Yet it was the American and British representatives in Moscow who bore most of the responsibility for reassuring the Soviets and carrying out the White House's wishes.

Before leaving Moscow, Harriman (and, through him, Hopkins in Washington) could not have been unaware of the potential clash between White House policy and attitudes in the U.S. embassy. Stalin brought the matter to Harriman's attention at their third Kremlin meeting when he vigorously criticized the U.S. ambassador. Steinhardt, according to Stalin, was a defeatist and a rumormonger. He also was disrespectful of the Russian government. Accordingly, Stalin indicated that he considered Steinhardt to be no longer useful in U.S.-Soviet relations.[123] Harriman also observed that the actions of the U.S. and British ambassadors were not conducive to building a healthy relationship with the Kremlin. British Ambassador Stafford Cripps and Steinhardt apparently bickered constantly, each accusing the other of failing to earn Soviet esteem. Harriman equated the situation with that found in a "girls school" and concluded it was "a bad situation in view of the determined policy on the part of the British and American Governments to get on a basis of mutual confidence with the Soviets."[124]

Steinhardt's days as U.S. ambassador to the Soviet Union were numbered. On his return to Washington, Harriman informed Roosevelt that Steinhardt was no longer useful in Moscow.[125] He was an excellent diplomat and was rewarded for his service with the ambassadorship in Turkey, but his attitudes toward the Soviet government and his recommendations for the conduct of

U.S. policy were out of touch with the administration's current agenda. Steinhardt resolutely clung to his view that relations with the Soviet Union must be conducted on a quid pro quo basis. Following the German invasion of the Soviet Union, the White House abandoned that approach and committed itself to a policy of unconditional aid to the USSR.

Although Steinhardt left Moscow, Thayer's comments to Harriman make it clear that belief in the necessity of a quid pro quo policy was widespread in the U.S. embassy in Moscow. It was relatively simple for Roosevelt to replace an ambassador, but as the history of U.S.-Soviet relations throughout the 1930s reveals, it was another thing entirely for the president to change the personnel of an embassy. Roosevelt was simply unable to do that. Thus, the administration resorted to its well-tested tactic of working around the existing bureaucracy.[126]

At the special request of Harry Hopkins, Philip Faymonville accompanied the Beaverbrook-Harriman mission to Moscow. Also at Hopkins' request, when Harriman departed the Soviet Union, Faymonville remained behind as a representative for the Division of Defense Aid Reports' Soviet supply division.[127] Faymonville's reappointment to the Soviet Union evoked no less controversy than had Davies' repeated attempts to have him remain military attaché. In the intervening period Faymonville had remained committed to his belief that the United States and the Soviet Union must cooperate. And he remained confident of Soviet military abilities. That brought him into direct conflict with much of the rest of the U.S. military, which, though awakening to the importance of the Soviet war effort, was still wedded to the interpretations of Yeaton and the Military Intelligence Division. Indeed, General Marshall forwarded the following report to Hopkins: "I don't know him [Faymonville] well, but I do know that competent men who have served with him, such as ex-Ambassador [William] Bullitt and Mr. [Loy] Henderson of the Russian Division of the State Department have serious doubts as to his judgement and his impartiality wherever the Soviets are concerned."[128] Hopkins had no greater respect for Marshall's man in Moscow. In early October he read one of Yeaton's cables from Moscow. Hopkins immediately shared his opinion of Yeaton and his views with Stimson:

There has been sent to us a copy of a report by our Military Attaché in Moscow dated October 10. This report in my opinion should be accepted with the greatest reserve.

When I was in Moscow, Yeaton was outspoken in his criticism of the Russian[s] and was insisting at that time—over ten to twelve weeks ago—that Moscow was going to fall at any time.

From my short observation in Moscow I can not see how any Military Attaché could get any reasonable expression of opinion from commuters or the general public which would be worthwhile.[129]

Thus, from the very beginning of American efforts to aid the Soviet Union in World War II, personnel on the ground in the Soviet Union generated strong and conflicting opinions among the higher levels of bureaucracy in Washington. As the war progressed, those responses would not lessen in intensity.

Conclusion

On 7 November 1941, Roosevelt publicly announced that he was placing aid to the Soviet Union under the lend-lease program. He thus fully committed his government to the policy of aid to the USSR. Even before November, however, Roosevelt had decided on that policy. Roosevelt's vision of the world was one in which Germany was the most pressing danger to the United States, and the defeat of Germany required U.S. cooperation with the Soviet Union. When Hopkins returned from Moscow in August 1941 with his declaration that Stalin intended to continue the war against Germany, Roosevelt pressed his government agencies to aid the Soviets as fully and rapidly as possible.

Despite repeated presidential interventions, there remained difficulties in the provision and transport of material for the Soviet Union. Some of the difficulties were practical, stemming from production shortages and a lack of knowledge of Soviet requirements. Other difficulties resulted from resistance among the personnel populating the vast bureaucracies charged with implementing the president's policies. Just as the State Department resisted Roosevelt's efforts to cooperate with the Soviet Union in the 1930s, so did the State and War Departments (and their constituent agencies) hesitate to follow the president's guidelines in the wake of Barbarossa. The military feared losing sorely needed material in a futile effort to prop up Russian resistance, while the State Department remained committed to their prewar belief that the only way to deal with the Soviets was on a strictly quid pro quo basis.

Roosevelt responded to this resistance in typical fashion. He attempted to work around his bureaucracies. His initial efforts to establish more harmonious Soviet-American relations involved sending special emissaries to Moscow to speak for him. Both Harriman and Hopkins met with Stalin alone, without the presence of the State Department's chief representative in Moscow. Harriman went one step further in the process of bypassing traditional channels. In his final meeting with Stalin, Harriman encouraged the Soviet dictator to communicate directly with Roosevelt.[130]

Roosevelt also bypassed his bureaucracies by establishing parallel organizations responsible only to the White House. The late July transfer of responsibility for Soviet assistance from the interorganizational committee to the Division of Defense Aid Reports under the control of Hopkins and his man, Burns, represents the first step in this process. The assignment of Faymonville to Moscow was the final step.

Bypassing the traditional policy-making and implementing apparatus held out the hope that institutional resistance would not slow down the provision of aid to the beleaguered Soviet armies. It also promised increased conflict and controversy. The reaction to Faymonville's appointment did not bode well for the future of Roosevelt's efforts to implement an aid policy toward the Soviet Union. This was particularly true because the controversial Army officer did not replace the existing officials in Moscow but was instead expected to work alongside them.

"All Aid to the Hilt": Developing a U.S. Policy Toward the Soviet Union, 1941–1943

Introduction

By fall 1941 Roosevelt was convinced that the United States must provide as much aid as possible to the Soviet Union while demanding nothing in return. He had both practical, immediate military reasons for this policy and long-term policy aspirations; and his commitment to this policy deepened as the United States moved from benevolent neutrality to belligerence in the global war.

Roosevelt's policy desires notwithstanding, it was clear to the president that the U.S. embassy personnel in the Soviet Union clung to their prewar perceptions of the Soviet Union and of what relations between the United States and the Soviet Union should look like. It was equally clear that their resistance to his policy could have a devastating effect on his ability to implement it. Consequently, Roosevelt resorted to his tactic of bypassing the bureaucracy by establishing a unique new structure with the sole mission of providing aid to and promoting cooperation with the Soviet Union. The heart of this new structure was the Office of Lend-Lease Administration (OLLA).

Although born of expediency, Roosevelt's decision to bypass the existing traditional policy-making structures and organs came at a high cost. As years went by and both old and new organs attempted to fulfill their assigned mission, the personnel who directed and manned each found themselves in growing conflict with each other. This clash became increasingly virulent and more difficult to keep private. Finally, by spring and summer 1943, it exploded into public view, placing the president's policy and the United States' relationship with the Soviet Union in jeopardy.

Implementing Soviet Aid

The emergence of Roosevelt's new policy to aid the Soviet Union was marked by two extraordinary presidential missions to Moscow: Harry Hopkins' in August 1941 and W. Averell Harriman's later that fall. The real implementation of the aid program, however, demanded regular, routine, and systematic action on the part of the U.S. government. Yet Hopkins and Harriman had both informed the president that the organization most directly responsible for implementing U.S. aid policy in the Soviet Union, the embassy in Moscow, was populated by individuals who ardently resisted a policy of providing unconditional aid to the Soviet Union. As a result, they argued, the provision of U.S. aid would continue to be plagued by the same difficulties that had prompted Roosevelt's late-summer bureaucratic shake-up in Washington.

By the time Harriman returned from his mission to the Kremlin in fall 1941, Roosevelt and Hopkins had already attempted to solve the problem of institutional resistance to aid to the Soviets. In Washington the White House tried to overcome bureaucratic snags by shifting the responsibility for providing aid to the Soviets from the State Department's Curtis Committee to the White House's Division of Defense Aid Reports. Soon thereafter, in late October 1941, Roosevelt established OLLA, which absorbed the Division of Defense Aid Reports and assumed full responsibility for administering the Soviet aid program. Roosevelt appointed Edward Stettinius as the new administrator of the OLLA, but Hopkins retained unofficial control of the organization.[1] The administration deliberately downplayed Hopkins' role because Stettinius was less controversial than Hopkins, who had incurred much enmity during his years as an aggressive New Deal administrator.

At the same time, Hopkins' decision to leave Faymonville in Moscow in order to establish a lend-lease office completed the creation of an entirely distinct organization for aiding the Soviet Union. From Faymonville in Moscow to Stettinius in Washington, this new organization was directly responsible to, and strictly controlled by, Roosevelt's White House.[2]

The mission of the new lend-lease office in Moscow reflected its direct relationship to the White House. General Burns later defined its role:

to assist in the execution of the aid program in order to achieve maximum effectiveness and by handling such problems as future modifications of the program items, quantities and design; maintenance; expedition; technical information; and, most important, teamwork between Russia and the United States.[3]

Significantly, Faymonville's new lend-lease office sought nothing from the Soviet Union in exchange for U.S. aid and strove mightily to avoid giving any appearance of exacting a quid pro quo. In this way the office underscored Roosevelt's firm belief that the only and most important compensation the United States would receive in exchange for its aid would be the defeat of Germany.[4]

While fulfilling its critical mission, Faymonville's Moscow lend-lease office was accountable only to Stettinius' OLLA and Roosevelt's White House. The lend-lease office did not report to the U.S. embassy in Moscow and was not under the jurisdiction of the American ambassador in Moscow. Nor was it responsible to Cordell Hull and the State Department or to Henry Stimson and the War Department. Thus, it operated entirely outside the existing U.S. foreign policy establishment.[5]

Aside from establishing new organizations to implement his Soviet aid policies, in 1941 Roosevelt left the traditional U.S. foreign policy-making and -implementing apparatus virtually untouched. The State and War Departments in Washington continued to provide advice to the White House and instructions to their officers in the field. In Moscow the U.S. embassy functioned much as it had before the Harriman-Beaverbrook mission. Foreign Service officers in Moscow dispatched their analyses and policy recommendations to Washington and attempted to carry out their diplomatic duties. The military attachés in Moscow likewise reported their assessments and recommendations to the War Department and continued their mission of gathering intelligence on the Soviet military. In short, despite Roosevelt's creation of new organizations for Soviet aid, the existing officials believed that their functions remained unchanged.

Thus by December 1941 Roosevelt had created a dual policy-making and -implementing structure for rendering U.S. policy toward the Soviet Union. Stettinius' OLLA and its office under Faymonville in Moscow were designed to carry out Roosevelt's policies aimed at closer cooperation with the Kremlin as expeditiously as possible. In contrast, the State and War Departments and their corresponding representatives in the Soviet Union remained firmly committed to their prewar belief that some quid pro quo should be exacted from the Soviet regime in return for this aid. These two structures essentially had fundamentally different and often conflicting missions. Roosevelt, however, had created these structures without clearly delineating the precise areas of authority of each. Consequently, as each organization attempted to fulfill its responsibilities, conflict between them inexorably increased.

A New War for Roosevelt

THE GERMANS AT THE GATES OF MOSCOW

Dramatic global developments in late fall 1941 temporarily overshadowed and masked the full ramifications of, and inherent contradictions in, Roosevelt's dual foreign policy structure in the Soviet Union. From late summer throughout the fall, the military situation along the Soviet-German front became increasingly dangerous for the Soviet Union and the Red Army, and by extension, for Roosevelt and the United States. Although not as precarious and potentially disastrous as U.S. embassy reports from Moscow indicated, the fate of the Red Army, major Soviet population centers in European Russia, and Stalin's Soviet state itself seemed perilous. The ebb and flow of this colossal military struggle shaped Roosevelt's foreign policy.

Even as Harriman and Beaverbrook prepared to embark on their supply mission to Moscow, German forces continued their advance eastward along the massive front: toward Leningrad in the north, Moscow in the center, and Stalingrad and the Caucasus in the south. Indeed, in September 1941, as Harriman and Beaverbrook were sitting down with Stalin to discuss the Soviet Union's material needs, the armies of the German Wehrmacht's Army Group South were completing their occupation of the Ukraine. Having destroyed the bulk of two Soviet *fronts*, including six armies and about 1 million men at Uman' and Kiev, in October, Army Group South captured Khar'kov, entered the Donbas industrial region, and occupied the Crimean Peninsula, isolating Red Army forces in Sevastopol' and the Kerch Peninsula.[6] By November, German forces in southern Russia were threatening Rostov and Stalingrad and the Caucasus beyond.

In the north, German Army Group North advanced to the suburbs of Leningrad and on 10 September captured Shlissel'burg on Lake Ladoga. It virtually encircled the city, leaving only a tenuous watery link across the surface of the lake connecting Leningrad and the rest of the Soviet Union. In October German Army Group North tried to sever Soviet rail lines east of Lake Ladoga by seizing the vital rail junction at Tikhvin, and although it failed to do so, it laid siege to the beleaguered city of Lenin.[7]

Satisfied that Leningrad would fall of its own weight, and jubilant over its victory in the Ukraine, in late September, German Army Group Center resumed its advance toward Moscow in the expectation of a quick victory. During the first two weeks of Operation Typhoon (the assault on Moscow) in October, German Army Group Center shattered, encircled, and destroyed the bulk of three Soviet *fronts* in the Viaz'ma and Briansk regions, including another six armies, killing or capturing about 1 million Red Army soldiers.[8] With its forward forces smashed, the Red Army had precious few forces with which to defend its capital. As the German juggernaut rolled forward, Stalin and his military staff ordered his forces to withdraw to a new defensive line at Mozhaisk, fifty miles west of Moscow, while the General Staff frantically accelerated the mobilization of fresh forces and raced them forward from the Soviet Union's vast interior.[9] While German forces pounded, outflanked, and seriously dented the Mozhaisk Line in mid-October, the Wehrmacht's forward progress slowed in the face of determined and often frantic Red Army resistance and the onset of the crippling autumn *rasputitsa* [rainy season], which turned Russian roads into seas of mud. Stalin summoned General G. K. Zhukov, who had just halted German forces at the gates of Leningrad, to Moscow in the hope that Zhukov could replicate his defensive feat once again. Assisted by the crippling rains and mud—as well as his characteristic ruthlessness—Zhukov restored stability to the city's defenses and marshaled the Red Army's reserves. At the same time, Hitler prepared to launch his final assault on Moscow once the winter cold turned the impassable mud to trafficable ice.[10]

Although Zhukov's actions and the onset of the rainy season had slowed German movement, in late October the Soviet capital still seemed imperiled. When Zhukov assumed command of the Red Army's threadbare western *front*, which was charged with the defense of Moscow, he discovered the *front* had few organized units and scarcely 90,000 men with which to defend the city.[11] While the General Staff ordered additional forces to the city, a desperate Stalin mobilized the city's civilian population, forming people's militia and volunteer workers' detachments to "fill gaps" in the defenses and enlisting hundreds of thousands of civilians to construct trenches and antitank ditches.[12] At the same time, on 13 October he ordered much of his government and the entire diplomatic community to evacuate Moscow; they fled to Kuibyshev and other cities to the east. This announcement, coupled with the civilian labor draft defense and unsubstantiated rumors about German tanks in a suburb of Moscow, contributed to an atmosphere of utter panic in the city, which only harsh Soviet internal security service (NKVD) action could quell.[13]

Reassured by Zhukov that the city could be defended successfully, on

17 October Soviet radio announced to the frightened Muscovites that despite the official evacuations, Stalin had decided to remain in Moscow to defend the capital with the Red Army against the German invaders.[14] Two days later Soviet authorities declared a state of martial law in the city. Alexander Werth, in Moscow as the correspondent for the *Sunday Times,* reported that the announcements combined to bolster civilian morale in October and November 1941.[15]

Improved morale alone would not, however, halt the German advance. Crawling forward through the muddy seas surrounding the Soviet capital, in early November the German Army Group Center continued its bid to envelop Moscow in anticipation of winter's arrival. Although Zhukov resisted this advance with a series of vicious attacks designed to slow the German forces, the arrival of the expected winter freeze on 15 November negated much of his desperate efforts. With the ground frozen solid, the feet of the German soldiers and the tracks of its panzers were freed from the grasp of the mud. By 28 November German armored spearheads had enveloped Moscow from both north and south. The lead elements of Third Panzer Group reached within twenty kilometers of the Kremlin, close enough for German officers to report spotting the city's center through their field glasses from church steeples north of the city.[16] On the opposite flank, the tanks of Heinz Guderian's Second Panzer Army bypassed Tula and approached Moscow from the south.

Driven on by Hitler, the German army began its final assault against Moscow from the north, west, and south on 1 December 1941. Having destroyed countless Soviet armies and millions of Red Army soldiers in their march across Russia, Hitler and his generals believed the Red Army, with no more reserves to throw into battle, was close to collapse. With the scent of victory so near, Hitler forbade the German Army to halt its offensive and withdraw into more defensible winter positions to resume the offensive in the spring. He intended to capture the Soviet capital immediately at any and all cost.

For the first few hours of the German attack, it appeared that Hitler's judgment might be correct. German forces penetrated up to a depth of about two kilometers into Soviet defenses west of the city. There they encountered stiff Soviet resistance as Zhukov again launched repeated spoiling counterattacks.[17] The Russian winter surrounded the invading Germans with biting temperatures and deep snow, the Red Army put up fierce resistance, and German units stretched their already weak supply lines. By the evening of 4 December this was all too much for the exhausted Germans, and they began to fall back to the positions they held on 1 December.[18] On 5 December 1941 the German offensive against Moscow sputtered to an exhausted halt.

Simultaneously, across a broad front from north of the city to its southern outskirts, a seemingly vanquished Red Army lashed out savagely against its tormentors with surprising and frightening effectiveness. Within hours, optimistic German field dispatches were replaced by desperate cries for help from beleaguered German front-line units.

As is often the case in war, appearances had been deceiving. Blinded by his optimism, Hitler had ignored the realities of a war in Russia. Despite the appalling toll that Soviet resistance and the rigors of winter took on the Wehrmacht's men and equipment, he ruthlessly urged his forces on. While Hitler was doing so, Stalin, his *Stavka,* the General Staff, and the entire cumbersome but immense Soviet military machine sprung into action, generating countless formations and units ultimately totaling nine reserve armies. It was these forces, mobilized and deployed secretly, that first slowed and then halted the Germans' final advance on Moscow. More important, it was these forces that began Zhukov's counterstrokes on 4 and 5 December, counterstrokes that Stalin then had the audacity to expand into a general counteroffensive in mid-December. By that time, for Stalin, Hitler, and, ultimately, for Roosevelt, the entire strategic equation had changed dramatically.

A NEW WORLD WAR EMERGES

The Wehrmacht's ignominious defeat at the gates of Moscow was not the only flicker of hope for the Kremlin in December 1941. No less significant from the geopolitical standpoint, dramatic events in the Far East that made the war truly global presaged further difficulties for the Berlin-Rome-Tokyo Axis. These developments also had a significant impact on Roosevelt's foreign policy agenda as the American president assessed the U.S. relationship with Japan in light of the Soviet position in its struggle with Germany. As the Berlin-Rome-Tokyo Axis knit separate conflicts into World War II, the new Axis impelled Roosevelt to formulate a coherent global foreign policy. Developments in the Pacific were inextricably linked to developments in eastern Europe, and all affected the president's policy decisions.

Relations between the Soviet Union and Japan had become increasingly tense throughout the 1930s. This tension erupted into open conflict when in July and August 1938 Soviet and Japanese forces clashed over the delineation of the Soviet-Manchurian frontier at Lake Khasan. Although they suffered high casualties, Soviet forces captured and held a disputed ridge.[19] One year later the Japanese sought to avenge this loss by seizing territory from the Soviet client state of Mongolia. On 11 May 1939, elements of the Japanese Kwantung Army based in Manchuria crossed the Khalkin-Gol River west of Nomonhan, where they occupied a small portion of Mongolian territory. The Soviets' mutual defense treaty with Mongolia compelled a Soviet response. After the struggle between Soviet-Mongolian and Japanese forces intensified during the summer, in late August a Soviet special corps under the command of G. K. Zhukov encircled and largely destroyed two Japanese divisions along the Khalkhin-Gol. The defeat forced the Japanese to sign a cease-fire with the Soviet Union on 15 September 1939.[20]

Relations between the Soviet Union and Japan became less strained after Khalkhin-Gol as both powers became absorbed with other serious problems: the Soviet Union with the German threat, and Japan with its relations with the United States. While Japanese strategy focused increasingly on Southeast Asia and the Pacific, the memory of Khalkhin-Gol served as a grim reminder of the Red Army's military capabilities.[21] This memory reinforced the Japanese inclination to avoid a further contest with the Soviet Union as Japan looked south and east. At the same time, Japan's Axis partner, Germany, signed a nonaggression pact with the Soviet Union and seemed to be pursuing a rapprochement with the Kremlin. In April 1941 Tokyo followed Berlin's lead and concluded its own neutrality pact with Moscow, on the premise that such a measure would secure its rear should it engage in a conflict in Southeast Asia and the Pacific. A few months later, on 22 June, Germany invaded the Soviet Union.

The advent of the Soviet-German War confronted the Japanese government with two strategic options. First, in a western (continental) strategy, it could reinforce its attempts to subjugate China by joining Germany in a war against the Soviet Union. Alternatively, it could pursue a Pacific strategy by moving south in search of vitally scarce resources. This option would risk war with Britain and the United States. It is clear that Roosevelt and Stalin were well aware of the dilemmas that Japan faced. In Stalin's case, because the fighting in European Russia provided ample evidence of the transitory nature of nonaggression pacts, he had to retain a significant military force along his Far Eastern border as he awaited the Japanese decision.

Not content to wait for Tokyo's decision, Roosevelt worked hard to develop his own policy in the Pacific. In fact, United States–Japanese relations had begun to deteriorate months before Germany turned on the Soviet Union. After Japanese forces advanced into northern Indochina in September 1940, signaling their intent to pursue Southeast Asia's critical natural resources—in particular, oil, tin, and rubber—the Roosevelt administration resorted to economic pressure in an attempt to discourage Japanese aggression. At the same time, however, because the United States was becoming more deeply involved in the war in the North Atlantic by dispatching vital military assistance to Great Britain, Roosevelt hesitated to provoke open conflict with Japan and cloaked his economic pressure with greater diplomatic contact.[22]

In the aftermath of the German attack on the Soviet Union, both the

United States and Japan struggled to define their foreign policies. Japan was the first to settle on a new course. On 2 July 1941 at an imperial conference, the Japanese government reconfirmed the decision it had made on 12 and 16 June to move into southern Indochina.[23] In the days after this conference, thanks to MAGIC intercepts—the American decryption of Japanese diplomatic codes—policy makers in Washington became aware of the Japanese decision.[24] This knowledge of Japanese intentions in Southeast Asia and, in all probability Malaya and the Dutch East Indies as well, neither resolved nor eased the Roosevelt administration's policy dilemma. The Japanese decision to attack to the south did not completely eliminate the threat of a Japanese attack on the Soviet Union. The historian Gerhard Weinberg argues that as of 3 July the United States was aware "that the Tokyo government had decided not to attack the Soviet Union."[25] Weinberg's assertion, however, is either based on the assumption that Germany would not defeat the Soviet Union, or should be qualified by the phrase "in the immediate future." As Weinberg points out in his analysis of the imperial conference that affirmed the decision to move south, Japan would consider attacking the Soviet Union "if it were obvious that that country was in a state of total collapse."[26] At the beginning of July the U.S. government, receiving dismal reports from Yeaton in Moscow, could not yet discount the possibility of Soviet collapse and a Japanese attack in Siberia.

As a result of this uncertainty, Roosevelt hesitated to adopt any concrete policy line. Instead, on 24 July, when Japanese intentions in southern Indochina became public knowledge, Roosevelt began implementing a three-tiered oil policy that maximized Japanese uncertainties as to both U.S. intentions and his own flexibility. The administration immediately froze Japanese assets in the United States; drew up new restrictions on the export of petroleum products to Japan; and established a system that would permit the president to halt shipments to Japan suddenly and without notice.[27]

Roosevelt's unwillingness to commit the United States to a definite policy in the Pacific clearly reflected his preoccupation with the war against Germany. Throughout the summer of 1941, Roosevelt remained committed to the principle that the most dangerous threat to the United States was Hitler. Increasing U.S. involvement in the naval struggle in the North Atlantic prompted Roosevelt to hesitate to take steps that risked a two-front war against two enemies simultaneously in Europe and the Pacific.[28] In June and July 1941, however, the strategic view from Washington began to change as Soviet military resistance seemed to belie the notion that Germany would inflict rapid catastrophic defeat on the Red Army. By late July 1941 Roosevelt reached the conclusion that the survival of the Soviet Union was vital to the security of the United States. That awareness led the president to pressure his government to increase aid to the Soviet military and to refrain from any steps that might encourage Japan to attack the Soviet Far East.[29] Roosevelt feared that shipping oil to Japan might encourage Japanese aggression against the Soviet Union. Consequently, by September the administration had secretly converted the freeze order into a de facto total oil embargo against Japan.[30]

By the time Roosevelt resolved to prevent Japanese aggression against the Soviet Far East and Siberia by economic means, these measures had already prompted the Japanese government to decide not to pursue military operations against the two regions in 1941. As Japanese leaders became aware of the U.S. oil embargo, a crisis atmosphere gripped the country. Japan's oil supply was diminishing, the resources required to replenish that supply lay to the south, and Japan's chief potential antagonist, the United States, had embarked on a naval building program that would only continue to increase its power relative to Japan.[31] As a direct result, by the fall of 1941, the Japanese government began actively to prepare for war with the United States and Britain unless diplomacy could exact concessions from the Anglo–American powers.[32]

Some hope, however faint, still existed in the fall that diplomacy could play some further role in improving United States–Japanese relations. In early November, for example, the Red Army seemed to have slowed the German advance significantly. Because most observers began to believe that Moscow might actually hold out, Japanese aggression against the Soviet Union seemed to become much less likely.[33] Accordingly, as the Japanese threat to the Soviet Union lessened, Roosevelt felt less impelled to divert Japanese attention from the north. At the same time, because the United States found itself increasingly enmeshed in the conflict in the North Atlantic, Roosevelt believed it would be best to avoid conflict with Japan. Hence, he began to show interest in finding a modus vivendi with the Japanese leadership.[34]

Roosevelt's interest in a diplomatic solution did not persist long. Once again it was the deteriorating situation in the Soviet Union that diminished Roosevelt's ardor for rapprochement with Japan. By the end of November, the Soviet military situation again looked desperate as German forces launched their final offensive against Moscow. In the Pacific as well, the Japanese were on the move, threatening the region adjacent to the South China Sea. An alarmed Roosevelt decided that a modus vivendi with Japan in the face of its aggression was akin to appeasement. Consequently he instructed Hull to inform the Japanese that any diplomatic settlement was predicated on a complete Japanese withdrawal from China.[35] As Roosevelt well understood, that condition was unacceptable to the Japanese regime. Unbeknownst to the American president, on 1 December 1941, the Japanese government affirmed their decision to go to war against the United States and Britain.[36]

On 7 December 1941, the Japanese navy launched a surprise attack against Pearl Harbor, Hawaii. Aircraft from 6 Japanese carriers damaged or destroyed 8 American battleships, 10 other warships, and most of the U.S. Army's aircraft on the island; they left in their wake over 2400 American dead and 1100 wounded.[37] The next day, President Roosevelt asked Congress to declare war against Japan, and Congress promptly voted for the declaration. Although not obligated by treaty, Germany and Italy joined Japan's conflict on 11 December by declaring war on the United States.

The United States of America was now a full belligerent in the global conflict. No longer restricted by the bounds of neutrality, Roosevelt gained the flexibility to prosecute the war and construct a peace largely as he saw fit.

ROOSEVELT'S WORLD MISSION

The Japanese attack on Pearl Harbor and resulting U.S. involvement in World War II had significant implications for U.S. foreign policy. The most immediate challenge to Roosevelt's stated prewar policy was to his definition of the greatest threat to American security. Throughout much of the 1930s Roosevelt had been convinced, and had argued, that Germany posed the greatest security threat to the United States. However, the treacherous and devastating Japanese attack on U.S. territory and military bases and associated Japanese assaults on U.S. territories in the western Pacific naturally challenged this position. Even though the U.S. public and Congress wholeheartedly supported the declaration of war against Japan, this did not necessarily translate into carte blanche support for a declaration of war against Germany. Hitler's ill-conceived 11 December decision to declare war against the United States eliminated Roosevelt's quandary. The Germany-first strategy was affirmed a month later at the Arcadia conference in Washington, D.C. Henceforth, faced with no other recourse than to wage a two-front war, Roosevelt's dilemma became strategic—namely, to determine U.S. priorities in a two-front war.

U.S. entry into the war also presented Roosevelt with the opportunity to play a more active role in global policy formulation, particularly regarding future peace, security, stability, and the spread of democracy. As had been the case during the final two years of World War I, American involvement in the war quickly took on the mantle of a crusade. Roosevelt and his administration seized the opportunity to reform the world along the same progressive lines embodied in his domestic New Deal agenda.[38] Roosevelt was not naive. A man who spent his formative political years in the Woodrow Wilson administration and who later campaigned for vice president on a platform centered on U.S. membership in the League of Nations, Roosevelt believed that establishing a fair and lasting peace was the most important outcome of war. Thus he was determined to overcome the impediments that had caused the Treaty of Versailles to fail.

From the very beginning of U.S. involvement in the war, Roosevelt believed that the key to avoiding another Versailles was to hold the wartime association between the United States, the United Kingdom, and the Soviet Union together.[39] Often that required adopting a type of "practical idealism." This meant that Roosevelt was prepared to compromise on some of his loftier principles (for example, the right of all people to determine their own government) in order to achieve his greater aim of lasting cooperation among the Big Three in structuring the postwar peace.

The Soviet Union was absolutely vital to Roosevelt's plans both in terms of winning the war and creating and maintaining the postwar peace. Before Pearl Harbor, the Roosevelt administration realized that effective Soviet military resistance to Germany was imperative if victory was to be achieved over Hitler's Reich. As Roosevelt formulated his other war aims, particularly regarding the establishment of a lasting postwar peace, he recognized that Soviet cooperation was essential for their attainment. It became obvious to Roosevelt that resolute continuation of his no-questions-asked aid policy was the key to fulfilling both goals.

1942: THE NADIR OF ALLIED FORTUNES

The deteriorating military fortunes of Allied forces in 1942 reinforced Roosevelt's belief that the survival of the Soviet Union and its Red Army was absolutely vital to the achievement of Allied victory.[40] Beginning in January 1942, Allied forces suffered defeat after defeat in virtually every theater of military operations around the globe. In the Pacific, after destroying much of America's Pacific Fleet at Pearl Harbor, the Japanese were able to exploit their initial success with impunity. They did so by launching consecutive assaults against the Philippines, Thailand, Malaya, and the Dutch East Indies. By May 1942 Japanese forces were approaching India and the shores of Australia, and they threatened to cut the British off from contact with their dominions.

The situation was little better on the other side of the globe. Europe was firmly in Hitler's hands, and British forces were relegated to operating in secondary theaters, where victories were also in short supply. All the while, German U-boats and surface raiders were threatening to win the Battle for the Atlantic. If they were successful, Britain might well be cut off from U.S. support. British forces in the Mediterranean theater and North Africa were faring poorly as well. After initial British successes against the Italians in North Africa in 1940, a short but violent campaign by Generalleutnant Erwin Rommel's Afrika Korps pushed British forces back into Egypt and threatened both the Middle East and Britain's vital Mediterranean supply lines to her Asian possessions.[41]

The most dangerous threat to Allied military fortunes in 1942, nevertheless, was the deteriorating military situation in the Soviet Union. After achieving his spectacular but unexpected victory over German forces at Moscow in December 1941, in January 1942 Stalin ordered the Red Army to embark on a general offensive to smash German forces along the entire Soviet-German front. Although the Red Army succeeded in inflicting embarrassing defeats on the Germans at Moscow, at Tikhvin near Leningrad, and at Rostov in the south, Stalin's grand winter offensive ended in April 1942 before the Red Army achieved any of his ambitious aims.[42] It was abundantly clear that when formulating his aims, Stalin had woefully overestimated the Red Army's strength and capabilities. Having lost manpower equivalent to its entire June 1941 strength, by April 1942 the bloodied and exhausted Red Army was deployed along a thousand-mile front from Murmansk to the Black Sea. Worse still, its forces were deployed in a crazy patchwork-quilt configuration of overlapping Soviet and German units located where the Soviet offensive had faltered. Because neither Hitler nor Stalin had achieved his strategic goals at Moscow, both resolved to do so in the ensuing spring and summer

Inspired by his partial victory at Moscow, an overconfident Stalin opened the spring campaign in May 1942 by attempting to conduct major offensives at Khar'kov and in the Crimea. Simultaneously, Hitler formulated his equally ambitious Operation Blau (blue), which required the German Army to achieve victory over the Soviet Union by means of a decisive thrust across southern Russia to seize Stalingrad and the oil-rich Caucasus region. Stalin's twin offensives struck German forces, which were themselves preparing to attack. Both ended in disaster. Having lost most of its strategic reserves in these spectacular failures, the Red Army was then ill prepared to deal with Hitler's new offensive onslaught.

With brutal efficiency, the German war machine struck Soviet defenses in southern Russia on 28 June 1942 and ground inexorably forward, crushing all Soviet resistance forces in its path. By late August 1942, German Army South (now formed into Army Groups A and B) reached the Volga River at Stalingrad and began a determined thrust southward into the Caucasus region. As had been the case in summer 1941, it seemed to the casual observer and military analyst alike that Hitler's Wehrmacht was unstoppable.

The Soviet military position in late summer 1942 was indeed precarious. Therefore, it was entirely understandable that Stalin would turn toward his western allies for assistance. From the very beginning of the war, Stalin had appealed to Britain to open a "second front" against Germany by invading continental Europe, thereby relieving Wehrmacht pressure on the Red Army. As the war continued, and particularly after the disastrous spring of 1942, the Kremlin's cries for the second front became more shrill and insistent. Nor was the second front Stalin's only demand. Given the Soviet Union's immense loss of resources and much of its prewar industrial base to the invading Germans, Stalin also requested increased Allied material assistance in the form of military equipment, vital raw materials, and essential supplies to sustain both the military and civilian population. Along with the military aid, Stalin also sought recognition of the Soviet Union's frontier as it had existed before the German invasion. The Soviet dictator demanded a sign of goodwill from his western allies.

Roosevelt fully appreciated the desperate nature of the Soviets' struggle for survival and both understood and feared the ominous implications if the Soviet Union did not survive. In short, he realized that if he did not strive to accommodate Stalin's demands, the Soviet Union might collapse or try to reach accord on a separate peace with Hitler. Given these stark prospects, Roosevelt found it increasingly difficult to turn a deaf ear to Soviet demands and decided to satisfy as many of them as possible. For example, in a private meeting with Litvinov on 12 March 1942, Roosevelt informed the Soviet ambassador that he did not expect any sort of difficulty with Soviet-desired postwar frontiers. Roosevelt further stated that he was fully in agreement with Stalin and had always considered it folly to have removed those provinces (the Baltic states and eastern Poland) from Russia after World War I.[43] Roosevelt asked Litvinov to inform Stalin that although the United States would not have a problem with Soviet territorial demands, for political reasons, it was best not to request a public commitment at that time.[44] In a later meeting with Molotov, Roosevelt again assured the Soviet leadership that the United States would not stand in the way of Soviet political demands, but he was concerned about U.S. public opinion.[45]

In early 1942, however, the question of military aid to the Soviet war effort was of far more immediate import. With Red Army forces under immense pressure in southern Russia and the Soviet Union's industrial base not tooled up for maximum wartime production, Stalin pressed his allies to commit themselves to opening a second front in Europe in 1942. At first, Roosevelt and his military advisers were willing at least to consider doing so. But after closer consultation with the British, it became clear to Roosevelt that it was impossible to open a second front in Europe in 1942. Both the United States and Great Britain lacked sufficient forces in Europe for a cross-channel invasion at that time. Thus, any second front would have to consist primarily of British troops.

After their near-disastrous departure from the continent two years earlier, Churchill was unwilling to risk what remained of his military.[46]

Given the Allied inability to relieve German pressure on the Soviet Union in direct fashion, it became even more vital that the Allies provide the Soviets with material necessary for them to continue their struggle. Thus, throughout the remainder of 1942 Roosevelt remained committed to his program to provide the Soviets with military aid. In fact, this aid was the only thing Roosevelt had to offer Stalin in exchange for continued Soviet military resistance to the Germans and for future cooperation in the process of formulating and ensuring postwar peace.

Antipodean Perspectives

American diplomatic personnel assigned to the U.S. embassy in Moscow played an integral role in the formulation and implementation of Roosevelt's wartime foreign policy during 1942. Because so much of the president's policy was predicated on the continuation of the provision of no–quid pro quo aid, the attitudes and actions of personnel in the embassy and lend-lease office in Moscow assumed an even greater importance than the normal routine influence of low-level government functionaries. The personnel's hostility and resistance toward the president's policy forced the president to modify his chosen course. It also forced Roosevelt to alter the way he formulated policy by increasing his reliance on advisers outside the traditional diplomatic structure. The specific roles Roosevelt's administration assigned to the officials in Moscow reflected the administration's awareness of this unique situation.

Hopkins had already underscored his appreciation of the unique circumstances in Moscow during the fall of 1941 when he established the lend-lease office in the Soviet capital in order to bypass the existing diplomatic structure. Because the provision of material assistance was now the focal point of American relations with the Soviet Union, this office overshadowed the U.S. embassy. When Stalin ordered the evacuation of most government organs and offices and the diplomatic community from Moscow to Kuibyshev and other locations in October 1941, Faymonville and the U.S. lend-lease office remained in Moscow. Similarly, Stalin himself never left the Soviet capital, where the most important state business was still being conducted.

Roosevelt's own resolve regarding the issue of military aid was evident in his selection of a new ambassador to replace Steinhardt. Roosevelt's first choice was Major General Burns, the head of the Soviet Division in the Office of Lend-Lease Administration, because of his ardent support for and familiarity with the policy of no–quid pro quo aid to the Soviet Union. However, Burns was too important to the Lend-Lease Administration to leave his post in Washington.[47] The president next turned to W. Averell Harriman, the man who led the U.S. delegation to the Moscow supply conference in September. Harriman argued that his work with Churchill was too important to be interrupted by transfer to the Soviet Union. Roosevelt also approached former ambassador Joseph Davies, who was too ill for a long stay in the Soviet Union.[48] Finally, Roosevelt settled on Admiral William H. Standley.

There were good reasons why Roosevelt chose Standley for the post. First and foremost, the admiral was a longtime friend of the president. He had been Roosevelt's chief of naval operations in the early 1930s. After retiring from the navy, Standley worked in the burgeoning military-industrial complex, where his military and industrial experience shaped him as an ardent proponent of military preparation as war appeared increasingly likely in Europe and the Pacific. This combination of advocacy and experience made Standley an appropriate choice for inclusion in the U.S. delegation in the Harriman-Beaverbrook Mission to Moscow. Thus, in late 1941 when he sought an ambassador who would emphasize the importance of U.S. material aid to United States–Soviet relations, Roosevelt's gaze finally fell on Standley. Although he did not have as much experience with the Soviet Union in particular and diplomacy in general as the three other candidates, Standley seemed to be a promising choice for ambassador.[49]

Roosevelt saw Standley's role primarily as an expediter of aid. In 1942 that was the only role Roosevelt envisioned for his representatives in Moscow. Thus, the president did not consider it important to share with Standley his overall policy vision and rationale for the aid policy toward the Soviet Union. Had he done so, Roosevelt would have realized Standley did not wholeheartedly share his view of the role of the ambassador to the Soviet Union. Standley believed that Roosevelt had chosen him for the post because he would "talk turkey" with the Kremlin.[50]

Unaware of Roosevelt's new focus in United States–Soviet relations, Standley left for Kuibyshev convinced that his ambassadorship would differ in no significant way from those of his predecessors. As an experienced and proud naval officer, he was not aware that other key figures in Roosevelt's administration viewed him as primarily a figurehead whose role was to expedite the shipment of essential military supplies to the Soviet Union.[51] Standley's growing awareness of the discrepancy between the way he and the administration perceived his mission would contribute to an atmosphere of tension and hostility that developed among American personnel in the Soviet Union.

Politics and Policy

The attitudes of officials in the State Department and the U.S. embassy in Moscow influenced Standley's view of the Soviet Union. Before his departure to his new post, Standley spent two weeks in Washington for what he described as "briefing and indoctrination."[52] Standley's "briefing and indoctrination" included several luncheon meetings with Roosevelt. At one of these he discussed the policy Roosevelt wanted to pursue toward the Soviet Union. In a brief outline of the development of United States–Soviet–British relations, Roosevelt explained that he was opposed to secret commitments "at this time" because they would violate the Atlantic Charter and the "basic principles for which we are fighting."[53] Elaborating on this summary, Roosevelt seemed to retreat a bit from his stated commitment to basic principles: "relations between the Soviet and American Governments must be based on mutual good faith and confidence, that our first objective was to win the war and that nothing should be allowed to arise at this time which might disturb the common front of the Allied powers."[54]

When Standley sought clarification of the possible discrepancy between a commitment to "basic principles" and a desire to avoid any conflict that "might disturb the common front," Roosevelt remained ambiguous. Standley recorded the exchange in a memorandum of the conversation: "I referred back to the basic principles of the Atlantic Charter and asked again if the entire matter was one of adhering to the basic principles for which we were contending. The President answered 'yes' and to good faith between nations."[55] Roosevelt was apparently not concerned about the ambiguity because he intended to resolve policy issues through personal diplomacy with Stalin. Even before dispatching Standley to the Soviet Union, Roosevelt instructed his ambassador to inform Stalin that if the two leaders could "arrange for a personal conference, all of the difficulties would disappear and he and Stalin would reach an absolute accord on all the questions at issue."[56]

Although Standley was briefed by the president, Roosevelt was vague about his policy toward the Soviet Union. Most of Standley's training actually occurred at the State Department.[57] During this period, when his closest contact at the department was Assistant Chief of the Division of European Affairs Loy Henderson, Standley studied the issues that affected United States–Soviet relations. Among those were the release of Polish officers captured by the Red Army in 1939, permission to fly planes across Siberia for delivery to the Red Air Force, coordination of intelligence activities, establishment of better radio communications between the Soviet Union and the United States, and a better exchange of information on technical and tactical matters.[58] In addition, Standley met U.S. citizens who had complaints against the Soviet Union. As a result, even before he left Washington, Standley sympathized with the Polish people affected by Soviet policy.[59] Overriding all concerns, Standley believed that it was his responsibility as ambassador to help develop a true partnership to defeat Germany by resolving the difficult issues that plagued United States–Soviet relations. Partnership, to Standley, implied an equal relationship in which each member gives as well as receives.

Standley arrived in Moscow and embarked on his mission by endeavoring to establish personal relations with Soviet officials. Eager to get to work, he was frustrated to discover that he had to wait twelve days to meet Stalin. During that period he received a telegram from the State Department advising him not to bring up with Molotov or Stalin any of the topics from his briefings. Standley was disgusted. Turning to Edward Page, one of the young Foreign Service officers assigned to the embassy, Standley exclaimed: "We can't get anywhere on such a basis. It's ridiculous on the face of it."[60] Rejecting the State Department's "suggestion," he had two uncomfortable interviews with Stalin and Molotov, during both of which he brought up "less pleasant matters."[61] These included the establishment of air shuttle routes, the shipment of raw materials from the Soviet Union to the United States, and the landing of an American air crew in Siberia after a bombing raid against Japan.[62]

Standley was not long in the Soviet Union before he experienced the same treatment as had his predecessors. The long delay before he was received by Stalin was just the beginning of a long series of slights and inconveniences heaped on the American ambassador. Standley's telegrams to the State Department began to echo the concerns of earlier U.S. ambassadors as he complained about the Soviet lack of cooperation with the U.S. embassy. By July Standley found the situation so distressing that he took it up with both Stalin and Molotov. Standley informed the State Department of his remarks to the Soviet leader: "I then stated that since my arrival here the Embassy in practically all aspects of its work had been continually subjected to delays, interference and indifference on the part of subordinate Soviet officials and that it appeared to me that almost a studied effort was being made to thwart the cooperative spirit which Stalin had agreed in my first interviews should exist."[63]

The new ambassador to the Soviet Union did not share the administration's attitude of how best to approach Soviet officials. He believed that efforts to avoid antagonizing the Soviets were perceived as signs of weakness. Consequently, he adopted a new approach: "In my dealings with the Russians, I came to believe in standing up to them, in being forceful and demanding. . . .

I had no hesitancy in speaking in a blunt, pointed and salty sailorman fashion."[64] Standley reached the same conclusion Steinhardt had reached years earlier. Although he was by now aware of Roosevelt's policy of "do not antagonize the Russians—give them everything they want," Standley believed that the United States should be exacting something from the Soviet government in exchange for material aid.[65]

The State Department bureaucracy and the Foreign Service were not monolithic organizations. Although most in the organization disagreed with Roosevelt's policy, individual personalities and ideologies did make a difference. There were some officials in the U.S. embassy who disagreed with Standley's recommendations. In particular, the chargé d'affaires (before Standley's arrival) and counselor of the embassy, Walter R. Thurston, dispatched several telegrams to the State Department advising what policy the United States should adopt toward the Soviet Union. In the first, dated 3 February 1942, Thurston described Soviet suspicions of America's intentions and proposed steps the United States could take to overcome them. Thurston essentially advocated the exact opposite of what Standley and others in the State Department would vociferously support in the coming years:

> If we have made our own vital decision to help the Soviet Union defeat Germany without reservations based upon fear of a victorious and powerful Russia, it should be possible to reduce the suspicions mentioned by the following two processes: First—positively—by exerting convincing efforts to supply the war needs of the Soviet Union to the satisfaction of the Soviet military observers and purchasing agents in the United States, who presumably should be given status and facilities comparable to those enjoyed by their British counterparts in so far as access to information is concerned; and second—negatively—by avoiding action which might be construed by Russians to indicate that we are holding back, or are seeking some ulterior advantage.[66]

First Secretary Charles E. Dickerson supported Thurston's position with a dispatch dated 20 March 1942. In this lengthy telegram, Dickerson specified what exactly the United States should avoid in order not to arouse Soviet suspicions:

> If, as is evident, it is to the immediate interest of the Allies that Russia should go on fighting the aggressor, then it is the essential task of the Allies to confine their activities in relation to the Soviet Union to the furnishing

of aid in whatever form the Soviets desire, as quickly as possible, at the points indicated by the Soviets, and in the largest volume possible within the terms of their own war effort. Advice on how to win their war is not regarded by the Soviets as a commodity of which they are in need, nor do they consider that they require very much instruction in the use of the matériel which may be furnished to them.[67]

This was the exact policy the Roosevelt administration and the lend-lease office in Moscow adopted. But with the arrival of Standley in the Soviet Union, Thurston and Dickerson became a dissenting minority in the U.S. embassy. Standley preferred the voices representing prewar attitudes.

STATE DEPARTMENT PERCEPTIONS

Standley's attitude coincided with that of many in the State Department. Despite the Roosevelt administration's intent to abandon any sort of reciprocal arrangement with the Soviet government, officials in the State Department were slow to discard their affinity for reciprocity. The question of reciprocity reared its head again in July 1942 when the Soviet Union suggested an exchange of notes to extend most favored nation status for consuls. Henderson objected that this was a bad idea because it would result in no measurable benefit for U.S. consuls in the Soviet Union. He argued that "the advantages accruing from a consular agreement of this kind would be of a unilateral nature."[68] A year later, Henderson warned the department about the folly of abandoning "a regime of reciprocity." He pointed out that America's unilateral lifting of travel restrictions on Soviet consular officers had not resulted in similar gestures by the Soviet Union.[69]

As the war progressed, State Department officials' concern for strict reciprocity gradually began to be overshadowed by a fear of Soviet policy motives. On 9 April 1942 Loy Henderson reported that the State Department was still worried about Soviet efforts to undermine the United States. He recommended the department send a telegram to Ambassador Standley to ascertain whether the Soviet Union had abandoned its policy of "endeavoring to [en]list persons emigrating to the United States from the Soviet Union as agents of the Soviet Government or of the Communist International and of treating relatives remaining in the Soviet Union as hostages in order to retain influence over persons enlisting as agents."[70]

In addition to its concern about Soviet espionage and communist influence, the State Department was disturbed by more overt Soviet foreign policy aims. Particularly distressing to State Department officials was Soviet incorporation of the Baltic states and insistence on their June 1941 frontiers. Henderson, whose early experience included stints in Latvia, where he met and married his Latvian wife, was outraged by Soviet actions in those three countries. In a memorandum dated 25 October 1941, Henderson warned against believing Soviet Ambassador to the United Kingdom Ivan Maisky's statements regarding Soviet-Finnish relations. Henderson warned of the Soviet precedent in the Baltic states: "Although in spite of its promises to the Baltic States that it would not infringe upon their integrity, the Soviet Government did not hesitate when the moment came to take full advantage of its bases in those countries in order to invade them, overthrow their Governments, and scatter the more intelligent sections of the population over Siberia and Asia."[71] Henderson's observations were correct, but his presentation of them reflected a simmering anger toward the Kremlin that would affect his response to every Soviet policy initiative.

Henderson pressed the State Department to adopt a policy of "firmness" toward the Soviet government with regard to the portions of Poland and the Baltic states that the Soviet Union claimed. He shared Standley's view of how the Soviet regime must be approached: "If we show the slightest weakness and equivocation in this regard the Soviet Government will at once bring tremendous pressure on us and in the end our relations will be more unfavorably affected than they would be if we display firmness at the outset."[72]

Leading officials in the State Department shared Henderson's perspective on Soviet territorial ambitions in eastern Europe. The issue came to a head after British Foreign Secretary Anthony Eden's visit to Moscow in December 1941. At that time Stalin proposed a treaty between the Soviet Union and the United Kingdom in which the United Kingdom would recognize the Soviet frontiers of June 1941. In response to that development, Hull had commissioned a memorandum that he sent to Roosevelt. In his preface to the memorandum, Hull rejected the premise that the test of America's good faith toward the Soviet Union should be recognition of their 1941 frontiers.[73] The memorandum Hull enclosed with his letter argued that acceptance of Soviet territorial claims in eastern Europe would destroy key principles of the Atlantic Charter. Instead of accepting these claims, the memorandum advocated a tougher approach toward the Kremlin: "It would seem that it is preferable to take a firm attitude now, rather than to retreat and to be compelled to take a firm attitude later when our position has been weakened by the general principles referred to above."[74]

Undersecretary of State Sumner Welles appeared outraged at the British consideration of Stalin's demands. On the surface, Welles' support of State

Department views in opposition to the president's may seem odd. Welles had a reputation as an intimate of the enigmatic president. Intimacy with Roosevelt, however, had limitations. It is arguable that Roosevelt confided fully in no one, not even his closest adviser, Harry Hopkins. Welles' position at the State Department may have also completely inhibited open conversation between the undersecretary and the president. Welles had some close friends in State. One of these was Adolf Berle, an ardent opponent of territorial concessions to the Soviet Union.[75] In 1942 Roosevelt wanted to avoid controversy over United States–Soviet relations. The best way to do that would be to avoid both public discussion of territorial issues and excessive State Department involvement in his conversations with the Soviet leadership. That required withholding his ideas from both foe and friend.

Even if Roosevelt had shared all his thoughts with Welles, they would not have affected Welles' initial response to the proposed Soviet-British treaty. When he met with British Ambassador to the United States William Frederick Lindley Wood, the first earl of Halifax, Welles laid out what he considered to be the administration's views on the proposed Soviet-British treaty:

> I said that I could not conceive of this war being fought in order to undertake once more the shoddy, inherently vicious, kind of patchwork world order which the European powers had attempted to construct during the years between 1919 and 1939. . . .
> Lord Halifax in his reply evidenced the worst phase of the spirit of Munich. He spoke of the need of having Russia to constitute the balance of power against Germany in the years after the war.[76]

Welles' perception was that the proposed treaty violated the principle of self-determination discussed in the Atlantic Charter.[77]

Berle shared this view. On 3 April 1942 he inserted himself into the discussions and sent a memorandum to Welles detailing his problems with the treaty. According to Berle, this treaty represented a "Baltic 'Munich.'"[78] To Berle (and many others) "Munich" was synonymous with foolhardy appeasement of aggression.

In his response to Berle's memorandum, Welles argued that the United States could be accused of nothing because the government had come out in opposition to the treaty. He did, however, concur in Berle's assessment of the agreement. He succinctly stated his attitude toward the territorial concessions embodied in the treaty: "In my own judgment, the treaty violated the clear terms of the Atlantic Charter and is indefensible from every moral standpoint, and equally indefensible from the standpoint of the future peace and stability of Europe."[79]

In August 1942, the State Department's Division of European Affairs briefed former Republican presidential candidate Wendell Willkie on official U.S. policy toward the Soviet Union. Acting Chief of the Division Atherton pointed out that policy was essentially the same as it had been in December 1941. Slight changes to the policy reflected a greater emphasis on the role of the Atlantic Charter and "the present unwillingness of the U.S. Government to enter into commitments at this time regarding specific terms of the post-war settlement."[80]

In marked contrast to Roosevelt, the State Department was consistently opposed to the recognition of any Soviet territorial claims. Throughout the early years of the Soviet-German War, State Department communications, particularly from the Division of European Affairs, reflected an unwillingness to brook any compromise of the principles for which State believed the United States was fighting. While the Soviet Union had its proverbial back to the wall in 1941 and 1942, there was little visible challenge to the State Department position. State Department officials were, after all, arguing against some future hypothetical. Their views were nonetheless on a path clearly divergent from that of the president. And the attitudes of State Department officials in Washington reinforced the attitudes of the State Department personnel in Moscow. In both Washington and Moscow, a dispute over the correct U.S. policy toward the Soviet Union developed rapidly from 1941 to 1943.

The Struggle for Information

Standley's mission in the Soviet Union was difficult not simply because of the developing policy dispute. From the moment Standley arrived in the Soviet Union, he felt himself in an awkward position. The Harriman-Beaverbrook mission had encouraged the establishment of direct channels of communication between Stalin and Roosevelt. As a result, Standley often remained in the dark, uninformed of developments, agreements, and negotiations between the two leaders. For example, on 3 May 1942, Standley sent a telegram to U.S. Secretary of State Cordell Hull complaining that he was not informed of discussions conducted by Hopkins and Marshall in London concerning the Soviet supply situation. Further, he noted that he was provided only incomplete information about a secret message that, through Maxim Litvinov, the Soviet ambassador to the United States, was passed from Hull to Stalin. In this instance, Standley concluded that "as a result of this situation the complete frankness which should have characterized this meeting with Stalin was lacking."[81]

Standley did not find any relief when later that month Molotov traveled to London and Washington. The State Department informed the ambassador that Molotov was visiting the two capitals in order to discuss the second protocol to the lend-lease agreement. Standley was unaware that Molotov, Churchill, and Roosevelt discussed the second front in Europe until BBC radio announced the details of a communiqué describing the talks.[82]

Standley sent the State Department a telegram on 22 July that repeated his complaint: "I have been handicapped in my conversations with Stalin and Molotov and in my interpretation of their attitudes and policies by the fact that I have never been fully informed of what took place or what commitments may have been made to Molotov while he was in London and Washington."[83] Despite Standley's concerns, the U.S. government continued to ignore him. On 12 August 1942, Churchill arrived in Moscow for discussions with Stalin. A few days earlier, Standley learned that Harriman would accompany the British prime minister. In fact, Harriman joined Churchill in his meetings with Stalin. Although the British ambassador was present at the Kremlin discussions, Standley was included in none except the traditional Kremlin dinner. Standley clearly resented Harriman's encroachment on his territory. The ambassador contended that he was led to believe that the Churchill-Stalin talks were a purely British affair. Upon learning that Harriman would be joining the prime minister, however, Standley believed that any agreements reached were "taken as tacit approval by the United States."[84] By not attending those meetings, Standley feared the U.S. ambassador would be unaware of what the United States had approved.

Later, while writing his memoirs, Standley spoke more candidly of his awkward position in the Soviet Union. Repeatedly, he complained about the lack of information he received, at one point describing it as "an opaque curtain."[85]

A Tangled Web: United States Representatives in the Soviet Union

Standley was floundering in Kuibyshev. The Roosevelt administration showed its ambassador the same lack of cooperation as did the Kremlin. Compounding this difficulty, Standley was hamstrung in his efforts to implement a reciprocal relationship with his Soviet counterparts. In order to exact a quid pro quo, he needed something to offer the Soviet government. Unfortunately for Standley, most of what the Soviet regime desired fell outside the ambassador's purview. The U.S. ambassador did not have jurisdiction over the U.S. lend-lease office in Moscow.

Standley's briefings before he left for Moscow included a description of the unique jurisdictional issues he would encounter in the Soviet Union.[86] As the United States–Soviet relationship matured, it became increasingly clear that the ambassador and the regular embassy personnel were marginalized, in particular regarding military assistance to the Soviets. The embassy personnel were aware of this marginalization and did not hesitate to advise the State Department to take steps to remedy the situation. On 5 March 1942 Thurston sent the department a telegram urging it to have all special organizations and agencies operate through the department and the embassy.[87] The Division of European Affairs supported this observation in a memorandum it drafted on 26 March.[88] Standley weighed in on this issue in April, when he sent the State Department a telegram in which he stated his position: "It is essential in my opinion that the head of the diplomatic mission be kept fully and currently informed at all times of the activities of other American agencies which might be operating in Russia."[89]

The issue of jurisdiction with Faymonville and the lend-lease mission also became an immediate bone of contention. Even before assuming his post, Standley had requested that Faymonville be attached to the embassy. The OLLA rejected this proposal, but it did agree that "Faymonville should check with Standley on all important Lend-Lease matters."[90] Hopkins agreed that although Faymonville would not be subordinate to Standley, the OLLA should copy Standley on all telegrams sent to Faymonville.[91] Despite these changes, before his departure for Kuibyshev, Standley had failed to resolve the Faymonville issue to his satisfaction.

Upon his arrival in the Soviet Union, Standley met with the U.S. military attaché, Colonel Joseph Michela, who informed him of his difficulties with Faymonville's office. Standley was aware that Faymonville fell outside his jurisdiction, so he had little recourse but to complain to the department about the problems.[92] In May 1942 Faymonville sent Standley a telegram that he asked to be forwarded to the State Department. Faymonville's message contained an analysis of Soviet press coverage of a speech by President Roosevelt. When he forwarded it to Washington, Standley added the following comments to the telegram: "The subject matter of this telegram is purely political and has little bearing on Lend-Lease or supply questions and I feel that it would have been more appropriate for Faymonville to have addressed to me for such unspecified use as I might see fit, the comments on American-Soviet political relations contained therein."[93]

Standley's complaint represented the mounting hostility brewing beneath the surface among U.S. personnel in Moscow at this time. In 1942 Standley and the American embassy personnel were situated in Kuibyshev, the Soviet city to which the diplomatic corps had been evacuated after the German invasion and advance to the gates of Moscow. Stalin, Foreign Minister Vyacheslav Molotov, and the majority of the Soviet government, however, remained in Moscow, as did Faymonville and the U.S. lend-lease mission. Therefore, because of his proximity to the real seat of power, Faymonville worked much more closely with high-ranking Soviet officials than did the U.S. embassy staff. Faymonville's work increasingly tended to encroach on the territory that traditionally had been reserved for the ambassador and his military attachés.

Accustomed to the prerogative of command, Standley had a difficult time accepting Faymonville's independent role. In his memoirs Standley recounted an encounter in his office:

> I remember looking across my small office at him one afternoon, standing militarily erect with his hand on the door knob and I thought, "If I were a captain of a ship or admiral of a division again and you were one of my officers, I'd know what to do, I'd say 'Damn it all, Faymonville, do what you're told or else.'"[94]

That, of course, was the heart of the problem. Standley was not a captain of a ship or an admiral of a division, and Faymonville was not one of his officers. They were both under the "command" of the White House, and both were charged with differing and often incompatible missions.

Unable to order Faymonville to follow his commands, Standley struggled to delineate clearly his areas of authority in the confused jurisdictional web. Unfortunately, the web was often so tangled that efforts to determine responsibility failed. Faymonville pointed out this problem in a conversation with Standley. Standley had expressed concern about Michela's inability to exchange information with his Soviet counterparts. Faymonville explained that he (Faymonville) was simply a conduit for lend-lease material. If Soviet officials asked for information, he had to pass that request on to Washington. If authorities in Washington decided to meet the Soviet request and sent the information back to Faymonville, Faymonville had to pass it on to the Soviets.[95]

Compounding the disputes over authority, Standley and Faymonville had different conceptions of what role the lend-lease office in Moscow should play.

Faymonville's orders from Washington, which he carried out effectively and without question, were: to provide the Soviets with anything they requested. In contrast, Standley expected that at the very least the Soviet government should show gratitude and appreciation for the material the United States supplied. The disagreement was apparent in a conversation the two had in fall 1942. According to Standley, he expressed no little concern at the lack of Soviet acknowledgment of U.S. lend-lease supplies.[96]

Overshadowing all, however, was Standley's concern about his lack of authority over Faymonville. In October 1942, when he was in Washington for consultation, Standley complained about a telegram the lend-lease office was sending Faymonville. Standley believed that the subject matter did not deal with supplies and should therefore be sent to the embassy, not Faymonville. The State Department had the telegram sent to Kuibyshev and repeated to Moscow, thereby acceding to Standley's demands.[97]

Standley's concerns were not limited to one telegram, however. During his visit home, Standley complained vociferously about his lack of control over Faymonville. Major General Burns outlined the dispute in a lengthy memorandum to Hopkins. Burns explained that Standley and the State Department wanted the OLLA to issue instructions that "General Faymonville report to Admiral Standley and thus become a fully regimented part of the latter's organization including operations and channels of communications." Burns warned Hopkins that this was a bad idea:

It is not believed that the concept outlined in the proposed instructions regarding the functions of the United States Supply Mission in the U.S.S.R. which are recommended by Admiral Standley and are indorsed by the State Department is sound or practical. These instructions would, in effect, regiment General Faymonville as a definite part of Admiral Standley's organization, and thus put the State Department in direct charge of the operations of Lend-Lease in Russia. This would be harmful to Lend-Lease for it would impose another operational level on top of the present set-up.[98]

Burns suggested that the OLLA issue a set of compromise instructions. He suggested that Faymonville be placed under Standley's overall supervision and coordination, and that he consult with Standley about any issues that did not fall under the rubric of lend-lease. Burns concluded, "Otherwise, General Faymonville would have independence of action."[99]

Standley was not pleased with the compromise. He demanded that the

OLLA adopt the policy suggested by him and the State Department. He even refused to return to Moscow unless the State Department placed Faymonville under his authority.[100] After much discussion, the government agreed to order the chief of the Supply Mission to report to the chief of the Diplomatic Mission.[101]

Standley returned to the Soviet Union determined to exert his hard-won, yet still ambiguous, authority over the lend-lease mission. The existence of Faymonville and the entire lend-lease supply structure outside the ambassador's chain of authority remained a continuing problem that ultimately became more public.

Roosevelt's Special Delegations to the Soviet Union and Their Repercussions

THE WILLKIE VISIT

Another continuing issue that seemed to Ambassador Standley to undermine his authority was the series of official visits by individuals or delegations of very important persons sent by Roosevelt to meet with Stalin. Roosevelt dispatched these special persons and delegations to help promote his personal diplomacy with Stalin, and each person and delegation operated almost wholly independently of the U.S. ambassador and his staff. The first such visit took place in August 1942 when Harriman accompanied Churchill on his visit to the Kremlin. On 2 September 1942 Standley reacted to that visit and Roosevelt's tendency to communicate directly with Stalin. In a letter to Sumner Welles, Standley expressed his concern: "But the method of dealing directly, or of sending special representatives to deal directly, with Mr. Stalin does not especially enhance the prestige and standing of the American Ambassador, nor is it helpful to him in his dealings with the Soviet authorities."[102]

Standley's concerns notwithstanding, in September 1942 Wendell Willkie, the defeated 1940 Republican candidate for president, embarked on a whirlwind global tour that included a stop in the Soviet Union. The tour was initially Willkie's idea. In July 1942 he sent a letter to President Roosevelt in which he asked permission "to take a trip to the middle east, into Russia and perhaps China."[103] One month later Roosevelt granted him permission to visit the Middle East and, if conditions were favorable, Russia and China.[104] Apparently no one in Washington kept Standley abreast of these developments; he was informed of the visit to Moscow only when Willkie's arrival was imminent.[105]

The purpose of Willkie's visit remains unclear. According to Standley,

Roosevelt sent Willkie to convey to Stalin the president's opinion on Polish-Soviet relations.[106] There is, however, no indication of this intent in the State Department's archives, and others contend that the visit was entirely unofficial: "Willkie was authorized to go on his own and 'say what I damned please' and he did."[107] In any case, it is clear in this instance as well that Standley remained cloaked in an "opaque curtain."

Actual developments during Willkie's visit improved neither Standley's position nor his attitude. In a memorandum he sent to the State Department about the visit, Standley pointed out that not only did Willkie refuse any advice or counsel from the embassy, but he also refused to include Standley in his meeting with Stalin.[108] Standley described his interpretation of these incidents in greater detail in his memoirs. For example, at one point during a dinner party with Soviet officials, Standley discussed an occasion when Willkie proposed a drinking bout between a young Soviet officer and the ambassador. This infuriated Standley, who felt it was not in keeping with the dignity of his position.[109]

Standley was also chagrined over being excluded from Willkie's meeting with Stalin. He was incensed that the Soviet government notified Willkie directly, rather than via the embassy, of his meeting with the Soviet premier. Showing no small amount of pique, Standley correctly surmised that he was not going to be included in the meeting. Later Standley asked Willkie if he had made a report to the president of his meeting with Stalin, to which Willkie replied: "Oh, no. There are other matters so secret that I can't trust them to coded messages or even to the Ambassador."[110]

The result of these and similar events heightened Standley's anger and frustration. As Willkie's visit concluded, Standley recalls deciding:

> His [Willkie's] activities and maneuvers in the Russian capital had left me in an untenable position; although the only officially accredited American Representative to the Soviet Government, I had been by-passed so frequently, my prestige was so low, that it seemed obvious to everyone in Moscow that I no longer enjoyed the confidence of my own government. Drastic action to reestablish my prestige or withdraw from my mission was imperative.[111]

On 28 September, Standley, his advisers on the embassy staff, and Loy Henderson, chief of the State Department's Division of European Affairs (who was visiting the embassy in Kuibyshev), conferred to determine what, if any, drastic action was required. They concluded that Standley must return to Washington to protest the continuing stream of special missions.[112] For his own part, Standley rightly feared that his role in United States–Soviet diplomacy had become utterly superfluous and, accordingly, decided to return to Washington.

While Standley was in Washington, direct communications between Roosevelt and the Soviets continued unabated; Stalin and Roosevelt exchanged notes that continued to bypass the U.S. embassy in the Soviet Union. As Roosevelt's speech writer later recorded: "Hopkins was now more than ever 'Roosevelt's own, personal Foreign Office.'"[113]

Joseph Davies, former U.S. ambassador to the Soviet Union and still a close confidant of both the president and Harry Hopkins, met with Standley while he was in Washington. In a long conversation, Standley revealed to Davies that the real reason he had returned to Washington was "to protect his 'position as Ambassador.'"[114] According to Standley, Willkie had seriously undermined it by elbowing him out of discussions with Stalin. Davies later wrote, "I was quite frank in telling Standley that I believed he was entirely right in that attitude."[115]

Unlike Davies, the Roosevelt Administration was not overly receptive to Standley's complaints, aside from agreeing to Standley's request that he receive copies of all correspondence between President Roosevelt and Stalin.[116] The fact was that both Harry Hopkins and the president were distressed by the ambassador's attitude.[117] Hopkins complained to Davies about Standley's reaction to the Willkie incident, declaring, "He [Standley] is concerned about his personal position in Moscow. He is sore over Willkie and does not want to go back unless, unless, unless, which he will not get."[118] Hopkins then asked Davies to replace Standley as ambassador to the Soviet Union if Standley refused to return, but Davies begged off, citing his doctor's concern for his health. Hopkins then asked what Davies thought of John G. Winant or Averell Harriman for the position. Davies explained in detail why he thought neither of them the best choice:

> Either would be good; but neither, in my opinion, has the best combination of qualities. Harriman is a hard-headed business executive—excellent, but might not have the imagination or the personality to either understand or command the confidence of the Soviets, which you have. Winant has the latter; but would be "starry-eyed" in the assessment of men and the practicalities necessary to [*sic*] dealing with these Soviet realists. What the job needs is a combination of the understanding and vision of Winant and hard-hitting business objectivity of Harriman.[119]

Davies suggested that Hopkins himself accept the appointment. Thus, the two men resolved nothing at this juncture, although it was becoming clear that the problems in Moscow could not be worked out without a change in personnel.

The Turmoil Becomes Public

STANDLEY AND THE PRESS

Standley's "drastic measure" of returning to the United States to discuss his position in the wake of the Willkie visit failed to make the administration more concerned with the difficulties embassy personnel encountered when dealing with special diplomatic missions to the Soviet Union. Indeed, it had the opposite effect by lessening the administration's faith in their current ambassador and increasing its dependence on trusted ex officio advisers. One of these advisers was none other than former Ambassador Davies, who himself maintained a steady stream of correspondence with the president and Harry Hopkins, advising them of his interpretation of many aspects of the Soviet situation.

Davies' role in the administration illustrated the developing clash between Standley and the White House. The dispute stemmed from two sources that became symbiotic as time passed. When Standley departed for the Soviet Union in 1942, he neither fully understood nor appreciated Roosevelt's policy toward the Kremlin. Roosevelt told the ambassador that relations should be based on the principles of the Atlantic Charter, but that "nothing should be allowed to arise at this time which might disturb the common front of the Allied powers."[120] The president focused on the nebulous phrase "good faith between nations," but Standley fixated on "adhering to the basic principles for which we were contending."[121] This differing interpretation of policy and mission was exacerbated by Standley's personality and his response to perceived (and real) slights. When Roosevelt and the Soviet officials began to offend Standley's pride, he reacted with increasing anger. That anger, in turn, hardened his opposition to the president's policies. Added to this volatile mix was the influence on Standley of State Department officials who had long been disgusted with Roosevelt's method and policy. By spring 1943 Standley had already expressed his outrage at the insults Roosevelt meted out to his position; he returned to Moscow reassured that the White House would take steps to address his concerns. Standley and Roosevelt had not, however, discussed the ambassador's increasing hostility to the White House policy. That issue would continue to fester.

On 8 March 1943 the simmering policy conflict exploded. Irritated by what he believed was a Soviet attitude toward lend-lease that seemed to obscure the source of assistance and belittle its value, the American ambassador turned to the press with his complaints. In his memoirs, Standley wrote that "it became increasingly obvious that the Soviet governmental authorities were attempting to conceal from the Russian people the nature of the extent of the aid." This is precisely what he said at the 8 March gathering of American correspondents at the embassy in Kuibyshev.[122] The press was amazed when Standley told them that the remarks were not off the record. They literally ran to their offices to break the news.[123]

The media's report of this story prompted an instant and significant reaction in the United States. Davies noted that he heard soon after midnight on 9 March on shortwave radio that the American ambassador had publicly criticized the Soviet government. Immediately he tried to contact high-ranking State Department officials. He reached Undersecretary of State Sumner Welles, whose first reaction was shocked disbelief.[124] It was not until the news made the newspapers the next morning that U.S. government officials began to accept it and to react to Standley's indiscretion. The reaction was swift and strong.

The same day, Davies prepared a memorandum for the president that assessed chronologically the development of Stalin's attitude toward lend-lease, seriously challenged the validity of Standley's remarks, and questioned his future usefulness as ambassador:

> The interview given out by Standley upon his return from Kuibyshev severely criticized the Soviet Government with failure to advise the Soviet public of American aid through Lend-Lease. Unfortunately, he was unsound on his facts, as extensive publicity and detail had been printed in the Soviet Press on the extent of American aid. It was resented as the unfriendly act of an ally to break out in public and 'wash dirty linen,' rather than to take the matter up at the Foreign Office as friends, and not as critics. The Soviets promptly retorted that the total Lend-Lease aid up to and including that time constituted but a very small percentage, between 5% and 10% of the total supplies, which were being required and used by the Red Army at that time. That Standley's usefulness in Moscow had been destroyed was generally proclaimed.[125]

The reaction to Standley's remarks was no less strident in the U.S. Congress. On 9 March 1943 Senator Tom Connally (Democrat, Texas), chairman of the Senate Foreign Relations Committee, stated: "Mr. President, I regret the necessity to criticize the ineptness of our Ambassador to Russia. I cannot understand why he should make such a statement as he did without having accurate information about the matter."[126] He added, "I trust that no unfavorable reactions may result from the incident provoked by the remarks of Admiral Standley in Moscow. I know that they came as a shock and a surprise to those who are in authority here in the United States."[127]

The public reaction to Standley's remarks was also rapid and harsh, so much so that President Roosevelt himself received numerous telegrams and letters from outraged citizens demanding Standley's recall.[128] Sentiment was not uniformly against the outspoken Standley, however. In fact, after hearing Standley's remarks, one journalist who had spent a great deal of time in the Soviet Union wrote that the more he knew of Ambassador Standley, the more impressed he was with him, and that Stalin was probably chuckling, "Good for you, Admiral," to himself as he heard of Standley's statement.[129] This journalist clearly thought Stalin would appreciate a tougher American approach.

Nor was Congress uniform in its criticism of Standley. Senator Alexander Wiley (Republican, Wisconsin) echoed the notion that Standley's statement was not as significant as administration officials apparently believed, stating: "In my opinion, all the 'fuss and feathers' about Ambassador Standley is only a tempest in a teapot."[130] Senator Burton K. Wheeler (Republican, Montana) took an even stronger stand in Standley's defense: "I do not know what was the purpose of Admiral Standley's statement. I must confess that I was surprised at his statement, but I have not the slightest doubt that his statement was correct and true, because otherwise he would not have made it."[131] These public and congressional defenders of Standley were few and far between.

As the public decried Standley's behavior and the debate raged on in Congress, the Soviet people and government reacted to the remarks. According to Alexander Werth, the Soviet censors were infuriated by Standley's statement and telephoned higher officials before deciding whether to allow the stories to be printed. The chief censor was enraged as he approved the statement. His mother had starved to death in Leningrad.[132] Other Russians were equally infuriated as they contrasted their mounting casualties—brothers, sisters, children, parents, friends—with Standley's complaint that they were not grateful enough for the material aid the United States sent. Werth described the reaction of one Russian: "We've lost millions of people, and they want us to crawl on our knees because they send us spam. And has the 'warmhearted' Congress ever done anything that wasn't in its interests? Don't tell me that Lend-Lease is *charity!*"[133]

The official Soviet reaction was less emotional, but no less critical. On 10 March 1943, Ambassador Litvinov met with Davies and stated that he could not understand the rationale for Standley's "attacks."[134] Foreign Minister Molotov then met with Standley on 19 March. In a message that he dispatched to the State Department the next day, Standley stated simply that Molotov "[d]id not question my right to make the remarks attributed to me but speaking frankly he did not agree with me."[135] Standley added: "In conclusion I stated that I hoped my remarks would not have a detrimental effect on American-Soviet relations. Molotov stated 'No, I do not believe so; perhaps they will have a useful effect in America.'"[136] Standley ended his telegram optimistically by stating that his remarks should help put the United States–Soviet relationship on a more "realistic" basis that could contribute to closer understanding.[137] Standley's interpretation was naive. On the very day that Standley took reassurance from his meeting with Molotov, the Soviet Foreign Ministry dispatched an angry telegram to its ambassador in the United States in which the Foreign Ministry asked Ambassador Litvinov to take the opportunity of a breakfast meeting with Stettinius to reply to Standley's "clumsy prank" and to refute all of Standley's charges.[138]

General Burns, who was now serving as the executive of the president's Soviet Protocol Committee, believed that Standley's remarks had branded Russia "an ingrate before the world" and "left a scar because it hurt Russia's pride."[139] Burns' assessment was probably closer to the mark than Standley's optimistic interpretation. Soviet officials had always expressed concern over hostility among U.S. government circles toward the Soviet Union.[140] After Standley's outburst, they appeared even more anxious. Indeed, former Soviet Ambassador to the United States Constantine Oumansky told Davies he believed the Standley incident was evidence that hostility had affected U.S. diplomacy.[141]

The official ramifications of Standley's public fit of pique were more far-reaching. The Roosevelt administration, which clearly disagreed strongly with Standley's opinion of the Soviet attitude toward lend-lease, publicly aired its displeasure. At a 9 March 1943 press conference, Sumner Welles stated that the U.S. government did not approve of Standley's remarks.[142] Hopkins was also distressed and contacted Davies to discuss the furor that Standley's remarks had caused in Congress. Great Britain even proposed that it act as a "friendly broker" to repair the Soviet-American relationship damaged by Standley's comments.[143]

Standley remained committed to his views. On 10 March he sent the State Department a telegram in which he again advocated the adoption of his policy recommendations:

I am becoming convinced that we can only deal with them [the Soviet government] on a bargaining basis for our continuing to accede freely to their requests while agreeing to pay an additional price for every small request we make seems to arouse suspicion of our motives in the Oriental Russian mind rather than to build confidence. . . .

Following the recent Soviet military successes it would appear that the Soviet policy of minimum collaboration is becoming more pronounced.[144]

To Standley it was manifest that the Soviet Union was not interested in collaboration. He repeated this belief in a telegram to the State Department dated 18 March 1943. In it he pointed out: "I have found few observers here who are willing to admit that real collaboration is likely even upon such an eventuality [the second front] or in the postwar period irrespective of what internal influences guide the destinies of this country."[145] The United States' generous lend-lease policy was thus foolish. It would never guarantee Soviet cooperation.

On 13 March Roosevelt moved to correct the unfortunate situation and met with Davies to renew his request that Davies go to Moscow as the new U.S. ambassador. Davies recorded that during the meeting Roosevelt pointed out to him that "Standley's usefulness there was ended. He would have him come home as soon as possible, without it being too obviously a recall."[146]

Continued Visits by Very Important Persons

Having requested that the administration refrain from sending over unofficial diplomats that would undercut his prestige and position in the Soviet Union, Standley was chagrined when on 8 April 1943 he learned of a planned visit by Major General Burns.[147] The OLLA sent Burns to Moscow to investigate the situation between the lend-lease office and the embassy. Because he was traveling to the Soviet Union on lend-lease business, Burns spent his time working with Faymonville rather than Standley. His visit thus exacerbated existing jurisdictional disputes.

Almost every aspect of the Burns visit infuriated Standley. Burns did not report to the ambassador, and he and Faymonville neglected to keep Standley informed of their activities.[148] In mid-May Standley complained to the State Department that Burns and Faymonville had departed Moscow for a trip to the front without informing him.[149] Standley confronted Faymonville about his activities, and Faymonville duly submitted a report to the ambassador. In a bitter telegram to the State Department, Standley denounced the lack of cooperation he received from Faymonville:

General Burns was ordered to report to me and presumably to keep me informed as to his activities while in Moscow. Since he failed to do so and since I felt it incumbent on myself to endeavor to keep the Department advised on the activities and accomplishments of American representatives sent on official missions to the Soviet Union I requested Faymonville, who also has received orders (Department's 407, of December 12) to keep me fully informed on all Lend Lease activities here, to submit to me in writing a full report on Burn's [*sic*] visit. As evidence of the type of cooperation I obtain from Faymonville I am submitting herewith excerpts from a report I received from him on May 29.[150]

Standley continued to describe a report that primarily addressed Burns' social and cultural activities. The remainder of Faymonville's report consisted of a list of the locations Burns had visited. He provided Standley no details about the visits.

The situation exasperated the American ambassador. Standley, however, was not merely angry at his lack of control over the lend-lease mission. By May 1943 Standley's views of Soviet policy sharply diverged from the OLLA's. Standley met with Faymonville and chastised the general. His confrontation only further frustrated him, however: "Spoke to Faymonville privately regarding his activities and political matters as they affected Lend Lease—did not make a dent. He gives Russian desires priority above all else."[151] Standley made similar observations of Burns. Standley complained to his wife: "General Burns is of the same belief as Faymonville; Russian interests come first, last and all the time; it's hopeless."[152] What Standley was railing against was not the pigheadedness of two American generals, but the policy of the Roosevelt administration.

Roosevelt was aware that he had to find a new ambassador to the Soviet Union, but for several reasons May 1943 was not the best time to recall Standley. Tensions in Allied relations with the Soviet Union in spring and summer 1943 demanded that the United States not be without an ambassador in Moscow. It was also important that Roosevelt find the right person for the job. Finally, although Standley received only limited support for his remarks, Roosevelt probably considered it unwise to anger the ambassador's supporters in Congress by recalling him.

With an ambassador so clearly opposed to the administration's policy toward the Soviet Union, however, Roosevelt continued to bypass the U.S. embassy in the Soviet Union until he could find a replacement for him. In an effort to expedite his personal diplomacy, Roosevelt resolved that it was time for another special diplomatic mission to Moscow. This time, he wanted Davies to lead it.

THE DAVIES MISSION TO MOSCOW

The purpose of Davies' mission was unclear to the U.S. personnel in Moscow. Annoyed by the furor created by his errant ambassador, Roosevelt also recoiled from Britain's notion that it should function as a friendly "broker" between the United States and the Soviet Union. Instead, Roosevelt wished to restore the primacy of the United States–Soviet relationship in the Allied camp and pursue his far-reaching goals vis-à-vis his important strategic partner. As before, he firmly believed that the best way to do so was by resuming his personal diplomacy. Specifically, he wanted to meet face to face with Stalin and restore a relationship of mutual good faith.[153] To keynote this new effort, Roosevelt provided Davies with a personal letter to deliver to Stalin.

Davies' arrival in Moscow, however, did not end the controversy that had erupted in Washington two months before. Shortly after his arrival on 22 May, Davies met with members of the American press corps in Moscow. What Davies did not know before this press conference, however, was that he had fallen into a trap set by Standley and his closest colleagues in Moscow, most of whom shared Standley's hostility toward Roosevelt's Soviet policy. By May 1943 both Army attaché Michela and naval attaché Admiral Jack Duncan resented continued and seemingly unconditional U.S. beneficence toward the Soviet Union. In addition, they were angry at the president's supporters, particularly lend-lease chief Faymonville, whom Standley, Michela, and Duncan openly despised. Thus, when he arrived on his special mission for Roosevelt, Davies strode into a virtual ambush in the form of a hostile press conference that his opponents had carefully organized in advance.

In fact, a subsequent investigation revealed that attachés Michela and Duncan had spent over a week preparing the newsmen, already friendly with and sympathetic toward the ambassador and his staff, for their meeting with Davies. When Davies said complimentary things about the Soviets, as expected, the journalists dutifully grilled him about why American diplomats did not receive much cooperation from the Soviets. The ensuing argument between Davies and the journalists lasted several minutes. Reportedly, Standley "[e]njoyed it thoroughly, 'chuckling and winking' at the reporters from time to time."[154]

Standley could not have wished for a less auspicious beginning to Davies' mission. In fact, he cabled Washington: "A protracted and exceedingly bitter controversy on the subject of Soviet cooperation ensued between the members of the press on one side and Davies on the other in which I fear unconsidered remarks were made and tempers almost lost."[155] Standley concluded: "As an aftermath I understand that the correspondents here with few exceptions are up in arms against Davies and are questioning the wisdom of sending here a man with such intolerant views."[156] One of the correspondents present at the press conference confirms Standley's interpretation: "his [Davies'] lack of knowledge regarding Russia shocked us all. . . . Like Standley we too think of Lend-Lease as a two-way street."[157]

Davies tried to place a more positive interpretation on the press conference. In his journal entry for 24 May, 1943, Davies wrote, "At a press conference, I urged upon our Press (some of whom I know well, and all of whom I know to be good Americans), that public criticism of our Soviet ally—even though in some instances, well-founded, might possibly be harmful to the war effort if it were to reach the top echelons of the Soviet Government."[158] In an early draft of this journal entry, Davies added: "It [the criticism] was quite generally accepted in the spirit in which it was offered."[159] Despite his optimistic tone, Davies was aware of the hostile atmosphere in Moscow.

Standley's successful ambush of Davies was not the end of his attempts to torpedo the Davies mission. Even as he feigned deep concern over Davies' poor performance in the initial press conference, Standley encouraged Michela and Duncan to take steps to guarantee similar results in Davies' subsequent press conference that was scheduled for the next day. According to the Federal Bureau of Investigation (FBI) account:

> Immediately after the conference, the reporters gathered in Admiral Duncan's apartment, and an agreement was made under which they were to secure additional ammunition for a second conference. . . . The Ambassador gave his approval, and Michela released to Eddy Gilmore and Bob McGaffin, both of the Associated Press, detailed information concerning the failure of the Soviet Liaison Office to give us the information concerning the common enemy which the United States Army has repeatedly requested.[160]

Davies, however, was astute enough to avoid walking into a second ambush. Forewarned by the reception he had received at his first press conference, Davies deliberately defused the tension at the outset of the conference by opening it with the admission that he had been mistaken in his criticism of the press corps the day before. Although it is doubtful that Davies was sincere in his apology, the remarks did prevent further public controversy.

The stormy press conference incident and the associated disagreement over Roosevelt's supposedly "soft" policy toward the Soviet Union was not the only bone of contention to surface between Davies and Standley during Davies' trip to Moscow. In addition, disputes arose between Davies and Standley about two lesser matters. First, Standley apparently resented people referring to Davies as "Mr. Ambassador," which he perceived as a breach of diplomatic etiquette (even though former ambassadors are entitled to use the title throughout their lifetime). Second, apparently satisfied that he had milked as much benefit as he could from these venues, Standley asked Davies' secretary, Stamm, not to organize any "press conferences" of his own. Although Davies acquiesced and informed Standley that he would ask his friends not to refer to him as "Mr. Ambassador," he denied that Stamm's meetings with the press were press conferences and refused to cease giving them.[161] Davies was so infuriated that he decided to cut his visit to Moscow short.[162] Evidently Standley was mollified, because he encouraged Davies not to cut short his visit to Moscow as he had planned.[163]

Davies indeed did not leave early. As a result, he had the opportunity to enjoy a dinner with Stalin at the Kremlin on the night of 23 May. Consistent with the remainder of his visit, controversy also swirled around Davies' dinner with Stalin. For his part, in a telegram to Secretary of State Cordell Hull, Standley characterized the dinner as "notable for the absence of spontaneous cordiality or genuine good humor."[164] According to Standley, Davies proposed a toast to the Soviet Union, which Standley believed "over-did his [Davies'] attempts to impress the Russians of his sincerity and love for them."[165] Thereafter, according to Standley, the company adjourned after dinner to a viewing of Davies' film *Mission to Moscow*, which Standley felt was ill-received and would do nothing to improve the relationship between the United States and the Soviet Union.[166]

Otherwise, the remainder of Davies' visit passed without further incident. Nevertheless, Standley could not resist a passing shot at Davies after his departure. In a summary of the visit, Standley sharply criticized Davies for obviously trying to publicize his film while on official business. Such behavior, Standley concluded, would reflect negatively on the president.[167]

Although many of the controversial incidents associated with Davies' mission may seem trivial, they did underscore two realities that dogged Roosevelt's attempts to achieve a lasting understanding with Stalin. First, they reflected the resentment on the part of many U.S. diplomats in Moscow, who believed that U.S. policies were too soft on the Soviet Union. Second, they highlighted the depth of hostility between competing U.S. diplomatic organs and figures in Moscow. More important still, the fact that the president of the United States had once again relied on a special emissary to conduct diplomatic relations with the Soviet Union rather than the accredited U.S. ambassador to that country escaped no one's notice. A member of the press, Quentin Reynolds, summed up the situation the best: "What bewilders us (and we are sure bewilders Stalin) is the fact that the President had sent Mr. Davies to deliver the letter. Our embassy is just across the street from the Kremlin and Ambassador Standley is never too busy to walk over to the Kremlin with a letter."[168]

In fact, Davies' delivery of Roosevelt's personal letter was a purposeful attempt to bypass the ambassador and was clear evidence that Standley was already in disfavor with the president. In the wake of the Davies mission, the damage to Standley's position and its resulting deleterious effect on the working atmosphere in the U.S. embassy grew. Consequently, in early June Roosevelt accepted the resignation Standley wrote to the president on 3 May 1943.[169] The turmoil in the implementation of U.S. policy toward the Soviet Union was simply too public to ignore.

Faymonville and Michela

While the situation with Standley was worsening to the point of becoming untenable, the equally hostile rivalry between the military attachés and the lend-lease group became more evident and finally reached the breaking point. From its inception, the relationship between Michela and Faymonville had been strained. The origins of their conflict were apparent in the starkly differing reports the two dispatched. As military attaché Faymonville had much greater respect for the Red Army than did Michela. As the war developed, Faymonville remained well known for his optimism regarding Soviet military performance. In contrast, Michela consistently expressed disdain for the Red Army.[170]

Michela's pessimistic outlook stemmed from two sources. First, like his predecessor, Yeaton, Michela was vehemently anti-Soviet. As a result, his hatred of the Soviet Union served as the filter through which he examined all his information about Soviet military performance and policy. In addition to skewing his perception of reality, Michela's hostility toward the Kremlin contributed toward Soviet unwillingness to share any information with him. Consequently, almost all of Michela's reports were based on "personal observations" or opinions.[171] In contrast, Faymonville was friendly toward and respected by Soviet military officials. Continuing the trend he began as military attaché in the 1930s, Faymonville conversed with Soviet officers, read

Soviet publications, and based his analyses on that evidence.[172] He also pursued the elusive goal of objectivity much more successfully than Michela. Faymonville was neither a passionate opponent, nor an ardent supporter, of the Soviet Union. In World War II he advocated a policy of support for the Soviet military because his observations as military attaché reinforced his assumption that it would be an important counterweight to Japanese power in the Pacific and German power in Europe. As a result, he was not blinded by prejudice, and his analyses and predictions were the ones that proved accurate. Michela never came close to Faymonville's understanding of the Soviet military, and his reports reflected this weakness.[173]

In November 1941 Michela parroted the Germans' inaccurate assessment of remaining Soviet resistance:

> I estimate there are no Soviet general reserves. . . . I believe there are no ammunition reserves and present factory output is below needs, quantity Soviet tanks remaining is negligible, serious shortage exists in signal equipment and material. No reliable information on far Eastern troops available but it is believed that all regular troops and equipment in Far East have been replaced with war conscripts and obsolescent material.[174]

One week later, Michela echoed his earlier assessment when he forwarded, to the Military Intelligence Division (MID), Polish General Wladislaw Anders' assessment of the Soviet-German war: "Extreme shortage all materiel and ammunition and replacements go to front without rifles, forty per cent all wounds are in left hand recalls same occurred during World War when he was tsarist officer. . . . Winter will retard but not stop Germans who now have two hundred division including four mtzd [motorized] and eighteen armored."[175] Michela added that he concurred fully with Anders' observations.

Even the successful Soviet counteroffensive outside Moscow did not change Michela's views. In a 21 December 1941 telegram to the MID, Michela discussed recent Soviet success outside Moscow. He incorrectly described the German withdrawal as "quiet and unhurried" and failed to note the serious crisis the Germans faced as a result of the Soviet counteroffensive.[176] Indeed, throughout January and February 1942, Michela and the MID continued to underestimate the scale of Soviet counteroffensive operations.[177]

When finally acknowledging the Soviet success outside Moscow, Michela attributed it to climatic conditions and defensive works.[178] In fact, the German advance slowed because of logistical problems and Soviet resistance. Michela held fast to his prewar belief that the Red Army was less efficient than the

German, and concluded that "the end of 1942 should find both Germany and the Soviet Union very much weakened."[179] In reality, the end of 1942 witnessed a seriously weakened Wehrmacht, but a resurgent Red Army.

The MID's analyses of the Soviet-German War reflected the pessimism of its military attaché in Kuibyshev. In a 20 July 1942 memorandum, the head of Military Intelligence, Major General George V. Strong, predicted future developments in the war. His estimate was wildly inaccurate. Most striking was his observation: "The likelihood of a large-scale successful Russian strategic counter-offensive is remote. Russia's strength lies in time and space."[180] The Red Army actually began to mount counterattacks in July and August, and launched full-fledged counteroffensives outside Moscow and Stalingrad (Operations Mars and Uranus) in November.[181] Strong also seriously misjudged Soviet military strength. He predicted: "The Russians will enter the winter 1942–1943 with approximately fifty-sixty per cent of the fighting power they now possess."[182] On 1 November 1942 the Red Army actually had 6,124,000 troops. On 5 May 1942 the Soviets had 5,449,898. In contrast to MID's estimate, the Soviet Union entered the winter of 1942–1943 with 112 percent of the fighting strength they had at the beginning of the summer.[183]

Even when it was no longer possible to ignore Soviet battlefield success, Michela allowed his anti–Red Army prejudices to pervert his reporting. On 18 January 1943 Michela reported to MID the observations of American correspondents who had just returned from the Stalingrad front. According to the correspondents, the Soviet offensive was genuine and not simply the result of a German withdrawal for the winter. The correspondents indicated that the Germans encircled in the city were "doomed." Michela added his own remarks to the end of this message: "Although I give above considerable credence generally there is possibility that German troops in Stalingrad were left there boldly and deliberately with reserve stocks supplied by rail before encirclement and supplemented by plane after encirclement to carry them over until predicted early Spring however no information available on this."[184] By 1943 Michela was so blinded by his prejudices that he was incapable of providing useful intelligence to the MID in Washington. He overstated German and underestimated Soviet capabilities. The military attaché also reported to the MID that the Soviets would remain on the defensive in summer 1943 because their offensive abilities were not equal to the Germans'. Summer 1943, in reality, witnessed the failed German offensive at Kursk and the subsequent successful Soviet offensives along the length of the front.[185]

Michela's attitudes toward the Soviet Union were evident as well in the increasingly political nature of his reporting. In a report dated 15 January 1942, Michela outlined his perceptions of Soviet-British-American relations at that time: "The fundamental precepts of the government of the Soviet Union are in direct contrast to those of the United States and Great Britain and we may in this respect separate the Soviets from the other two. The political ideologies of Red Russia have been, are, and will be, repugnant to the United States and Great Britain."[186]

Michela argued that "force of circumstances" had forced the three powers to cooperate. He raised a hypothetical question, however, that was based on the assumption that the leaders of the Soviet Union had "not discarded their ambitions to make Red Russia a dominant factor in post war world affairs." Michela posed the question, "Shall our aid, therefore, be free and all out, or shall it be carefully gauged—so carefully that both Germany and the Soviet Union will find themselves completely exhausted and neither can be a dominant factor after the war?"[187] Michela left this question unanswered.

Michela's hostility toward the Soviet government reemerged in a report he submitted on 24 May 1942. Analyzing the Soviet presence in Iran, Michela was vitriolic in his condemnation of the United States' unconditional aid policy and Soviet foreign policy:

To believe Soviet propaganda that world revolution is no longer on their agenda is to be caught off guard. The Soviet Union has been greatly weakened by this war, but on the very day that this war ends, when the united nations will relax for a few hours to congratulate themselves on their victory, great caution will have to be exercised to see that Red forces do not at once start moving to improve their position at the expense of her former allies. If such opportunity presents itself, she will be quick to seize it.[188]

Michela's assessment of Soviet policy aims did not change. By February 1943 his concern with Soviet postwar goals combined with his anger at the Roosevelt administration's aid policy to produce a fantastic theory about the Soviet unwillingness to share military intelligence:

A reason [for their unwillingness to share intelligence], however, must exist, and it does! It is the post war aims of the Soviet government; the pursuance of which the Soviets well know will meet opposition from both the U.S. and England, and this observer is convinced that the Soviets intend to push their claims in Europe, even to the extent of resorting to armed force, the day the war with Germany ends.[189]

Ironically, Michela now appeared to notice improved Red Army efficiency but ascribed it to sinister postwar motives: "Call it World Revolution or call it

Soviet 'Imperialism'—the net result is that the Soviets are determined to control Europe if they can."[190] In Michela's mind, the solution to this looming threat was clear. The United States must cease the policy of unconditional aid and adhere to a strictly quid pro quo relationship.

Michela despised the Soviet Union and the Roosevelt administration's Soviet policy. Powerless to change the United States' unconditional aid policy, Michela turned on its representative in Moscow. His struggle with Faymonville became so bitter and so personal that Michela was unsatisfied with anything less than the destruction of Faymonville's career. This struggle eventually became so public that it threatened the continuation of Roosevelt's policy.

It was apparent to observers that elements in the U.S. Government opposed the administration's lend-lease policy toward the Soviets. Even before leaving for Russia, Davies became aware of openly hostile feelings toward the policy. In April 1943 he had a conference with David Bowes-Lyon of the British embassy. At this meeting, Bowes-Lyon told Davies of hostility to Soviets in "high and authoritative U.S. circles" and even quoted the head of the Office of Strategic Services (OSS), William Donovan, as "being so violent as to say he himself would fight with the Poles against Russia."[191] In addition, Davies observed on his arrival in Kuibyshev that some people "low down" in the State Department were being deliberately obstructionist to Roosevelt's policy.[192] This observation was also made by others, including Burns, who wrote to Hopkins, "We now have a number of United States representatives in contact with Russian representatives who do not trust Russia and who do not follow a national policy of the 'good neighbor and a sincere friend' to Russia. They obviously do not develop mutual trust and friendliness. These should either be replaced or they should be required to pledge loyal support to the above policy."[193] Most striking, because subsequent developments confirmed the accuracy of his observation, was Davies' journal entry of 24 May 1943:

> From what I am reliably told by American journalists here, there are two camps at the Embassy, one headed by the Ambassador and General Michela, the Military Attaché, and stimulated by Captain Duncan, the Naval Attaché, directed against the Lend-Lease group, headed by Major-General Burns, who happens to be here from Washington, and General Faymonville, who is here permanently in charge of Lend-Lease matters. As I get it, there is a lot of sniping going on, principally conducted by Captain Duncan.[194]

The sniping was much worse and more long-standing than Davies had imagined. It dated to 1941 when Michela began to experience serious difficulties in obtaining information from the Soviet authorities. Since the beginning of the German-Soviet war, the military attaché's office in the Soviet Union had requested intelligence from the Red Army and permission to visit the front. The attachés had been largely unsuccessful and demanded that the United States adopt a policy of reciprocity in its dealings with Soviet officials.[195]

Soon Michela argued that the cause of his difficulties was America's lend-lease aid.[196] MID was unmoved, however, and instructed the military attaché to cooperate fully with Faymonville and to allow the lend-lease mission to handle all lend-lease-related matters.[197] Cooperating with Faymonville did not resolve Michela's problems. On 3 March 1942 Michela reported that the Soviet authorities had asked Faymonville if he desired to visit the front. Faymonville declined and suggested they make the offer to Michela. The Soviets did not follow Faymonville's suggestion, and an infuriated Michela requested that he be withdrawn from the Soviet Union because he could "not accomplish anything worthwhile."[198] MID again rejected Michela's request, citing the importance of his post in the Soviet Union, and ordered him to remain there.[199]

The frustration was taking its toll on what little remained of Michela's objectivity. Later in March he began to keep a file of regular reports on the status of his relationship with the Soviets. The first report, dated 31 March 1942, began by stating that "the attitude of the Soviet Government toward this office is not satisfactory."[200] In it Michela added the Soviet offer to Faymonville to a litany of complaints against the Soviet authorities. Michela was angry that British General Mason-MacFarlane visited the front; that Soviet officials had planned and precipitously abandoned a trip to the front for Michela; that the Soviet government restricted the travel of America's embassy staff; and that Soviet authorities had turned down a series of other requests. Michela concluded the report by calling for the United States to get "tough" with the Soviet Union.[201]

In this first report, Michela credited Faymonville with attempting to help him get a visit to the front. By June 1942 Michela identified Faymonville and his office as a source of the problem: "The Soviets have therefore treated our supply mission in the same manner as the British military mission and have taken up matters with General Faymonville which do not concern him. It can be frankly stated with practical certainty that General Faymonville has not discouraged this procedure."[202]

In his September 1942 report, Michela repeated his assertion that the organization of U.S. military representation in the Soviet Union hindered his mission.[203] One month later Michela submitted a memorandum on his position to General Strong. Michela argued that Faymonville's staff was a valuable source of intelligence that was not accessible to the military attaché, and that Soviet officials approached Faymonville about issues that were not in his jurisdiction. Michela proposed that the solution to the bureaucratic confusion was to place all activities under the control of Ambassador Standley.[204]

By 1943 Michela complained more frequently and aggressively about Faymonville's activities. In March he complained to the MID about Faymonville's use of communication facilities: "It is my opinion that Faymonville considers himself subject to Lend Lease control only and that he is exercising what he believes his right to select what ever channels are available."[205] Later that month he complained to the MID: "Am unable to get any cooperation from Lend Lease Administration here."[206] In April Michela attempted to place his complaints against Faymonville in a broader context: "Soviet methods of playing one US agency against another gives them all advantages."[207]

By May it was becoming difficult for Michela to hide his rancor toward Faymonville. On 12 May 1943 he sent the MID a telegram reporting on Burns' visit to Moscow.[208] Michela began the telegram with a complaint: "General Burns and Faymonville departed 2 days ago for destinations not reported even to Ambassador." He then recounted his efforts to explain to Burns the difficulties he was having with the lend-lease office. Burns apparently did not evince any sympathy for the military attaché. According to Michela, he replied: "it was useless to attempt acquisition information." Michela was flabbergasted by Burns' reply:

> Am unable to understand Gen Burns [*sic*] attitude here in isolating himself and party socially as well as officially from everyone including Ambassador all being completely ignored.
>
> From this end it appears that 2 uncoordinated US Governments are represented here.[209]

Although puzzling to Michela, Burns' attitude can be explained by the military attaché's continued struggle against White House policy—a policy Burns had helped to author. Michela was reminded in March that "White House Policy does not permit using Lend Lease as a basis of bargaining."[210] Despite this admonition, Michela persisted in his efforts to place lend-lease on a reciprocal basis. On 17 May 1943 Standley and Michela intercepted a telegram from Faymonville to Stettinius. Faymonville informed Stettinius that Soviet officials were going to request a new type of parachute. He recommended that the OLLA approve the request. Michela was beside himself. He and Standley wanted the Soviet authorities to submit the request through the military attaché's office on a "reciprocity basis." He concluded the telegram: "Such procedure remains the only bargaining means available to me."[211]

By June Michela's animosity toward Faymonville was becoming public knowledge. The military attaché gave a cocktail party for the visiting flier Eddie Rickenbacker; he refused to invite Faymonville.[212] The struggle between Michela and Faymonville had become so public that the FBI and the Army chief of staff's office investigated it. As a result, the FBI developed a large file on Faymonville, and the chief of staff's office received a comprehensive report on the issues among U.S. military personnel in Moscow.

The FBI investigation originated as a result of a request by Michela. Unable to shake Faymonville's determination to carry out White House policy, General Michela attacked Faymonville personally. He accused Faymonville of being a homosexual and requested an investigation of him.[213] As a result, in September 1942, the FBI began an investigation of Faymonville on "morals charges."[214] Agents investigating Faymonville's background in San Francisco found nothing except witnesses who had the utmost respect for the general. Most, in fact, assumed Faymonville was being investigated before being appointed ambassador to the Soviet Union.[215]

The FBI agent in Moscow uncovered more disturbing evidence against Michela than against Faymonville. His description of Davies' press conference hinted at a plot against Faymonville: "For some time before Davies' arrival there had been conferences between Michela and Duncan and the newsmen, and during the week of May 5 an agreement was reportedly reached that they would interview Faymonville at what was to be 'the most difficult hour Faymonville had ever had.'"[216]

Despite his suspicions of Michela's intentions, the FBI agent in Moscow was required to investigate every potential lead. The most promising was given to him by somebody in Moscow. In 1938 one of Faymonville's clerks in Moscow resigned. The NKVD had photographed this man in a homosexual act and threatened to blackmail him. He resigned after discussing the matter with Faymonville.[217] Faymonville respected the man, and wrote him a letter of recommendation.[218] FBI Director J. Edgar Hoover sent a telegram to his agent in Moscow reporting that "illicit relations" between Faymonville and this man were not admitted, but were implied.[219] Although the FBI never uncovered any concrete evidence against Faymonville, Michela had succeeded in casting a shadow over his reputation. In summer 1943 that shadow widened as the army undertook steps of its own.

In July 1943 the Army chief of staff's office completed its investigation. The report to the chief of staff was initiated because General Marshall had "received information charging that Gen. Faymonville was refusing to cooperate with other U.S. missions in Russia and that his personal and official conduct was so pro-Soviet as to raise the question on some persons' minds as to whether he was being blackmailed by the Soviet Government."[220] The report is lengthy and replete with rumor and innuendo. Furthermore, much of the report was written on the basis of information given by General Michela, "General Faymonville's principal opponent in American diplomatic circles in Moscow."[221]

The report encompassed a wide variety of issues, ranging from the specific suspicion that Faymonville was working with the Soviets to Michela's worry "about the 'pinks' who surround the President" and the possibility that if Michela resigned, one of the "pinks" would be appointed military attaché.[222] Given the personal animosities involved, it proved impossible for the report's author to determine the truth as to who was or was not a Soviet spy. Thus, the author recommended the Solomon-like solution of removing both parties from their posts. He recommended that "[t]he War Department immediately relieve Brigadier General Joseph A. Michela and his assistant, Colonel Roswell, and that as soon as this is done, the papers be transmitted to Mr. Hopkins requesting his assistance in removing General Faymonville and replacing him by a competent civilian."[223]

The anonymous author of the report on Faymonville was not alone in his conclusions. Major General Strong met with Davies and discussed his thoughts on the situation. Strong stated that he thought he had to replace both Faymonville and Michela. Davies argued strongly for Faymonville's retention, even broaching the subject the next day with Harry Hopkins. Although Hopkins deeply regretted that the situation had reached this point, he declared that matters were now "beyond anything he could do."[224]

General Burns, however, reacted angrily to the malicious report. In a six-page handwritten memo, Burns decried the injustice of the investigation, criticized what he termed as gross inaccuracies in the report's observations and conclusions, and formulated a series of succinct concluding judgments based on his perception of the report's contents:

Apparently without his knowledge and any opportunity to defend himself, Faymonville has been secretly investigated upon request of the War Dept. on the suspicion that he is guilty of such charges as:

1. Indulgence in homosexual practices
2. Personal debauchery and responsibility for debauchery in his Lend/Lease organization

3. Being blackmailed with result he is unduly friendly and helpful to Russia and therefore not properly protecting the interests of the U.S.
4. Failure to cooperate properly with other American representatives in Russia.

The report contains much worthwhile information and analysis with reference to Faymonville but it also contains much gossip and hearsay evidence for which Gen. Michela seems largely responsible. These latter refer not only to Faymonville but to a number of individuals who are not sufficiently anti-Faymonville to suit Michela. Such individuals are therefore likewise subjected to a secret one way attack.[225]

Burns concluded his memorandum by defending Faymonville and praising his adherence to official U.S. policy. While doing so, he emphasized the disturbingly high level of animosity toward the Soviets so evident in many American personnel and linked this animosity to the vicious infighting now occurring among them.

The strong and amicable relationship that Faymonville had developed with the Soviets primarily motivated the support Burns and Davies accorded to Faymonville. Both understood that Faymonville's attitudes and efforts were in full accord with Roosevelt's wishes. Faymonville's views was particularly important in light of the anti-Soviet views expressed by Standley at his ill-considered 8 March press conference. Although the nature and extent of Soviet reaction to the recall of Faymonville remain unknown, a conversation between the Soviet ambassador to Mexico, Constantine Oumansky, and Davies sheds some light on the Soviet reaction. To Oumansky, Faymonville's "punishment" was indicative of the existence of a "certain clique in the [U.S.] Army, who were opposed to the President's policy of Lend-Lease which Faymonville was directing."[226] Of course, one statement cannot be judged to reflect in toto the Soviet reaction to the resolution of the Faymonville-Michela dispute. However, Oumansky's comment is likely to have typified the Soviet response, because Faymonville was one of the few who did get along well with the Soviets during a period when the United States and the Soviet Union were allies. Surely the fact that Faymonville had been accused of treason as a result of his warmth to the Soviet Union could not have gone over too well in the Kremlin.

On 19 October 1943 the *New York Times* published an article that illustrated that this dispute and the issues involved in it were well known to the public. The article stated, "For some time it has been an open secret in Moscow that there has been a conflict in the ideas and aspirations of the Lend-Lease administration on the one hand and the embassy and its military attaché officer on the other."[227] On September 28, 1943, the War Department recalled both

Faymonville and Michela to the United States and returned them to their permanent ranks of colonel.[228] The administration now sought to put an end to the division and hostility among its personnel in the Soviet Union.

The Shifting Tide of War

While Roosevelt was working to attain his policy objectives and U.S. personnel in the Soviet Union struggled among themselves for a dominant position in the formulation and implementation of that policy, the military struggle shifted in the Allies' favor. Although the true turning point in Allied military fortunes began as early as June 1942 at Midway Island in the central Pacific, the Axis suffered a serious defeat in October 1942 at El Alamein in North Africa and then, in November 1942, an outright disaster at Stalingrad. In the European theater of war, the United States and Britain followed up the victory at El Alamein with Operation Torch, an amphibious invasion of North Africa. Soon after, British and American troops conquered Sicily and prepared to land in Italy.

In the Pacific, in 1942 the Japanese learned just how fleeting and incomplete their victory at Pearl Harbor had been. In May 1942 the ascendancy of the aircraft carrier in naval warfare began to emerge at the Battle of the Coral Sea. The Japanese and the Americans both suffered carrier casualties in this battle, but it was a loss the United States was far more capable of overcoming. One month later, in June 1942, the United States won a clear victory at Midway Island. Again the United States lost one carrier, but this time the U.S. Navy sank four Japanese carriers. In that single battle, the United States recovered from the setback at Pearl Harbor and achieved rough parity with the Japanese naval forces. The Japanese would never regain their advantage.[229]

Despite these dramatic events in North Africa and the Pacific, the most telling change in Axis fortunes occurred on the Soviet-German front, where the bulk of Hitler's armies were engaged. The first eight months of 1942 had indeed been a period of extreme peril for the Red Army and the Soviet state. Driven on by Hitler's insatiable appetite for natural resources and military victory, the Wehrmacht's vast legions had reached the banks of the Volga River and foothills of the oil-rich Caucasus Mountain region. As in 1941, however, while pursuing his aims, Hitler severely overreached himself. Neither his armies nor the resources of the German state were sufficient to fulfill the ambitious tasks Hitler assigned them.

The German armies' long and costly summer campaign, followed by the brutal city fighting at Stalingrad, sapped the strength of the Wehrmacht and accorded the beleaguered city an importance to Hitler and Stalin that it scarcely warranted. By October 1942 the German assaults expired along the banks of the Volga in utter exhaustion. By this time the Wehrmacht's strength had seriously eroded, forcing Hitler to cajole his allies into committing inadequate forces into combat to satisfy missions that were beyond their capability. Hitler's grand offensive creaked to a halt; the tide turned.[230]

As had been the case at Moscow the year before, during the German onslaught, Stalin and his High Command had carefully marshaled their reserves, seeking an opportunity to strike back at their tormentors. The opportunity occurred in mid-November 1942, when, once again, the Soviet High Command prepared and conducted massive multiple counteroffensives designed to achieve what they had failed to accomplish in the winter of 1941–1942—the collapse of German forces in the east.

A galaxy of fresh Soviet offensives surprised and stunned the Wehrmacht in November 1942, altering once and for all any hopes on Hitler's part for victory in his crusade against Bolshevism. Stalin first unleashed a massive force of five *fronts* totaling fourteen armies and well over 2 million men against Wehrmacht forces west of Moscow and in the Stalingrad region through twin operations code-named, respectively, Mars and Uranus. Although the Red Army failed to crush German Army Group Center west of Moscow in Operation Mars, Operation Uranus successfully encircled, destroyed, or severely damaged three Axis armies and tens of divisions in the Stalingrad region.

The Red Army then unleashed operation Little Saturn in mid-December 1942, destroying yet another Axis army and clearing the southern bank of the Don River west of Stalingrad of German and other Axis forces. In February 1943, after destroying the once-proud German Sixth Army in the ruins of Stalingrad, Stalin ordered the Red Army to commence a general offensive along the entire front from the Baltic to the Black Sea. Within a month, eight Red Army *fronts* with over forty armies were assaulting shaky German defenses from Leningrad to the northern shores of the Sea of Azov. Only by serious exertions and at considerable cost were German forces able to halt the determined Soviet drive. Largely as a result of the skill of the new commander of German Army Group Don, Field Marshal Erich von Manstein, and the exhaustion of the Red Army's overextended attacking forces, German forces were able to halt the Soviet juggernaut in mid-March 1943.[231]

In midsummer 1943 Hitler's unrequited ambition prompted him to launch one last effort to defeat the Red Army on the field of battle. Hitler unleashed that final effort in early July 1943 at Kursk, only to suffer another defeat, for the first time at the height of the summer. Kursk turned out to be a disaster for the German cause. Scarcely had the Wehrmacht tasted defeat at Kursk when the

Red Army opened yet another massive offensive across a broad front. Under unrelenting assault, Hitler's legions had no choice but to initiate an unprecedented strategic retreat to its highly touted Panther Line, which stretched from the Baltic Sea along the Dnepr River to the Sea of Azov and the Black Sea. This defense line did not hold out for long. In fact, by October 1943 Red Army forces had pierced the vaunted German defenses and were fighting for possession of Belorussia and Kiev and Krivoi Rog in the Ukraine.[232]

By late July 1943, if not earlier, it was abundantly clear to the world, and to the Roosevelt administration in particular, that it was just a matter of time before the Soviet Union won its war against Germany. More telling still, although ultimate Soviet victory over Hitler was a near certainty, America's military forces were still months away from engaging the German Army to any significant extent. By summer 1943 the Allied offensive in Italy had bogged down in the mountains halfway along that peninsula, and no Allied ground forces had yet to invade France.[233] Therefore, the "second front" in Europe that Stalin was arguing for remained a fiction. Worse still for those who took a pessimistic view of future relations with the Soviet Union, without a second front, it was increasingly possible to envision the Red Army unilaterally liberating central, and perhaps even western, Europe.

Meanwhile, on the other side of the world, the war with Japan was becoming increasingly violent and prolonged. Although it was essential to achieve victory, the painful island-hopping operations that U.S. forces were undertaking were time-consuming and brought U.S. forces closer to the Japanese mainland in a painfully slow fashion.[234] Moreover, once those operations were completed, the United States faced the grim prospect of attacking Japanese forces entrenched in their homeland, to say nothing of the vast regions of Japanese-occupied China. Therefore, it was also realistic to ponder the positive role the Soviet Union might play as an active military ally and participant in military operations in the Pacific rim region.

Thus, the situation in the fall of 1943 required Roosevelt to reassess America's ongoing and future relationship with the Soviet Union. This need coincided with the necessity of resolving conflict among U.S. diplomatic personnel within the Soviet Union. The year 1943 would be a turning point in the United States–Soviet relationship.

Conclusion

When Roosevelt launched his policy of unconditional aid for the Soviet Union in 1941, the Soviet position was precarious at best. The first two years of the war were a terrifying roller-coaster ride for those who hoped the Red Army would defeat Hitler. In summer 1941, very few of Roosevelt's professional military and diplomatic advisers believed the Soviet regime would survive the German onslaught. Reassured by a few voices in the wilderness, however, Roosevelt staked his future hopes and plans on Soviet success. He sent shiploads of war material desperately needed for an American military buildup. In exchange, he asked only that the Red Army and the Soviet people continue their horrific struggle against the German aggressors.

In implementing this policy, however, Roosevelt faced constant and increasing opposition from within his own government. Many individuals in both the War and State Departments clung to their prewar hostility toward all things Soviet. From the chief of the Division of European Affairs in the State Department to the military attaché in Moscow, these people became increasingly concerned with issues such as information acquisition, treatment of diplomats, and territorial delineation, and sought concessions for the vast quantities of supplies the United States delivered to the Soviet Union.

Their pleas failed to persuade the president. Unconcerned by issues of daily diplomacy and military attaché work, Roosevelt kept his gaze firmly fixed on his goals. First and foremost, he wanted the Soviet Union to continue to fight Germany. A separate Soviet-German peace was by no means out of the question in 1941, 1942, or early 1943. The historical precedents were significant. In 1918, the Bolshevik regime had signed the Treaty of Brest-Litovsk with Germany, thereby ending their involvement in World War I even as their allies continued to fight in France and Belgium. More recently, in 1939, Molotov and Joachim von Ribbentrop had concluded the infamous nonaggression pact that sparked World War II.

Roosevelt was also concerned about the war with Japan. By 1943 the Soviet Union was still not at war with that country, and the United States was engaged in vicious combat across the Pacific. Roosevelt hoped that the Soviet Union would help the United States defeat Japan after the defeat of Germany.

Thus, a successful conclusion of the present war was of the utmost concern to President Roosevelt. Roosevelt, however, was also concerned with the results of the war. He did not want a repeat of the conclusions of World War I. The Treaty of Versailles was supposed to prevent that sort of war from ever occurring again. It failed miserably. Roosevelt was determined to form a partnership that would construct and enforce a peace. The Soviet Union was vital to his goals. Roosevelt sought to forge a wartime partnership between Moscow and Washington that would endure the end of the struggle against the common enemy.

From 1941 to 1943, while the fate of the Soviet Union hung in the balance,

Roosevelt was unwilling to do anything that might risk either Soviet survival or Soviet cooperation. U.S. aid to the Soviet Union had to be unconditional.

By 1943 it was painfully obvious that most United States officials in the Soviet Union did not share their president's views. It was equally clear that they would stop at nothing to undermine Roosevelt's policy. The situation in Moscow had become so heated that it threatened to damage the tenuous partnership Roosevelt was developing. Roosevelt had to resolve that conflict. He did so through a sweeping reorganization and replacement of the personnel conducting the United States' relations with the Soviet Union.

At the same time global developments prompted a reassessment of Roosevelt's Soviet policy. By the end of the summer of 1943, the Soviet Union was no longer teetering precariously on the brink of destruction. As Soviet fortunes improved, so did the necessity to discuss postwar plans. From 1943 until his death, Roosevelt finally was able to conduct his personal diplomacy. He sat down with Stalin and Churchill to discuss the big issues. More importantly, he sat down with them as equals. The Soviet Union was no longer a weakened state that needed to be handled with kid gloves. The time for bargaining had arrived.

6

Forging Peace: Relations Between the United States and the Soviet Union, 1943–1945

Introduction

As the geopolitical and military situation in fall 1943 developed, Roosevelt resolved to strengthen the relationship between the United States and the Soviet Union. No longer a supplicant fighting for its survival, the Soviet Union assumed the role Roosevelt had long imagined for it: a necessary partner for ensuring victory over Germany and Japan and for guaranteeing the lasting peace he hoped would follow. Although he still rejected the strict quid pro quo policy advocated by the State Department and the military, Roosevelt believed by this time that the establishment of an enduring postwar peace required some reasonable give and take by both the United States and the Soviet Union. In short, in Roosevelt's view, if both powers shared common global interests in the postwar world and aspired for peaceful coexistence in some postwar global security system, both had to pay more than lip service to cooperation and compromise. While requiring reasonable give-and-take on both sides, this policy and the altering geopolitical context that it addressed also compelled Roosevelt to fine-tune his contacts between the United States and the Soviet Union at every level.

At the summit of the relationship, Roosevelt hoped to embark on a course of personal diplomacy with Stalin. He understood, however, that productive cooperation could not consist only of agreements made at rare encounters between the two leaders. The sort of relationship Roosevelt envisioned required sustained activity and contact at every level of the foreign policy apparatus. It demanded a bureaucracy capable of organizing and coordinating numerous and diverse activities; it meant more active cooperation between personnel at the embassy level.

This subtle change in policy was accompanied by a change in the way the United States implemented its Soviet policy. The State Department slowly emerged from a decade of Roosevelt-imposed exile to participate systematically in policy making and implementation with regard to the Soviet Union; and Roosevelt changed the way the United States was represented in the Soviet Union. He recalled the bickering and often obstructionist military attachés, diplomats, ambassador, and lend-lease representatives. In their stead, Roosevelt created a streamlined organization designed not only to eliminate jurisdictional conflict, but also to generate more active support for the president's Soviet policy.

Removing intransigent individuals and even restructuring the bureaucracy would prove insufficient to resolve the conflict between the White House and the U.S. embassy in the Soviet Union. Although these changes appeared promising during the halcyon days of fall 1943, when the American, British, and Soviet foreign ministers met in Moscow and when Churchill, Roosevelt, and Stalin met at Teheran, that promise proved illusory.

Despite Roosevelt's best efforts to create new representation in Moscow, completely eliminating opposition to his Soviet policy proved impossible. Carrying out Roosevelt's expanded program of cooperation with the Soviet Union required experienced diplomats in the U.S. embassy. That experience came at a price. Foreign Service officers who had trained with Kelley in the 1920s and 1930s returned to positions of influence in Washington and Moscow in 1944 and 1945. They, in turn, impressed on an increasingly embittered ambassador their views of a correct policy toward the Soviet Union. Within a matter of months, the embassy and the president resumed their journey down divergent paths. By 1945 the president and his ambassador to the Soviet Union were again struggling against each other over whether to pursue a firmer or a friendlier posture toward the Kremlin.

Cleaning House

Above all, Roosevelt's new approach toward the Kremlin required a supportive and efficient structure to implement it. Thus, as the president prepared in 1943 for his first face-to-face meeting with the Soviet premier, he instituted a comprehensive reform of those organs involved in the conduct of relations between the United States and the Soviet Union. In Washington, he created the Foreign Economic Administration, whose mission was to work much more closely with the State Department rather than to compete against it. At the same time, he enacted several personnel changes in the State Department designed to lessen the influence of the anti-Soviet clique trained by Robert Kelley in the 1920s. The State Department, for example, dispatched Loy Henderson to Iraq, where his role in United States–Soviet affairs was negligible.[1]

Because they were aimed at resolving both jurisdictional and attitudinal disputes, the changes Roosevelt made to U.S. representation in Moscow were even more dramatic. To avoid future conflicts over authority, the administration created a new structure in Moscow: the United States Military Mission to the Soviet Union (USMM). The entire organization fell under the control and authority of the U.S. ambassador to the Soviet Union. At the same time, the War Department abolished the position of military attaché to the Soviet Union for the duration of the war. Instead of serving as intelligence officers in the embassy, all military personnel in the Soviet Union henceforth became part of the USMM. The president also assigned the USMM a task that was strikingly different from that of its predecessor agency. Although the USMM's primary responsibility remained to expedite the provision of material assistance to the Soviet Union, it was now required to foster more active and extensive cooperation between the United States and the Soviet Union.[2] In carrying out its assignments, the military mission would engage in a wide variety of activities that went beyond the task of supplying material aid.

His selection of personnel to direct the new organizations also reflected Roosevelt's concerted effort to resolve attitudinal disputes. In fall 1943, army attaché Michela, naval attaché Duncan, lend-lease chief Faymonville, and Ambassador Standley all departed from the Soviet Union. To replace them, the State and War Departments and the Foreign Economic Administration appointed less controversial individuals who shared a more moderate view of the Soviet Union. They neither viewed the Soviet Union as an inevitable future enemy, nor believed that the United States should provide the Kremlin unconditional aid. Instead, they shared Roosevelt's emerging belief that the United States and the Soviet Union should act as partners in constructing a relationship that would survive the defeat of Germany. Partnership was predicated on a give-and-take on both sides.

The new ambassador to the Soviet Union, W. Averell Harriman, embodied this concept. In doing so, he also reflected the transitional nature of Roosevelt's

Soviet policy in 1943.[3] In September 1941, when he and Beaverbrook traveled to Moscow, Harriman revealed himself to both Roosevelt and Stalin as an ardent supporter of no-questions-asked aid to the Soviet war effort. After meeting with Stalin, Harriman concluded that the United States should take no action that Stalin might conceive of as a demand for reciprocity.[4] In 1941 the establishment of a cooperative relationship between the United States and the Soviet Union demanded that the United States persuade Stalin of American goodwill.

Harriman had no illusions about the nature of Stalin's Soviet Union and the ease with which the United States could form a partnership with Stalin. On 22 January 1942, Harriman met with Ray Atherton, the acting chief of the State Department's Division of European Affairs, and discussed U.S. policy toward the Soviet Union. Harriman advocated a policy of "firmness" toward the Kremlin: "Harriman said when these deliveries [lend-lease shipments] were being made on schedule, naturally our position would be stronger but at no time should we compromise, especially with such an opportunist and hard bargainer as Stalin, or begin any sort of territorial compromises. Stalin would respect any person that looked him in the face and said 'no.'"[5] Harriman's firm line, however, did not involve attaching conditions to aid for the Soviet war effort. Indeed, he stressed that the United States should be friendly and treat the Soviet Union as a partner in the world.[6] What Harriman envisioned was a firm distinction between U.S. policy regarding efforts to defeat Germany and Japan, and U.S. policy regarding postwar political and territorial issues. Creating a partnership with the Soviet Union in effect demanded a dual policy. The United States should continue to provide material aid for the war against Germany and Japan on a no–quid pro quo basis. On every other issue between the two powers, however, the United States should maintain a firm bargaining posture.[7]

As the war progressed, Harriman remained consistent in these beliefs. In February 1943 he advised Hopkins that "I believe when we are on sound ground nothing is gained with the Russians by letting them kick us around."[8] Two months later he repeated this assertion to Edward R. Stettinius, the lend-lease administrator: "My experience is that the Russians are brutally and bluntly frank with us, and we can well afford to be equally so."[9]

Harriman's views on the United States–Soviet relationship were no secret to the Roosevelt administration. Harriman's relationship with the president and Eleanor Roosevelt dated back to his school days, when he attended the Groton School with Eleanor's younger brother, Hall Roosevelt. The relationship between Harriman and Roosevelt became closer during the New Deal years, when Harriman actively supported much of Roosevelt's business legislation. Harriman was also a close friend of Roosevelt's confidant, Harry Hopkins.[10] The correspondence between the two is peppered with Harriman's observations on U.S. relations with the Soviet Union.[11] Furthermore, Harriman was not reluctant to air his opinions beyond the confines of the White House. In his notes for 7 May 1943, he remarked on how he had disseminated his views:

> Beaverbrook is for the appeasement policy toward Russia, to which I am dead opposed. I feel strongly that we must be friendly and frank but firm when they behave in a manner which is incompatible with our ideas. Otherwise we are storing up trouble for the future. I am also convinced that Stalin will have greater confidence and respect for us, as an ally in the war and postwar. These views I have held and expressed for at least 18 months.[12]

Roosevelt thus appointed an ambassador who he knew advocated a modification of the no-questions-asked aid policy toward the Soviet Union. On the surface, this situation differed little from the circumstances surrounding Roosevelt's earlier appointment of Steinhardt and Standley to their position as ambassadors. All three men shared the belief that the United States should be friendly but firm in its relations with the Kremlin. Yet Harriman's ambassadorship was different in two significant ways. First, unlike his predecessors, Harriman perceived a distinction between policy for winning the war and policy for structuring the postwar peace. Second, whereas Roosevelt had deliberately bypassed Steinhardt and Standley, the president actually intended for Harriman to play an important role in the implementation of U.S. policy toward the Soviet Union.

These differences are significant because they signaled a change in Roosevelt's own policy and the methods he used to implement that policy. By restructuring the U.S. foreign policy apparatus in the Soviet Union in 1943, Roosevelt demonstrated that he intended to create a tool that he could use, rather than just another organization he would work around. Furthermore, Roosevelt placed Harriman in a position to wield more power than any U.S. ambassador to the Soviet Union had had since at least June 1941. If Harriman's views were irrelevant to Roosevelt because the White House intended to ignore the bureaucracy and persist with a no–quid pro quo policy, restructuring U.S. representation in the Soviet Union made no sense. Harriman's views were important to Roosevelt, and his appointment signified Roosevelt's agreement with Harriman's dual approach.

The president intended to meet with Stalin and forge a cooperative relationship, and he needed a representative in Moscow who would help ensure the relationship's implementation. The administration's repeated struggles with Steinhardt and Standley amply testified to the difficulty ambassadorial hostility could create for the president. With the expanded workload that increased cooperation entailed, Roosevelt could not afford to be crippled by resistance from his own representatives. Thus, it was important that Roosevelt select an ambassador who shared his vision for the development of U.S. policy toward the Soviet Union.

To that end, Roosevelt turned toward his close and trusted personal friend, Harriman. The president personally briefed Harriman on his mission to the Soviet Union. In several lengthy conversations, Roosevelt explained that he hoped to negotiate the territorial issues personally with Stalin. Roosevelt hoped to persuade the Soviet leader to adopt the United States' positions, but he also believed he had some leverage to use with the Kremlin. This leverage included participation at the council table with the great powers, American support for measures to strengthen Russian security, and help for the postwar reconstruction of Russia.[13] Thus, Roosevelt intended to bargain with Stalin, and he wanted Harriman aware of the policies he would be expected to support.

In advising Roosevelt he would accept the post, Harriman informed the president that he was optimistic about the future of the Soviet-American relationship.[14] At the same time, he was determined to be firm with his Soviet counterparts.[15] Thus, shortly after settling into Spaso House, the ambassador began to advocate new policies toward the Soviet Union.

Thanks to his long relationship with Roosevelt and several presidential briefings, Harriman arrived in Moscow with a firm idea of his mission's priorities. He understood that his general goal was to build a strong relationship between the two powers. Harriman knew, however, that the most immediate aim of his mission was to ensure that the Soviet Union entered the war against Japan early enough to make a difference.[16] The new ambassador also believed that Roosevelt's primary political objective was to gain Stalin's participation in the establishment of a postwar international organization.[17]

Although Harriman had long advocated a get-tough approach toward the Kremlin, he was aware that attainment of his mission goals required a bit more delicacy. Thus, not long after he arrived in Moscow, he described to his staff his plan for approaching the Russians: "We want to show them that (1) we are for the war first; (2) we accept them as equals, and (3) we have an intense interest in their reconstruction."[18] Point number 3 would prove to be the heart of Harriman's new approach to the Soviet Union. Unlike his predecessors, he did not advocate bargaining over lend-lease material essential to the war effort. He did, however, believe that postwar reconstruction aid should be a fundamental part of United States–Soviet diplomatic relations. On 5 November 1943,

Harriman met with Soviet Commissar for Foreign Trade Anastas Mikoyan as a tentative first step in implementing his new policy.[19]

The new head of the U.S. Military Mission, Major General John R. Deane, also reflected the president's views. When he arrived in Moscow in October 1943, Deane was optimistic and eager to implement Roosevelt's policy.[20] He agreed with the White House's earlier policy of providing the Soviet Union all aid it requested on a no-questions-asked basis. He also believed that so long as the Soviet Union was fighting for its survival, no-questions-asked aid was the only policy the United States could realistically support. Like Roosevelt, however, Deane recognized that during the course of summer 1943, the situation had changed. Because the Soviet position was no longer precarious, Deane believed the United States could afford to adopt a new and somewhat firmer approach toward the Kremlin.[21]

The transfer of new personnel to Moscow was not the only indication of a change in Roosevelt's policy. The structure of U.S. organizations in Moscow itself revealed that Roosevelt was now ready to bargain with Stalin. By placing the USMM under the control of the U.S. ambassador, Roosevelt also placed it under the control of the State Department. And in 1943, as it had in 1941, the U.S. Department of State was committed to a quid pro quo policy toward the Soviet Union. Despite their unchanging advocacy of a policy of reciprocity, Roosevelt was now ready to permit the department to exercise greater influence on the formulation and implementation of his Soviet policy.

Final Acts of World War II

MILITARY EVENTS

It is impossible to understand Roosevelt's evolving attitude toward the U.S.-Soviet relationship outside the context of developments on the world's battlefields. During the period from November 1943 through spring 1945, Allied forces continued their advance in all theaters of the war. In the war against Japan, U.S. forces conducted a two-pronged offensive across the central and southern Pacific that reduced and captured Japanese island bastions ever closer to the Japanese mainland. By November 1944 American forces had conquered New Guinea, landed in the Philippines, and commenced a massive bombing campaign against Japan proper. Between January and April 1945, U.S. forces completed their island-hopping advance, seizing Iwo Jima and Okinawa, Japan's final bastions on the road to Tokyo.[22]

In the European theater, 6 June 1944 marked the arrival of the long-anticipated "second front" in northern France. On that date, U.S., British,

Canadian, and other Allied forces landed at Normandy and began their most direct assault against Hitler's fortress Germany. After an arduous two-month-long struggle to break out of the confines of the Normandy bridgehead, in August 1944 Allied forces lunged forward, shattering German Army Group B, capturing Paris, and reaching the western borders of Hitler's Reich by late November. Despite enduring Hitler's final strategic offensive in the west during the Battle of the Bulge, by 1 February 1945, Allied forces reached the vaunted German Western Wall and lower Rhine River, 320 miles from Berlin.[23]

On the Soviet-German front, after breaching German defenses along the Dnepr River in November 1943, the Red Army piled up victory after victory on its inexorable march westward toward Germany. In late December 1943, the Red Army resumed its massive twin offensives against German forces in Belorussia and the Ukraine, expanding and then exploiting its lodgment deep in the Ukraine. When the Belorussian offensive stalled, Stalin reinforced his efforts in the Ukraine and then launched a series of massive offensives that shattered German defenses in the region. By April 1944 Red Army forces plunged into the Crimea, southern Poland, and northern Romania.[24] Early during the winter campaign, the Red Army also commenced the tedious process of defeating German forces in northern Russia, liberating Leningrad, and advancing toward and into the Baltic region.[25]

In June 1944, Stalin and his Stavka began a series of summer offensives designed in part to relieve German pressure on the Allies in the west and, more importantly, to smash German forces in the east, expel them from Soviet territory, and begin the liberation of central Europe.[26] With grinding relentlessness, Soviet forces destroyed or severely damaged three German army groups in Belorussia, eastern Poland, and Romania, recaptured huge tracts of territory, and reached and breached the Vistula River in central Poland and the Carpathian Mountains in western Romania. As the Red Army crossed the 1941 Soviet frontier and advanced on Riga, Warsaw, Bucharest, Belgrade, and Budapest, political issues moved to the forefront of Allied concerns.[27]

The striking successes the Red Army recorded in the winter of 1944–1945 only exacerbated existing Allied political apprehension. Responding to Allied requests to help relieve German pressure on their forces in the Bulge, on 12 and 13 January 1945, the Red Army struck German defenses in East Prussia and central Poland, vaporized Wehrmacht resistance, and lunged toward Königsberg on the Baltic Sea and Berlin. By 1 February, Soviet troops stood on the Oder River, only thirty-six miles from the capital of Hitler's Reich. There, while Roosevelt and Churchill were meeting with Stalin at Yalta, the Red Army suddenly halted its advance after seizing bridgeheads across the river, ostensibly to consolidate its gains and prepare a future climactic offensive on Berlin.[28]

When Stalin halted his offensive against Berlin in early February, the Red Army remained menacingly poised along the Oder River until mid-April 1945. In the meantime, Stalin transferred sizable reserves to Hungary, where, after defeating the final German offensive of the war at Lake Balaton, in mid-March the Red Army mounted a decisive westward drive that culminated on 13 April with the capture of Vienna.[29] Three days later, the Red Army began its final drive to capture Hitler's capital and destroy his Reich.

SOVIET FOREIGN POLICY

Developments on the battlefield inevitably were reflected in the adaptation and implementation of policy by all Allied powers. Nonetheless, there was a remarkable degree of continuity between Soviet prewar and wartime foreign policy. If anything, the Soviets' experience in what they called their Great Patriotic War seemed to strengthen rather than alter certain tendencies in the Kremlin's foreign policy. The most significant tendency was Stalin's desire to preserve and protect the Soviet Union as the engine of world revolution. In the 1930s Stalin had dramatically broken with the ardent proponent of socialist world revolution, Leon Trotsky, choosing instead to build "Socialism in One Country." According to this theory, only after socialism had become strong and secure within the Soviet borders would the Kremlin be able to spread revolution around the globe.[30]

Thus, it was not surprising that after the German invasion in June 1941, the security and survival of the Soviet Union remained the most vital of all Soviet interests.[31] In addition to recognizing the necessity of defending the small socialist "seed," by the mid-1930s Stalin had already begun to associate the security of the Soviet state with his own personal survival and his regime's security.[32] Consequently, throughout the war the Soviet dictator demanded certain concessions from his allies at the peace table.

Stalin's most basic concern—indeed, the prerequisite to Soviet acceptance of any peace settlements—was for secure Soviet frontiers. This meant British and American acceptance of the borders the Soviet Union had established as a result of the Molotov-Ribbentrop pact of 1939. Stalin made no secret of the importance he attached to these borders. When British Foreign Secretary Anthony Eden arrived in Moscow in December 1941, Stalin suggested Britain and the Soviet Union sign a treaty containing a secret codicil guaranteeing the Soviet Union's frontiers as of 22 June 1941. Eden refused to agree at that time, citing the necessity to consult with the United States. A series of meetings and an exchange of correspondence among the three powers followed, during which the United States (or at least the State Department) expressed its concern about acquiescing to territorial arrangements so early in the war. Nevertheless, Stalin refused to be deterred and continued to press the issue through-out the remainder of the war.[33]

Nor did the Kremlin limit its demand to just the expansion of its borders. For security, the Soviet Union also wanted a weakened Germany and Japan. At their first meeting, Stalin warned Roosevelt that Germany could pose a military threat to the Soviet Union in the future. Citing the history of Germany's past three wars (the Franco-Prussian War, World War I, and World War II), Stalin declared that within fifteen to twenty years Germany would again threaten the peace if the Allies did not take steps now to prevent it.[34]

In addition to the issues of Soviet frontiers and the fate of Germany, the future of Poland was also of vital interest to the Soviet Union. Specifically, Stalin demanded two things of Poland after the war. First, he wanted the Polish-Soviet and Polish-German borders moved about a hundred miles to the west. Poland's eastern frontier would accord roughly with the line recommended by the Briton George Nathaniel, the first Baron Curzon, at Versailles in 1919. Stalin also insisted that any future Polish government be "friendly" to the Soviet Union. Stalin reminded Roosevelt and Churchill that twice in recent history a weakened Poland had served as a corridor for German invasion. Under no circumstances did he want to permit this to occur again.[35]

Although these concerns were certainly the centerpiece of Soviet wartime foreign policy, they were not the limit of it. In a process that the historian Vojtech Mastny has identified as security through empire, Stalin also sought to ensure Soviet security through the expansion of Soviet influence whenever and wherever the opportunity arose.[36] This opportunism, however, was pragmatic. Stalin balanced it carefully against the necessity of cooperating with his western allies. Indeed, he believed that postwar cooperation among the Big Three was indispensable to the attainment of security for the Soviet state.[37] Reports by three important figures in the Soviet foreign policy apparatus support this view. In a memorandum dated 10 January 1944, the former ambassador to Great Britain, Ivan Maisky, outlined his view of Soviet foreign policy.[38] Maisky's report was lengthy, but he summarized the policy he advocated in his conclusion: "strengthening of friendly relations with the United States and England; exploiting to our benefit the Anglo-American contradiction with the prospect of a closer contact with the British; expansion of Soviet influence in China; making the USSR a center of gravity for truly democratic countries and forces in all countries, especially in Europe."[39] The belief that cooperation with the United States and Britain was not only desirable but necessary to the attainment of Soviet foreign policy aims was central to Maisky's reasoning.[40]

Andrei Gromyko, Soviet ambassador to the United States, reached a similar conclusion in his report to Molotov dated 14 July 1944. After describing opportunities and conflicts that might emerge in the United States–Soviet relationship, Gromyko reached the following conclusion: "In spite of possible difficulties, which from time to time may emerge in our relations with the United States, the necessary conditions are clearly present for a continuation of cooperation between our two countries in the post-war period. To a great degree these future relations would be determined by the very nature of the relationship which has already been shaped and is still being shaped during the war."[41]

Former ambassador to the United States Maksim Litvinov also believed that cooperation among Britain, the United States, and the Soviet Union was possible in the postwar world. Litvinov did not believe that the United States and the Soviet Union would engage in much "positive political cooperation" after the war, but he did believe that their common interest in the preservation of peace would lead to some collaboration among the three powers.[42]

Thus, from 1943 to 1945, as the leaders of the three major wartime allies met and began to discuss the structure of the peace, there was remarkable congruence in the most significant postwar aspirations of both the United States and the Soviet Union. As the war ground to a close, there was every reason to expect cooperation among the powers to continue.

Roosevelt's Personal Diplomacy

Roosevelt hoped that he could establish a solid foundation for postwar cooperation in a face-to-face meeting with Stalin. This desire for a summit meeting with the Soviet premier was a natural development of Roosevelt's hostility toward the professionals in the State Department. He had never trusted their opinions of the Soviet Union and was unwilling to entrust the establishment of the wartime and postwar relationships with the Soviet Union to them. Beginning with Hopkins' mission to Moscow in summer 1941, Roosevelt endeavored to establish direct contact with the Kremlin. W. Averell Harriman reinforced that effort when he encouraged Stalin to contact Roosevelt directly. The series of special emissaries that so antagonized the embassy throughout 1941 to 1943 were more examples of Roosevelt's desire to foster personal diplomacy with the Soviet Union.

When Davies traveled to Moscow in May 1943 and delivered the letter from Roosevelt to Stalin suggesting a meeting in summer of that same year, it initially appeared that Davies was successful. Roosevelt suggested a small meeting between the two leaders. He told Stalin he imagined he would bring an adviser (Hopkins) and an interpreter, but he would leave State Department officials out of it. Stalin accepted Roosevelt's suggestion of a meeting in Alaska, and Roosevelt prepared to engage in his long-sought personal diplomacy with the Soviet Union.[43]

The meeting of the two leaders was increasingly important. Despite Roosevelt's intention that nothing be done to provoke Soviet suspicion, the course of the war thus far had resulted in the emergence of several areas of tension among the three great powers. The president had indeed overcome (or bypassed) the resistance in his foreign policy apparatus and carried out his no–quid pro quo aid policy toward the Soviet Union. Nevertheless, the best intentions of the White House could not prevail over all the exigencies of war. By summer 1942 Allied supply convoys to Murmansk were suffering near-disastrous casualties. The Germans had fortified their naval and air forces in northern Norway to interdict the vital northern supply line to the Soviet Union. As a result, Allied losses were tremendous. Aware that tanks and supplies rusting on the bottom of the sea were of use to no one, the western Allies suspended convoys along the northern route. In July and August 1942, they attempted to replace these shipments with increased convoys through the Persian corridor and Siberia, but those routes could not make up the loss of the northern route. The British attempted to send a convoy to Murmansk in September 1942, but heavy losses forced them to cancel convoys in October and November. By summer 1943 the Allies had still not resumed the scheduled deliveries through the Soviet north. Thus, at the height of the titanic struggle between the Soviet Union and Germany outside Stalingrad, the Allies reduced the flow of supplies to the Red Army.[44]

During the same period, the issue of the absence of the second front in northwestern Europe continued to exacerbate relations among the three Allied nations. Almost since the first German went into battle against the Soviet Union in June 1941, the Kremlin had pressed Britain, and later the United States, to open a second front against Germany by a cross-channel invasion of the continent. For almost as long, Britain and the United States had promised to do so as soon as requisite forces and landing craft were available. First they assured Stalin that they would invade northern France in 1942, but then the United States and Britain informed Stalin it would be delayed until spring 1943. When that deadline approached, in February 1943, Roosevelt and Churchill informed Stalin the second front would be delayed until August or September 1943. A few months later, they informed the Soviet leader that the invasion of northern France would not be launched until spring 1944. By that point Stalin was furious over what he perceived as deliberate Allied inactivity. He was convinced his allies were determined to see the Soviet Union and Germany fight each other to exhaustion. This belief, combined with his awareness that the Wehrmacht was preparing a massive offensive for summer 1943, caused a rupture in Soviet-American relations. In July 1943, Stalin wrote to Roosevelt informing him that it was impossible for him to keep his promise to Davies. Stalin would not meet Roosevelt in summer 1943.[45]

Either dramatic Soviet success at Kursk in July and August 1943 reassured the Soviet premier that the Soviet Union would not exhaust itself against Germany, or it merely convinced Stalin that he had more to gain than lose from a meeting with Churchill and Roosevelt. In any event, Stalin informed Roosevelt that he would like to arrange a meeting among representatives of the Soviet Union, the United States, and the United Kingdom.[46] The resultant foreign ministers' conference was scheduled for October 1943 in Moscow. Roosevelt, however, still wanted a face-to-face meeting with Stalin, and the Soviet leader finally granted this wish. After much haggling over a location for the meeting, Churchill, Roosevelt, and Stalin agreed to meet at the end of November in Teheran.[47]

The Teheran conference was vitally important to Roosevelt's Soviet policy. For the first time, at this conference Roosevelt shared his vision of the postwar world with Stalin. Without the advice or interference of State Department officials, the president met the Soviet premier and explained in detail what he hoped to achieve through the war, and what he was willing to concede to attain his goals. Having established his friendly intentions toward the Kremlin with two years of unconditional aid, Roosevelt now indicated he was eager to begin the delicate bargaining process to achieve lasting postwar cooperation between the two countries.[48]

In meetings with Roosevelt at Teheran, Stalin promised Roosevelt that the Soviet Union would join the war against Japan after the defeat of Germany. He also agreed to participate in an international organization based on Roosevelt's concept of the "four policemen." Consequently, by the time the conference adjourned, Roosevelt believed he had ensured victory over the Axis powers in the present war and had received adequate commitments to avoid repeating the mistakes of the last war. Roosevelt believed the agreements would safeguard the peace for at least the next fifty years.[49]

In exchange for Stalin's pledges of support, Roosevelt acquiesced to Stalin's demands for territorial acquisition and the creation of a Soviet sphere of influence in eastern Europe. Roosevelt only asked that for the sake of public opinion, and in light of the upcoming U.S. presidential election in 1944, Stalin find some way of allowing the people in the Baltic states and Poland to express their will. Stalin assured Roosevelt he would. According to the Soviet minutes of the meeting, after Roosevelt explained his concern for public opinion and Stalin explained that he understood, Stalin said to Roosevelt, "This, of course, does not mean that the plebiscites in these republics should be held under some form of international control." Roosevelt replied, "Of course not. It would be helpful to declare at the appropriate moment that in due course elections in these republics will take place."[50]

Interpreting the transcripts of the conversations at Teheran is much like analyzing poetry. One gets the sense that there was much winking and nudging going on, and that the words used were chosen largely for their symbolic and metaphorical value. Thus, it is impossible to be certain what each leader actually meant. Nevertheless, when placed within the context of previous and subsequent communications, one can discern the most likely interpretation of the respective remarks. It is also necessary to consider the position and intent of each leader at Teheran and thereafter within the context of the military situation in the European theater of war. The Red Army had won the Battle of Kursk, advanced into eastern Belorussia, and crossed the Dnepr River into the Ukraine. In contrast, the western Allies were stalled in Italy and had yet to launch a cross-channel invasion of Europe. Thus, it was abundantly clear to all three heads of state that the Red Army would liberate large chunks of eastern and central Europe with or without Allied assistance. First and foremost, this included Poland and much of the Balkans.

This reality conditioned Roosevelt's policy with regard to both the Polish question and Stalin's requests for territorial gains. Therefore, consistent with his previous and subsequent comments on the Polish issue, although Roosevelt did expect Stalin to acquiesce to elections in Poland and the Baltic states, he also expected those elections to be less than free and unfettered. He repeatedly informed the Soviet Union that Poland must of course have a government friendly to Moscow; yet at the same time he insisted that the elections appear free so as not to offend world public opinion. For example, according to Soviet Ambassador Maksim Litvinov in an early May 1943 meeting with Roosevelt, the president declared that "in his opinion neither the U.S.A. nor England should take it upon itself to defend Polish interests in the Union." Two months later Roosevelt's trusted representative, Harry Hopkins, met with the Soviet chargé d'affaires, Andrei Gromyko, to advise him that Stalin would be surprised at how far Roosevelt was prepared to go in recognizing Soviet rights.[51] Some historians have suggested that it is evidence of Roosevelt's naïveté that he could expect a free election in these countries to return a government friendly to the Soviet Union.[52] Roosevelt was not naive; he fully understood what it meant for the Soviet Union to be guaranteed a friendly government in a neighboring country. He also understood that for the sake of world public opinion, the election must appear to be free. Roosevelt wanted Stalin to take appearances into consideration.

Whatever his personal feelings about the principle of self-determination and the sensibilities of the Polish and Baltic peoples, Roosevelt was not about to sacrifice his goal of postwar cooperation with the Soviet Union in a futile effort to challenge what the westward march of the Red Army would guarantee. He understood that Soviet armies would liberate Poland and much of eastern Europe. Furthermore, when Roosevelt and Churchill accepted the surrender of the Italian government in September 1943 and welcomed Charles de Gaulle as the leader of the French, they also accepted the principle that liberating countries would retain the dominant influence in the countries they liberated. By excluding the Soviet Union from this process in the west, they tacitly excluded themselves from similar processes in the east.

Overall, the Teheran conference was a successful beginning to Roosevelt's personal diplomacy with Stalin. The two had indeed "got along fine," and found they agreed on much. They both realized they were working toward the common goal of creating a sustainable peace.[53] The details of that peace, however, required further arduous bargaining. The road toward victory remained rutted.

In the months after their meeting, the three allies struggled to implement the agreements reached at Teheran. On 6 June 1944 the long dispute over the second front came to an end when Allied forces landed on the beaches of Normandy, but new disputes soon emerged to replace the old. In the east, Soviet forces crossed the 1941 frontier and began their occupation and liberation of eastern Europe. Applying the same principles as his western Allies had applied in Italy, Stalin unilaterally dictated the terms of the surrender in the former Axis countries Romania, Bulgaria, and Hungary.[54]

Even more heated controversy erupted in late summer 1944 over Poland. Relations between the Polish government-in-exile in London and the Soviet Union were essentially nonexistent. In spring 1943 the Germans had discovered a mass grave of Polish officers in the Katyn Forest near Smolensk. During their occupation of Poland in 1940 and 1941, Soviet security forces detained and murdered tens of thousands of Polish officers. When Germany discovered their bodies, it orchestrated a propaganda coup, correctly accusing the Soviets of the atrocity and calling on the International Red Cross to investigate. On the very same day, the Polish government-in-exile made a similar appeal. The Soviet government feigned outrage and broke off its relations with the London Poles.

As the months progressed, Britain and the United States urged the Soviets and London Poles to resume diplomatic relations, but to no avail. The Kremlin insisted that as a prerequisite to resumed relations the Polish government in London must recognize the Curzon line as the Polish-Soviet frontier. The

London Poles demurred. As the Red Army marched further west, Soviet demands increased. The Kremlin soon wanted the Polish government in London to replace certain ministers. Finally Stalin began working with the Polish Committee for National Liberation (the Lublin Poles) that he had created as an alternative government to the London Poles. By the end of 1944, despite Roosevelt's appeals that Stalin wait until he and Roosevelt had an opportunity to discuss the issue in person, the Soviet Union recognized the Lublin Poles as the provisional government of Poland.[55]

Other issues emerged as irritants in American-Soviet relations at the highest level. Closely related to the problem of the Polish government was the problem of the Warsaw uprising in August–September 1944. In August 1944, when the Red Army was advancing westward through Belorussia via Brest and toward the Vistula south of Warsaw via Lublin, the Polish Home Army (a military organization linked to the Polish government-in-exile in London) began an uprising against German forces in Warsaw. The timing could not have been worse. Although the Red Army dispatched a tank army toward Warsaw, forces operating in Belorussia and eastern Poland were stretched to the limit after over a month of heavy fighting. The Soviet tank force reached within fifteen miles of Warsaw's eastern outskirts in early August, when German counterattacks decimated the armored force.[56] Fresh Red Army forces approached the city but were unable to dislodge the German defenders on the Vistula River's eastern bank until mid-September.[57] Subsequently, a Polish force subordinate to the Red Army assaulted in vain across the Vistula into Warsaw in late September but failed to prevent the Germans from crushing the Poles in Warsaw, which they did in extremely brutal fashion.[58]

Churchill and Roosevelt wanted to attempt at least token efforts to assist the Poles. They asked Stalin for permission to use Soviet air bases to drop supplies to the beleaguered Home Army. However, Stalin refused to do so until mid-September, citing the danger to the aircraft and the likelihood that the Germans would capture the supplies.[59] Soviet historians have since argued with some validity that any effort to assist the Warsaw Poles militarily would have required altering the direction of the Red Army's main attacks north and south of the city, and have cited the difficulties involved in a wholesale regrouping of Red Army forces at the end of major offensive operations. Military assistance around Warsaw, they claimed, would have ignored the fact that Red Army forces were engaged in heavy fighting for bridgeheads across the Bug and Narew bridgeheads north of the city and the Magnushev and Pulavy bridgeheads over the Vistula River to the south and would also have disrupted the conduct of future operations. Notwithstanding these military realities, however, it is extremely doubtful that Stalin had any genuine wish to assist the Warsaw Poles even if he could.[60] For the Polish Home Army and its supporters, Warsaw was and still remains an example of Stalin's unconscionable desire to crush an independent Poland. Despite the validity of Stalin's military reasons for refusing to aid the Poles, the Warsaw uprising became a public relations disaster for the Kremlin.

Other irritants emerged as Roosevelt and Stalin bargained for a viable and lasting postwar settlement. Although Stalin agreed with Roosevelt about the need for an international organization to preserve the peace, the details of how that organ should function remained in dispute. At the Dumbarton Oaks conference in October 1944, the Soviet Union and the United States debated concrete aspects of a new United Nations organization such as the need for unanimity among the great powers and the number of member votes each state should receive in the organization's General Assembly.[61]

By late 1944 these and other issues made it clear that another summit meeting among Churchill, Roosevelt, and Stalin was essential. Again after much dickering as to the conference's time and location, the three leaders resolved to meet on Soviet territory at Yalta on the Crimean Peninsula in February 1945. There, Churchill, Roosevelt, and Stalin essentially consolidated and expanded on the decisions reached at Teheran. This time with the presence of State Department representatives at the conference, Roosevelt continued to follow the course he had set when he launched his personal diplomacy in fall 1943. Roosevelt bargained with Stalin in another effort to ensure Soviet participation in both the war against Japan and in the creation of a sustainable peace.[62]

As in their previous bargaining sessions, both Roosevelt and Stalin won concessions from each other. Stalin reaffirmed his promise to enter the war against Japan three months after the defeat of Nazi Germany, and in return, Roosevelt agreed to certain territorial concessions in the Far East, including Soviet annexation of southern Sakhalin Island and the Kurile Islands, a Soviet lease on Port Arthur on the strategically important Liaotung Peninsula, and the internationalization of the port of Dairen on the same peninsula.[63]

The Yalta participants also addressed key issues emerging in the war against Germany. Churchill, Roosevelt, and Stalin reached agreements on the question of the occupation and control of Germany, on reparations from Germany to compensate the Soviet Union and other states for the damage it had inflicted during the war, and on the future frontiers and government of Poland.[64] In addition, Stalin permitted France to be included as the fourth power in the occupation and administration of Germany, even though he insisted France's projected sector be carved from British- and American-controlled territory.

Finally, all three agreed to participate in the formation of a "general international organization to maintain peace and security."[65]

At the time, the conference appeared to be a success. Three countries with vastly different political and economic systems and goals managed to focus on their common aim of defeating the Axis and creating a lasting peace. In doing so, they reached agreement, albeit a fragile one, on a series of volatile issues. Predictably, one of the most controversial agreements concerned Poland.[66] Although Churchill and Roosevelt recognized Stalin's territorial claims in the region, they asked that the Soviet Union support a call for the "reorganization" of the existing provisional government in Poland. Although the Declaration on Poland called for reorganization on "a broader democratic basis with the inclusion of democratic leaders from Poland itself and from Poles abroad," the formula accepted by the three was deliberately vague.[67] For his own part, Roosevelt was aware that he was asking Stalin for a concession without having any leverage in the matter. The Red Army had occupied virtually all of Poland, and as a result, Stalin was essentially free to do whatever he liked. When Roosevelt's chief of staff, Admiral William D. Leahy, advised the president that "this is so elastic that the Russians can stretch it all the way from Yalta to Washington without ever technically breaking it," Roosevelt reportedly replied, "I know, Bill—I know it. But it's the best I can do for Poland at this time."[68]

What Roosevelt had gained from Stalin at this conference was a commitment to a continued relationship among the great powers. As long as all were participants in an effective postwar international organization, discussions aimed to resolve conflicts among them would continue. In addition, Roosevelt was open to using economic leverage as a bargaining chip after the war. The innocuous phrase "at this time" indicated that Roosevelt remained committed to his policy of friendly bargaining with the Soviet Union. The key to his policy was the maintenance of a "friendly" relationship within which bargaining could occur.

In the weeks after the Yalta conference, Roosevelt's pursuit of his "friendly" policy became ever more difficult. Secret German military approaches to U.S. officials in Bern, Switzerland, regarding a possible German surrender produced an extremely heated exchange of telegrams between Roosevelt and Stalin.[69] Nonetheless, Roosevelt refused to allow this dispute to damage the overall relationship between the two powers. In the last telegram he sent to Stalin, Roosevelt advised the Soviet premier:

> Thank you for your frank explanation of the Soviet point of view on the Berne [*sic*] incident which it now appears has faded into the past without having accomplished any useful purpose.

In any event there must not be mutual distrust, and minor misunderstandings of this character should not arise in the future.[70]

The Bern incident was not, however, the only source of "misunderstanding" in relations among Britain, the United States, and the Soviet Union. Roosevelt was angered by Soviet unwillingness to allow U.S. planes to enter Poland to help liberated American prisoners of war.[71] Roosevelt also remained concerned about developments in Romania, where, after the Red Army's march into that country, the Soviet Union peremptorily reorganized the country in accordance with the Soviets' own wishes.[72]

In the winter of 1945, however, no issue was as threatening to Allied harmony as the issue of Poland. As Leahy had warned the president, the Yalta agreement on Poland was extremely elastic. The problem that emerged after the conference, however, was not simply one of the Soviets stretching the elastic as far as they pleased. It was also a matter of conflicting interpretations over the meaning of the agreement. Essentially, all parties in the dispute struggled over what precisely the "reorganization" of the Polish government meant. The Soviet government argued that it meant the continuation of the existing provisional government (based on the Lublin Committee) with the inclusion of a few members of other parties. The British government and the U.S. ambassador to the Soviet Union, Harriman, contended that it required a completely new government including members of all parties.[73] Concerned with public opinion, Roosevelt would have preferred a more liberal interpretation of "reorganization" than the Soviets were offering. Consequently, he sent Stalin a telegram on 1 April 1945, pleading with the Soviet premier to understand the importance of United States public opinion:

> In the discussions that have taken place so far your Government appears to take the position that the new Polish Provisional Government of National Unity which we agreed should be formed should be little more than a continuation of the present Warsaw Government. I cannot reconcile this either with our agreement or our discussions. While it is true that the Lublin Government is to be reorganized and its members play a prominent role, it is to be done in such a fashion as to bring into being a new government. This point is clearly brought out in several places in the text of the Agreement. I must make it quite plain to you that any such solution which would result in a thinly disguised continuance of the present Warsaw régime would be unacceptable and would cause the people of the United States to regard the Yalta agreement as having failed. . . .
>
> You are, I am sure, aware that the genuine popular support in the

United States is required to carry out any government policy, foreign or domestic. The American people make up their own mind and no government action can change it.[74]

Despite his concern over the Polish government, Roosevelt did not share Churchill's willingness to risk postwar cooperation with the Soviet Union over the Polish issue. The San Francisco conference scheduled to establish the United Nations was rapidly approaching, and the western Allies still lacked the leverage to force Stalin to do anything.[75] By no means does this indicate that Roosevelt was pursuing a no-questions-asked policy of support for the Kremlin. He remained firmly committed to his new policy of reasonable bargaining. Ever the practical idealist, however, Roosevelt understood that he could only really bargain when he had something to bargain with. On the matter of Poland, Roosevelt had nothing to offer. On 6 April 1945, he telegraphed Churchill to support the prime minister's forceful refutation of Soviet complaints against his allies and clearly underscore his view that the tripartite relationship was a relationship among equals:

We must not permit anybody to entertain a false impression that we are afraid.

Our Armies will in a very few days be in a position that will permit us to become "tougher" than has heretofore appeared advantageous to the war effort.[76]

Roosevelt's practicality also prompted him to keep a firm grasp on his priorities. As angry as he became over Soviet actions in Poland, Roosevelt never lost sight of his primary aims: victory in war and the preservation of the peace. Thus, in one of his last messages to Churchill, Roosevelt summarized his perception of his disputes with Stalin:

I would minimize the general Soviet problem as much as possible because these problems, in one form or another, seem to arise every day and most of them straighten out as in the case of the Bern meeting.

. . . We must be firm, however, and our course thus far is correct.[77]

Until his death, Roosevelt would remain committed to the course he had first charted in the heady days of fall 1943. The three victorious nations could bargain and quarrel over all the controversies emerging as they marched toward the heart of Germany, but they must remain committed to preserving their partnership.

The Machinery of Diplomacy

Roosevelt's commitment to cooperation notwithstanding, preserving the partnership among the three Allied powers would prove exceedingly difficult. Roosevelt thought that he had eliminated most of the obstacles to his policy when he restructured and reorganized U.S. representation in the Soviet Union. Certainly his appointment of an ambassador who was not only a close personal friend but also an advocate of his policies would have encouraged the president to believe he could now work with, rather than against, his foreign policy bureaucracy. Eliminating resistance to his policies, however, was not that easy.

THE FOREIGN SERVICE OFFICERS

Ambassador Harriman arrived in Moscow determined to begin the delicate process of bargaining for a postwar settlement. Although he had some experience in Soviet affairs, it was limited, and his new approach toward Soviet officialdom required expert knowledge of the Soviet system. In that regard, the embassy housecleaning was an ineffective response to resistance to White House policy. Although it had succeeded in removing from Moscow people clearly hostile to the president's policy, it had left the embassy lacking in Soviet expertise. Worse still, it had failed to address one of Roosevelt's fundamental problems: the persistence of an anti-Soviet ideology among the department's Soviet specialists. Thus, when Harriman realized he needed a Soviet expert to help run the embassy, he was forced to turn to the very people Roosevelt had bypassed for over a decade.[78]

Harriman turned to Charles "Chip" Bohlen and George F. Kennan. The State Department refused to assign Bohlen to the position of counselor of the embassy because he lacked the rank and experience required. Nonetheless, as he was preparing for the position of Roosevelt's interpreter at the Teheran conference, Bohlen served in Moscow for a short time with Harriman. Unable to gain Bohlen as a permanent member of his mission, Harriman insisted on the higher-ranking Kennan. In July 1944 the State Department transferred Kennan from London to Moscow.[79]

The two experts on the Soviet Union brought to their positions years of experience as well as extensive knowledge of the Soviet Union and the Russian language. They also brought the attitudes and ideologies instilled during their training under Robert F. Kelley. Kennan and Bohlen had both been students in Kelley's Russian-language training program. Kennan attended classes at the University of Berlin's Oriental Seminar, and Bohlen was a student at the Paris School of Oriental Languages. In both Paris and Berlin, the diplomats studied

Russian history and culture as taught by Russian émigrés. The young Soviet experts emerged from their training with a perspective emphasizing the negative aspects of the Soviet system.[80] Kennan's and Bohlen's perspectives were reinforced by their experiences in Moscow during the 1930s period of show trials and purges.[81] By World War II both diplomats were firmly aligned with the group of bureaucrats opposed to Roosevelt's policy toward the Soviet Union.[82]

Bohlen's direct influence on Ambassador Harriman was short-lived. The two worked together before and during the Teheran conference, but after the conference Bohlen returned to Washington to serve as the head of the Division of European Affairs. As part of Roosevelt's reorganization in 1943, the State Department removed Loy Henderson from his position as chief of the Russian Section of the Division of European Affairs. The war had not altered the views Henderson had held since his stay in Moscow in the 1930s. From his position in the State Department, Henderson continued to lead the struggle against the White House's policy toward the Kremlin. As a result, in June 1943 Roosevelt named Henderson American minister to Iraq.[83] Bohlen returned from Moscow to replace Henderson.

Bohlen later commented that the changes this wrought within the department were inconsequential. He agreed with Henderson that U.S. policy toward the Soviet Union was more emotional than realistic, but before summer 1943 Bohlen did not advocate changing that policy. "[G]iven the military facts of the war," Bohlen saw no alternative.[84] However, as those military facts began to change, so too did Bohlen's perceptions. Shortly after the Teheran conference, Bohlen sent Harriman a memorandum in which he explained that Soviet intent was to "be the only important military and political force on the continent of Europe."[85]

Bohlen continued to play an active role in American-Soviet relations throughout the remainder of the war. In December 1944, as the administration was preparing for the upcoming Yalta conference, Roosevelt appointed him liaison between the White House and the State Department. Bohlen later argued that close contact with Roosevelt and Hopkins during this period tempered his hostility toward Bolshevism with the knowledge that there was no political alternative to cooperation with the Soviet Union.[86] Nevertheless, he remained wary of Soviet intentions, especially in the wake of the Yalta conference.[87] By the time Roosevelt died, Bohlen shared many of the more passionately anti-Soviet Kennan's views.

Kennan became counselor-minister of the embassy in summer 1944. Kennan, not at all shy about expressing his opinion, warned Harriman that Kennan's views on U.S. policy toward the Soviet Union differed from those of the administration.[88] Unlike Bohlen, Kennan attained his experience in Soviet affairs exclusively under the purview of the State Department. As a result, he was never exposed to the political realities that served as a moderating influence on Bohlen when he worked with Hopkins and Roosevelt. Nor was Kennan constrained by the influence of public opinion. Consequently, Kennan became a vociferous critic of what he described as an unrealistic policy toward the Soviet Union. Indeed, he soon became a most eloquent spokesman for the futility of attempting a friendly relationship with Stalin.[89]

A few short weeks of service in Moscow during the summer of 1944 were enough to convince Kennan that the perceptions he had developed during his service in Moscow in the 1930s were indeed correct: "What I saw during that time was enough to convince me that not only our policy toward Russia, but our plans and commitments generally for the shaping of the postwar world, were based on a dangerous misreading of the personality, the intentions, and the political situation of the Soviet leadership."[90]

As a result of this apparent validation, Kennan prepared a lengthy memorandum for Harriman. In this epistle entitled "Russia Seven Years Later," he discussed the nature of the Soviet system and the development of Soviet foreign policy under Stalin. Kennan insisted that Soviet machinations in eastern and central Europe were predicated on one aim: the ruthless expansion of Soviet power. He warned U.S. leaders not to be naive when dealing with the Kremlin:

> [T]houghts of international collaboration settled down only too easily beside dreams of empire in minds schooled from infancy to think and deal in even sharper contradictions than these. As long as no second front existed, expediency suggested that the idea of collaboration be kept rather to the fore, the idea of spheres of interest rather in the background. But when the second front became reality, there was no longer any need for excessive delicacy. The resultant bluntness of Soviet policy has caused some surprise and questioning in the West.[91]

Kennan concluded his memorandum by advising western policy makers that it would be futile to attempt to establish truly friendly relations with Stalin's Kremlin.[92]

Over the next few months Kennan became more convinced of his estimate of Soviet policy. In January 1945 he sent his friend Bohlen a letter lamenting the state of the United States–Soviet relationship. Soviet political aims, according to Kennan, were "not, in the main, consistent with the happiness, prosperity or stability of international life on the rest of the continent." Kennan described a Kremlin that was not just a threat to Europe: "Not only are these Russian aims inconsistent with the main currents of central and western European tradition but they are in conflict with our own interests." Kennan's concern over Soviet policy was therefore evident.

Just a few months after penning "Russia Seven Years Later," he described a much expanded version of Soviet aims. The Soviet Union was "a jealous Eurasian land power, which must always seek to extend itself to the west and will never find a place, short of the Atlantic Ocean, where it can from its own standpoint safely stop." The only realistic policy the United States could adopt in the face of this expansion, according to Kennan, would be the denunciation of cooperation with the Soviet Union; instead, the Allies should partition Europe into two spheres of influence.[93]

By spring 1945 Kennan had already begun to conceptualize what would emerge in 1947 as the "containment" policy. This was a policy based on an acknowledgment that cooperation with the Soviet Union was impossible, and that the Soviet Union's inevitable attempts to spread its influence globally must be resisted. Kennan shared this conception with his State Department colleagues in a memorandum entitled "Russia's International Position at the Close of the War with Germany."[94]

Kennan's and Bohlen's views both reflected the attitudes that had been present among Foreign Service officers since the United States initiated diplomatic relations with the Soviet Union in 1933. Ingrained hostility toward the Soviet Union was the filter through which these specialists viewed the Soviet regime. As the Red Army marched victorious across Europe, the Kremlin did much to reinforce the Soviet specialists' worst expectations.

The Teheran conference had been a celebration of optimism for many of the participants.[95] Roosevelt returned to the United States with agreements to all his major objectives. The Soviet Union would enter the war against Japan; the Soviets would participate in the creation of a United Nations organization; and the Soviets would undertake a variety of cooperative military projects in the Soviet Union. Roosevelt summed up his satisfaction with the conference in his Christmas Eve fireside chat when he explained that he "got along fine" with Stalin.[96] Despite the heady atmosphere, the lone State Department representative at this conference, Bohlen, was not convinced by Stalin's gestures. In a memorandum shortly after the meeting, Bohlen informed Harriman he believed that Stalin was planning for a postwar Europe dominated by the Soviet Union.[97]

Even if the Foreign Service officers had been disposed to optimism regarding the Kremlin's intentions, Soviet actions soon would have discouraged it.

By January 1944 the good feelings generated by the heads-of-state meeting had dissipated, and diplomatic interaction in Moscow returned to normal. Unfortunately for the diplomats, "normal" meant accustomed difficulties that inhibited the conduct of fruitful business. On 9 January 1944 Harriman reported to the State Department that, despite Stalin's promises, there were difficulties implementing the military cooperation discussed at Teheran.[98] In addition, he reported that Soviet authorities also refused to provide any information regarding their lend-lease requests.[99]

By far the greatest strain on United States–Soviet relations remained the question of Soviet relations with Poland. Soviet attitudes and actions toward Poland confirmed the Foreign Service officers' worst fears, and posed the greatest threat to the aspirations of those who believed in postwar United States–Soviet collaboration. Despite apparent agreements between Roosevelt and Stalin at Teheran, it became increasingly clear throughout 1944 and 1945 that the Soviet Union would act unilaterally if necessary to achieve its goals in Poland.

HARRIMAN EMBITTERED

As the war approached its end and the frustration of U.S. diplomats increased visibly, Harriman's views began to reflect those of his diplomatic staff. Clearly Stalin's actions and overt intransigence were factors that prompted the ambassador to change his attitude. Indeed, the deterioration of Harriman's belief in prospects for friendly cooperation with the Kremlin reflected Stalin's evolving foreign policy. In hindsight, Harriman later remarked that Soviet-Polish relations contributed most to damaging his hopes for Soviet-American cooperation.[100] His correspondence with the State Department makes this fact evident. For much of his first few months in Moscow, Harriman worked to reestablish sounder relations between the Soviet Union and the Polish government-in-exile in London. At that time, he believed that if the Polish government in London would just agree to some concessions, Stalin was willing to work with them.[101]

However, Harriman's optimism began to wane in August 1944, after the Polish Home Army launched its uprising in Warsaw. Like many others, Harriman concluded that the Red Army deliberately halted its advance at the Vistula River outside Warsaw and he judged that Stalin, despite pleas from the Poles and the western Allies, intentionally left the Poles to their gruesome fate. Harriman's concern was only exacerbated by Stalin's refusal to permit U.S. and British aircraft to land on Soviet territory after dropping supplies to the Home Army. He duly reported these concerns to the secretary of state:

For the first time since coming to Moscow I am gravely concerned by the attitude of the Soviet Government in its refusal to permit us to assist the Poles in Warsaw as well as in its own policy of apparent inactivity. If [Andrei]Vyshinski correctly reflects the position of the Soviet Government, its refusal is based not on operational difficulties or denial that the resistance exists but on ruthless political considerations.[102]

The Warsaw uprising and Stalin's response marked the point at which Harriman's and the White House's views of the correct policy toward the Soviet Union began to diverge.

Before the Warsaw uprising, Harriman was committed to fulfilling the mission Roosevelt had assigned to him—namely, to obtain Stalin's assent to Soviet participation in the war against Japan and in a postwar international organization. Like Roosevelt, Harriman believed that bargaining was an appropriate means to achieve these ends. As a result, he advocated using U.S. economic assistance in the postwar reconstruction of the Soviet Union as an enticement for postwar U.S.-Soviet cooperation.[103] Although Harriman was optimistic that this new approach would lead to greater Soviet cooperation at all levels, his priority still remained the attainment of the two goals Roosevelt assigned him. Thus, he informed Hull in January 1944 that the United States should "make every effort to avoid the Polish question becoming a definite issue between the Soviet Government and ourselves."[104] Harriman pointed out that reasonable resolution of this issue would be in the interests of a future world security organization, but it was clear that the United States should not allow a relatively small issue to derail progress on far greater ones.

By September 1944, however, Harriman's attitude had markedly changed, largely due to his discomfiture with Soviet behavior at Warsaw. In a letter to Hopkins that either Standley or Steinhardt might have drafted, Harriman proposed an entirely new policy toward the Soviet Union. Rather than using only postwar aid as a bargaining chip, he now argued that the United States should pursue a strictly quid pro quo policy toward the Soviet Union in every respect:

> I am convinced that we can divert this trend but only if we materially change our policy toward the Soviet Government. I have evidence that they have misinterpreted our generous attitude toward them as a sign of weakness, and acceptance of their policies.
>
> Time has come when we must make clear what we expect of them as the price of our good will.[105]

Although Harriman was still careful to avoid inflicting any damage to the

Soviet war effort, he believed that Stalin should feel the consequences of his unwillingness to cooperate on various matters.[106]

As was the case with his predecessors, a variety of other influences contributed to Harriman's hardening views toward the Soviet Union and his divergence from Roosevelt's policy. Of course Harriman was outraged over Soviet behavior. However, outrage alone was insufficient justification for his metamorphosis. Roosevelt too was repeatedly angered by Stalin's actions, yet he never permitted his anger to obscure the goals he sought to achieve. Unlike Roosevelt, Harriman's relative isolation in Moscow seemed to weaken the ambassador's sense of perspective. As had been the case with his predecessors, Steinhardt and Standley, Harriman became so immersed in daily diplomatic issues and disputes that he almost lost sight of Roosevelt's primary goals of obtaining Stalin's cooperation in the war against Japan and Soviet involvement in a postwar security organization. In addition, the attitudes of those who surrounded Harriman, in particular Kennan and the British ambassador, Sir Archibald Clark-Kerr, clearly affected the ambassador's outlook.

Harriman's optimism began to fade shortly after Kennan, who was the ambassador's principal Soviet expert at the embassy, arrived in Moscow. Indeed, Kennan prepared his lengthy exposition on the ominous nature of Soviet foreign policy at about the same time as Harriman began reassessing Soviet motivations. Harriman also developed a close relationship with Clark-Kerr, who himself advocated a firmer policy toward the Soviet Union and had been a supporter of Standley.[107] Finally, Harriman developed an extremely cordial relationship with Major General Deane, the head of the USMM, who, for a wide variety of reasons, was also keenly disappointed by his frustrating experiences in the Soviet Union.

DEANE AND THE FRUSTRATIONS OF MILITARY COOPERATION

When General Deane arrived in Moscow in October 1943, his views and goals accorded with those of the ambassador and the president. While he advocated a firm policy toward the Soviet Union, he was also convinced that it was possible to forge a friendly and cooperative relationship between the two countries. In many respects, Deane succeeded in achieving these goals. For example, he managed to implement several important aspects of military cooperation, including procedures for the release of interned American aviators who had crash-landed in Siberia and closer intelligence collaboration between the U.S. Office of Strategic Services and the Soviet internal security service (NKVD).[108] However, other attempts to effect military cooperation achieved only mixed results and left Deane increasingly frustrated and disillusioned. Among the most serious, contentious, and frustrating aspects of military cooperation were the U.S. use of Soviet bases to bomb German military installations; the establishment of weather stations in Siberia necessary to facilitate the war in the Pacific; the repatriation of Allied prisoners of war liberated from captivity by the Red Army; Soviet unwillingness to agree to mutual military coordination measures, such as bombing lines between Allied and Red Army forces; and perceived Soviet wastage of lend-lease material.

During the summer of 1944, at U.S. request Stalin permitted the Fifteenth U.S. Army Air Force (USAAF) to begin flying shuttle bombing missions over Axis territory to and from bases in the Soviet Ukraine. The project, code-named Operation Frantic, represented the longest sustained contact between Soviet and U.S. military personnel in World War II. Nonetheless, the operation proved to be far less than a complete success. Ostensibly, the project's purpose was to enable the USAAF to engage strategic targets inaccessible from existing bases in Britain and Italy, thus helping to revive Allied strategic bombing efforts. Additionally, the operation was designed to convince the Soviet Union of the value of strategic bombing and therefore induce it to permit the United States to conduct air attacks against Japan from bases in Siberia.[109]

Under the auspices of Operation Frantic, the USAAF established three air bases in the Ukraine, including bomber bases at Poltava and Mirgorod and a fighter base at Piriatin, for which the Soviets were to provide air defense. Although the USAAF flew several successful missions to and from these bases, difficulties constantly plagued the operation. First, the Americans experienced problems working with the Russians and perceived the Soviets to be hindering rather than expediting the mission by placing overly stringent restrictions on USAAF activities.[110] Furthermore, once these problems surfaced, Soviet authorities used bureaucratic procedures to block any attempts to resolve them. The Soviets also seemed to delay the shipment of supplies and personnel to these bases.[111]

Controversy over the shuttle bombing reached a head on the night of 21–22 June 1944, when the German Luftwaffe bombed the U.S. air base at Poltava, destroying a large number of U.S. aircraft on the ground without losing a single plane to Soviet antiaircraft defenses. This incident created an atmosphere of mutual distrust and recrimination that thereafter soured the entire cooperative effort. Although the summary report on the incident prepared by Major General Robert L. Walsh, the commander of the USAAF Eastern Command, avoided blaming the Soviets for their failure to repulse the German attack, the USMM's chief of staff (and the majority of U.S. personnel at the bases) thought differently: "Our base commander and General Deane had previously pleaded for permission to station night fighters for just such a contingency, but the request was disapproved by the Kremlin, which stated that Russian anti-aircraft batteries would provide adequate protection."[112] Subsequent U.S. attempts to convince Soviet authorities to permit the deployment of U.S. anti-aircraft units and night fighters to the bases proved unsuccessful.

Soviet archival materials provide an altogether different perspective on the incident. These indicate that Germans acquired detailed information about the Poltava air base from a photo a captured American airman had forgotten to turn over to Soviet security forces. They also indicate that, after spotting a German reconnaissance plane that had followed U.S. aircraft back to the base, the Red Army Air Force commander, General A. R. Perminov, requested U.S. commanders to transfer their aircraft from Poltava to other bases. Because U.S. officials agreed to relocate only a small portion of their aircraft, the majority were lined up along the airstrip, making them easy targets when the Germans launched their attack.[113]

The Soviet military considered its defense of the base adequate and turned down American requests for night fighters as unnecessary. In addition, permission to station night fighters at the airfields would have added little to the overall defense of Poltava; unlike their American and German counterparts, Soviet night fighters did not use airborne radar sets.[114] But as the Soviet archives indicate, the Soviets do not bear sole responsibility for the attack. U.S. forces at Poltava were complacent. American commanders took few precautions to ensure the security of their bases. The camps and airfields were designed as if they were operating in peacetime conditions. In addition, U.S. commanders disregarded both Soviet advice that they disperse their aircraft and Soviet warnings that the Germans were very familiar with Poltava, having used it as a Luftwaffe airfield until 1943.[115] The successful German air raid of 21–22 June would shake the Americans out of their complacency, but not without contributing to heightened tension between U.S. and Soviet officials.

In the wake of this incident, by October 1944 the United States decided to withdraw from the shuttle-bombing project but to leave approximately 200 personnel at Poltava. After the conclusion of active operations United States–Soviet relations declined even more precipitously. The Soviets increased the restrictions on U.S. personnel at Poltava, hostilities between the American and Russian personnel intensified, the Russians began to loot the American warehouses, and Americans engaged in behavior that angered or annoyed the Soviets.[116]

These problems were the result of a multitude of factors, but the greatest problems were inherent in the nature of the mission itself. The Soviets did not share British and American faith in strategic bombing. Furthermore, even if they did believe in the efficiency of that type of air operation, the advance of Allied forces elsewhere in Europe during late summer and early fall 1944 made the U.S. request for the bases in the Ukraine superfluous. By August and September, for example, the Allied advance in France provided more than adequate bases in range of Axis targets in northern and eastern Europe. Thus, in the Soviet view, the American desire to maintain a physical presence in the Soviet Union appeared increasingly political in nature. In fact, General Walsh underscored this point: "I cannot help but feel there is too much promotional scheming in our ventures and not enough realism. We cannot fool the Russians. They are very realistic and without question practical when it comes to watching the work of others. Artificial situations do not appeal to them."[117]

In his final report on the Poltava incident, Walsh also listed additional factors that he believed contributed to the difficulties with the Soviet authorities. Among these were repeated requests for flights that were not made; last-minute changes in operational procedures; tendencies to play up publicity on cooperation; shuttle missions that were run for no reasons other than political; continued attempts to expand the number of personnel in the Soviet Union; and numerous visiting delegations.[118]

A second point of contention associated with United States–Soviet military cooperation was the U.S. Navy's desire to establish weather stations in Siberia. The development of controversy surrounding this effort paralleled the development of problems with Operation Frantic. The U.S. Navy established two weather stations, in Khabarovsk and Petropavlovsk. Although these stations were vital for the provision of weather forecasts that assisted the American strategic bombing offensive against Japan, they would also provide vital information in the event of a U.S. invasion of Japan. Initially the Soviets were positive about the establishment of these stations and approved their creation without hesitation.[119] However, as the war with Japan neared a conclusion, the Soviets gradually cooled to the idea of U.S. personnel being based in Siberia. They began to accuse the American personnel of espionage.[120] Soviet distrust mounted throughout 1945, until the navy closed the weather stations in December 1945.

A third aspect of United States–Soviet military cooperation that frustrated Deane was the issue of repatriating American prisoners of war (POWs) liberated by the Red Army. As head of the USMM, Deane attempted to take steps to assist the liberated Americans. According to existing agreements, Soviet authorities were supposed to transfer liberated Americans to the port of Odessa for the trip to the United States. However, Soviet transportation to the port was insufficient, and many Americans simply hitchhiked and walked to Moscow. When returning POWs told Deane that there were sick and wounded Americans in Poland awaiting transport to Odessa, Deane proposed that he take a team by plane from Poltava to Lublin to collect the Americans. The

Soviets rejected this proposal.[121] The situation became so frustrating that Deane appealed to the president to intervene on behalf of the POWs. Roosevelt did this in a letter to Stalin dated 4 March 1945: "[I request] that instructions be issued authorizing ten American aircraft with American crews to operate between Poltava and places in Poland where American ex–prisoners of war and stranded airmen may be located."[122]

Stalin responded that there was no need to use the U.S. aircraft because Soviet authorities had already sent virtually all of the POWs to Odessa.[123] Evidently this was incorrect because Roosevelt wrote to Stalin again on 18 March, stating that a number of sick and injured Americans were still in Poland and asking why the Soviet leader would not permit a contact team of American officers to assist them.[124] Stalin replied that the president's information was inaccurate and that American POWs were being treated better than Soviet POWs in American hands.[125] This incident did little to allay increasing distrust between the two parties.

Heated controversy also grew between Stalin and his western allies over the matter of instituting joint military coordination measures, such as bombing lines necessary to prevent accidental air and, eventually, ground clashes between advancing Allied and Red Army forces. In Allied eyes, the establishment of such measures was absolutely vital because Allied and Red Army forces were nearing one another. Without such measures, argued the United States and Britain, armed incidents were bound to occur. For his part, a suspicious Stalin rejected these proposals as unnecessary, even though one serious incident occurred south of Belgrade in October 1944, when the USAAF bombed the headquarters of an advancing Soviet rifle corps, killing the corps commander and many of his men.[126] This incident, which was handled by General Deane and General A. I. Antonov, the chief of the Red Army General Staff, also involved General George C. Marshall and, undoubtedly, Stalin and Roosevelt as well.

Other issues did not merit the intervention of the president but proved equally trying to Deane's patience. For example, shortly after arriving in Moscow Deane became concerned about Soviet wastage of lend-lease material. In particular, Deane discovered that the Soviets possessed a large number of diesel engines that were rusting away for lack of hulls in which to install them.[127] Deane was horrified, and proposed to Marshall an immediate change in lend-lease policy. He argued that "we must insist on some data to support Soviet requests, particularly if items are in short supply." Further, Deane suggested that lend-lease aid should be used as "a lever to force Soviet acquiescence to any operational proposals which we submit."[128]

Deane's suggestion that lend-lease be used as a lever reflected his growing discouragement over prospects for future cooperation with the Soviet Union. By September 1944 the general even began to fear that he would fail to fulfill his primary mission of ensuring Soviet collaboration in the war against Japan.[129] Three months later Deane sent Marshall a letter advocating a radical change in U.S. policy toward the Soviet Union. He pointed out that the current policy was detrimental to U.S. prestige and should be replaced with a much more restrictive aid policy. The United States should provide the Soviet Union all aid it requested if it contributed to winning the war. If it did not contribute to winning the war, the United States should insist on a quid pro quo.[130]

YALTA AND BEYOND

By spring 1945, the situation in the bureaucracy making and implementing the U.S. policy toward the Soviet Union was beginning to resemble the situation that had existed before fall 1943. The individuals involved were less volatile and there was more unanimity among personnel in the Soviet Union, but there was still a developing split between the president and the people charged with implementing his policies.

The souring attitude among U.S. personnel in Moscow was paralleled by a growing wariness among their counterparts in Washington. Many in the U.S. Army General Staff rejected the premise that postwar cooperation with the Soviet Union was possible. In July 1944, Army G-2 insisted that there would be a major clash of policy between the Soviet Union and the United States.[131] In fact, that clash seemed to be materializing in late summer and fall 1944, when Stalin ignored his allies' pleas to aid the Poles. Thus, when Deane sent his December 1944 letter to Marshall, the chief of staff forwarded it to Stimson saying he fully agreed with Deane's conclusions.[132] By January 1945, the Joint Intelligence Committee also viewed the Soviet Union with deepening suspicion.[133]

Despite Roosevelt's repeated efforts to reorganize resistance out of the State Department, it never abandoned its concern over Soviet aims or its advocacy of a firmer policy toward the Soviet government. Consequently, emboldened by the pessimistic dispatches from Moscow, State Department officials approached the Yalta conference armed with a battery of demands they wished Roosevelt to present to Stalin. Although the president was prepared to bargain to obtain his two major aims, his diplomatic corps wanted him to seek a variety of other concessions as well.[134]

Each individual who attended the Yalta conference did so with different objectives and different perceptions of what could realistically be accomplished. Even though Roosevelt considered Yalta a success, he was aware that some of the apparent Soviet concessions were not as complete as his advisers would have liked. With regard to the most inflammatory issue—that of Poland—Roosevelt recognized that Soviet agreement to a "free and independent" government was tenuous. He told Leahy as much when he said it was the best he could do for Poland at this time. Unfortunately, Roosevelt did not share this observation with all of his officials. Thus, Harriman and the representatives from the State Department returned to their posts determined to implement the letter of the Yalta agreements without understanding that their interpretation of what had occurred and the Soviet interpretation were almost diametrically opposed.[135] Worse still, they did not know about Roosevelt's reservations and ultimate intent.

It would be fallacious to contend that the Yalta agreements caused the breakdown in the United States–Soviet wartime relationship. Although the ensuing deterioration of the relationship did indeed coincide with increasingly open conflict over the meaning of the Yalta accords, it is difficult to comprehend any other outcome for the conference. The mind-set in which key figures approached the meeting predetermined the results of the conference. On the one hand, Roosevelt went to Yalta determined to gain, at whatever cost, Soviet participation in the war with Japan and the creation of a viable postwar security organization. When he departed, he believed he had accomplished his mission, and he understood what price he had paid for it. On the other hand, Harriman and his State Department colleagues arrived in Yalta determined to obtain other concessions from the Kremlin. They left the Crimea convinced that they had obtained them and they should hold the Soviets to them. The problems caused by these conflicting interpretations are most evident with regard to Poland. The key passage in the agreement on Poland's government was a compromise between the Soviet Union, which wanted Poland governed by the provisional government it had already recognized, and the United States and Britain, which desired a completely new provisional government consisting of representatives from a variety of parties. Although the deliberately vague wording of the compromise satisfied Roosevelt's aims, it misled Harriman and the State Department.

From February through April 1945, Harriman and Clark-Kerr worked in Moscow to ensure that the Kremlin delivered on what they perceived were its promises regarding Poland. Molotov, however, resisted their efforts every step of the way.[136] At the same time, Roosevelt's personal relationship with Stalin deteriorated. After a heated exchange of telegrams, it appeared that Roosevelt was prepared to agree with his ambassador that it was time to get tough with Stalin. Yet despite his frustration, Roosevelt remained wedded to his hopes for lasting cooperation between the Soviet Union and the United States at a time when his diplomatic colleagues were not. As he wrote to Churchill on 11 April 1945: "I would minimize the general Soviet problem as much as possible because these problems, in one form or another, seem to arise every day and most of them straighten out. We must be firm, however, and our course thus far is correct." His actions and this firm statement of perspective and purpose stand as proof of Roosevelt's lasting faith that the war could be won and a lasting peace could be forged and preserved.

Roosevelt steadfastly persisted in working for his principal goals of gaining Soviet participation in the war against Japan and Soviet cooperation in forging a new United Nations. To achieve his goals, in 1943 Roosevelt had intervened to place the U.S. embassy in Moscow back on the same course as the White House; in 1945 Roosevelt was unable to accomplish that feat again. On 12 April 1945 Roosevelt complained of "a terrific headache" and slumped over in his chair. A few hours later, the president was dead.

Roosevelt's Slippery Legacy

When Harry S. Truman became president in April 1945 he was determined to continue Roosevelt's policies. To ensure continuity in U.S. foreign policy, he resolved to contact key State Department officials and the many U.S. ambassadors. With regard to United States–Soviet relations, Truman turned to Harriman for an explanation of Roosevelt's policy.[137]

Throughout spring 1945, Harriman had unsuccessfully urged Roosevelt and Secretary of State Edward Stettinius to allow him to return to Washington and lobby for a firmer quid pro quo policy toward the Soviet Union. Only after Roosevelt's death did Stettinius relent and decide it would be appropriate for the ambassador to brief the new president. Harriman thus returned to the United States to meet with Truman before the president's first meeting with Molotov. Truman asked for and received a briefing on the existing state of Soviet-American relations, and in the process, Harriman shared with him the attitudes of the U.S. embassy personnel in Moscow. He complained to Truman that the Soviet Union was violating the Yalta agreements, especially with regard to Poland. He advised the president that the United States had to take a more forceful stance toward the Kremlin. In short, Harriman persuaded the president to adopt the very course that Roosevelt had been struggling against throughout the war.[138]

Truman adopted the line advocated by Harriman, and subsequent U.S.-Soviet relations were characterized by this firmer approach.[139] Even though Truman briefly consulted with Hopkins and Davies, he never established a close rapport with Roosevelt's unofficial advisers, many of whom had either died or were too ill or infirm to play any role in government any longer.[140] The formulation and implementation of foreign policy reverted to the very bureaucracy Roosevelt had ignored and mistrusted for twelve years. In the end, it was the bureaucrats who shaped policy, simply by outliving the president and all his men.

Conclusions

Truman and a New Beginning?

There is no straight line from Harriman's April 1945 conversation with Truman to the adoption of Kennan's policy of "containment" of the Soviet Union. At least initially, Truman's course veered often from the cooperation advocated by the last vestiges of Roosevelt's administration to the competition supported by the new cabinet and the bureaucracies they controlled. Yet as 1945 drew to a close, the outlines of a coherent policy toward the Soviet Union were emerging. The United States would stand firm against the further expansion of Soviet influence.[1]

To argue that Truman adopted this new policy solely as a result of the influence of Ambassador Harriman and the U.S. diplomats in Moscow would be a simplification of the complex process of policy formulation. A variety of factors, domestic and foreign, contributed to the pursuit of a more competitive relationship with the Kremlin. These factors are numerous and their relative importance has been debated since the inception of the cold war itself. Among the more notable are a shift in public opinion away from support of the Soviet Union, United States commitment to a global open door to trade, and Soviet actions in eastern Europe and the Middle East.[2] Nonetheless, it is impossible to ignore the often pivotal role of lower-level officials in the policy formulation process.

Many of the men who served in Moscow before and during World War II went on to hold important and influential positions in the U.S. government. W. Averell Harriman, George Kennan, and Charles Bohlen were among the diplomats who influenced subsequent policy toward the Soviet Union. Harriman became Truman's secretary of commerce.[3] Kennan and Bohlen both became ambassadors to the Soviet Union. Bohlen became a special assistant and principal adviser on the Soviet Union to Secretaries of State James F. Byrnes and George C. Marshall.[4] Kennan established and chaired the Policy Planning Staff at the State Department, where he played an important role in the formulation of the Marshall Plan.[5] Even Loy Henderson returned from exile in Iraq to contribute to the shaping of Truman's policy. As chief of the Division of Near Eastern Affairs, in February 1947 Henderson chaired a committee created to study the "problem of assistance to Greece and Turkey." That committee recommended providing aid—a decision that contributed to Truman's enunciation of the Truman Doctrine.[6]

Several of the military officers who served in Moscow also continued to shape policy under the new administration. Michela and Yeaton both worked in the Military Intelligence Division after their return from Moscow. There they helped formulate the military estimates on the course of future conflict with the Soviet Union. Michela served as military attaché in Czechoslovakia, where he died in 1949, and for a time Yeaton served as chief of the U.S. Army section in charge of technical information exchange with the Soviet Union.[7]

In contrast, the officers and officials who supported Roosevelt's policy disappeared quickly from government circles as the war ended. Harry Hopkins withdrew from government service in August 1945.[8] Joseph Davies continued to advise Truman on Soviet issues, but by mid-1947 Truman was no longer interested in Davies' opinions.[9] Even before the war ended, Burns retired from the military because of illness.[10] Faymonville served out his military career in relative obscurity at an Ordnance Division in Arkansas before retiring in 1948.[11]

Thus, the fresh faces and new interpretations that rushed in with Roosevelt as he sought to offer a New Deal to the American people and to chart a new course in U.S. history returned from whence they came. The people in control of the apparatus of foreign policy making under Truman could trace their lineage to the people in control of the apparatus under Hoover and earlier. Their presence ensured a continuity in policy unmolested by the vagaries of presidential elections.

Theoretical Explanations

Theoretical approaches to the making of foreign policy in the United States are extensive.[12] Many of the theories developed by political scientists and diplomatic historians are instructive in explaining the development of U.S. foreign policy toward the Soviet Union during the Roosevelt administration. The complexity of the history, however, belies the notion that there could be a monocausal or single-theory explanation for the development of international relations.

One of the most obvious explanations for the development of U.S. policy toward the Soviet Union is found in the theory of bureaucratic politics. Most identified with Graham T. Allison's study of the Cuban Missile Crisis, *Essence of Decision,* this theory explains that the president's ability to formulate foreign policy is limited by the bureaucracy charged with implementing the president's decisions.[13]

In the case of Roosevelt and the Soviet Union, the influence of the bureaucracy was clear. From the moment that Roosevelt sat down with Litvinov to discuss the establishment of diplomatic relations, the State Department struggled to define and implement its own policy toward the Kremlin. Indeed, bureaucratic resistance became so stiff that at crucial moments Roosevelt turned to unofficial representatives to carry out his policy. The most important moments in the wartime relationship between the two powers were indeed those characterized by extrabureaucratic activity. Hopkins flew to Moscow to launch the president's aid policy; Harriman traveled as a special emissary to formalize the aid policy; Davies hand-delivered a letter to Stalin inviting him for personal talks with the president; and at Teheran and Yalta it was Roosevelt himself who forged the compromises designed to construct a workable peace. Every step of the way, Roosevelt was aware of his struggle with the bureaucracy and sought unconventional ways to overcome it.

In the end, however, the bureaucratic-politics theorists were proven correct. The bureaucracy outlived the president, and it was the voice of the bureaucrats that shaped the outlook of the new president. During the transition from Roosevelt to Truman, the State Department succeeded in pressing its views on the new president. Truman turned to Ambassador Harriman for his opinion of the correct policy to pursue toward the Soviet Union. In the person of Harriman, State Department influence was immediate and dramatic.

The State Department was not the only bureaucracy against which Roosevelt struggled. When Roosevelt worked so hard to bypass the traditional foreign policy bureaucracy, he included among that body not just the State

Department, but also the War Department, particularly the Military Intelligence Division and its military attachés. Although Roosevelt for the most part chose to ignore those agencies in carrying out his Soviet policy, the military bureaucracy flourished during the war and emerged as a dominant bureaucracy in postwar foreign policy.[14]

The history of U.S. relations with the Soviet Union under Roosevelt thus goes a long way toward establishing the validity of the theory of bureaucratic politics. What it reveals even more strikingly, however, is the importance of individuals to history. In this era immediately preceding the explosion of foreign policy bureaucracy, it is easy to study the individuals who make up the bureaucracy. Bureaucracies may be institutions, but they are institutions made up of large numbers of individuals. And those individuals matter. In order to understand why and how bureaucracies behave, it is vital to understand why and how the people who populate the bureaucracies behave. It is insufficient to argue that "where one stands depends on where one sits." Philip R. Faymonville and Joseph A. Michela both sat in the same place: they were career army officers. Yet they could not have stood in greater opposition to each other.

The explanation for how these individuals behaved is not contingent merely upon their institutional mission. Their behavior derived from two very different, but equally important areas: psychology and ideology. Understanding the psychology of the actors in a foreign policy environment is extremely important; it is also extremely difficult.[15] This study raises—and, by necessity, leaves unanswered—many important questions. What in Michela's and Standley's psyche led them to respond in so hostile a manner to the administration's policies? Why did they take policy differences as personal affronts? What in Roosevelt's psychology led him to believe that he could accomplish anything if he simply sat down with the Soviet dictator? In the case of Stalin, the need for a psychological interpretation of his behavior is obvious to many. Several historians have already sought to examine the question of Stalin's paranoia and how it affected his policies.[16] The historian Frank Costigliola used the same analytical framework to study George Kennan and the early cold war. He concluded that Kennan's emotions and personality played an important role in the development of foreign policy.[17] The same approach should be taken with the other men and women developing and implementing U.S. foreign policy.

Although psychology is an important tool for understanding the behavior of individuals, it supplies only partial answers. Yet another explanation for the development of U.S.-Soviet relations under Roosevelt lies in ideology. Michael H. Hunt has defined ideology as "sets of beliefs and values, sometimes only poorly and partially articulated, that make international relations intelligible and decision making possible."[18] Ideology is derived from a cultural context. On that level, identifying contrasting ideologies seems somewhat simple. The Soviets must have had an ideology derived from Soviet culture, and the Americans must have had one derived from American culture. Unfortunately, culture is not that simple. One can argue that there is a dominant national culture at work in the United States, but it is not the only culture from which individual Americans derive their ideologies. At work in the case of the individuals involved in U.S.-Soviet relations during Roosevelt's presidency were a number of often contrasting cultures. The ideology of the career Foreign Service officers who served as Soviet specialists was influenced by a bureaucratic culture developed in the corporatist environment of the 1920s. But these individuals each brought to that bureaucratic culture differing outlooks from their youth. Henderson was the child of a minister; his experiences were far different from those of his more economically privileged Foreign Service colleagues.[19]

Cultural influences that shape ideology are also generational. The formative events in Roosevelt's foreign policy experience were World War I and the failure of the Treaty of Versailles.[20] In contrast, the younger Foreign Service officers were more influenced by the Munich agreement and the Nazi-Soviet nonaggression pact. The historian Daniel Yergin identifies a cultural split along generational lines, but he defines it as those who believed in what he called the "Riga axioms" (a belief that the Soviet Union was motivated by a desire to spread revolutionary communism throughout the world) and those who held views he called the "Yalta axioms" (a belief that in foreign policy the Soviet Union would behave like any other great power and could be dealt with the same way).[21] A more striking evolution, however, is the transition from references to the failure of Versailles in the rhetoric of Roosevelt and Hopkins, to the references to Munich-style appeasement in the rhetoric of the younger Foreign Service officers.

For the Foreign Service officers who served in the embassy throughout Roosevelt's tenure, their complex and often dissimilar ideologies shared a significant element: a distrust of and hostility toward the Soviet Union. For some, like Henderson, this was simply anticommunism. Others, like Kennan, couched their antipathy in terms of basic power political realities: they were opposed to Soviet imperial-style expansion. All, however, shared the belief that the Soviet Union represented a real and immediate threat to the United States' way of life.

In contrast, Roosevelt's ideology, stemming from a horror of war, was predicated on a belief in the necessity of peaceful coexistence. In this regard, his world outlook was more similar to that of the Kremlin. As William Appleman Williams and others have argued, the United States was committed to a policy of open doors and free trade.[22] The Soviet Union was no less committed to socialism and its eventual expansion. By 1945, however, Roosevelt and Stalin shared a belief that the most important requirement for the attainment of either of their ultimate aims was the preservation of peace. They also shared the belief that peace demanded the cooperation of the United States and the Soviet Union in the postwar era.[23]

Thus, the history of U.S. policy toward the Soviet Union under Roosevelt reflects the important role of ideology in both the development of U.S. policy and in the interaction between the United States and the Soviet Union. It also reveals the importance of personality and psychology. Finally, it underscores the contention of the bureaucratic-politics theorists that foreign policy is not simply the prerogative of the president. It is the result of a complex process of action and interaction among a variety of government institutions.

Roosevelt had a vision and a plan for United States–Soviet relations. He envisioned a world in which the two great powers would cooperate to ensure the peaceful resolution of conflicts. He imagined it possible to prevent war for at least fifty years. In implementing his policies, Roosevelt faced countless difficulties. As he tried time and again to explain to Stalin, conducting foreign policy in a democracy is a complex and difficult struggle. The president was not a dictator. He constantly had to consider and work with public and congressional opinion. This necessity prevented him from implementing his policies as quickly and completely as he often desired. Roosevelt had to pursue a careful policy toward the Soviet Union. He had to ensure that the public and the Congress supported his actions before he plunged forward. Indeed, it was these considerations that led him to request compromises from Stalin regarding Poland; and it was for these reasons that he worked so diligently at shaping U.S. opinion through his radio addresses and press conferences.

But public and congressional opinion was by no means the most recalcitrant difficulty facing Roosevelt. His greatest problems were found in his own executive branch. Many within Roosevelt's vast government did not share his vision of the future, and they resisted the president's actions in numerous ways. The role of U.S. personnel in the Soviet Union during Roosevelt's administration is a striking illustration of the variety of issues to be studied in foreign policy making and implementation.

This history demonstrates that it is not enough to study the ideas and plans of the president. What Roosevelt wanted was not always what he got. In addition, this detailed analysis of the struggle between Roosevelt and his bureaucracy clarifies some contentious elements in the study of Roosevelt. The president may not have left a written record of his thoughts and goals, but a reconstruction of the actions he took indicates a consistent and coherent policy toward the Soviet Union and, after the war began, a coherent vision of the postwar world. From the appointment of Bullitt to the appointment of Harriman as ambassadors to the Soviet Union, Roosevelt showed a desire to reach out and establish a working relationship with the Kremlin. With the sole exception of Steinhardt, Roosevelt appointed a series of ambassadors initially committed to cordial relations with the Soviet Union. When the ambassadors became disillusioned and diverged from Roosevelt's course, the president replaced them.

Roosevelt was aware of the resistance of the career Foreign Service officers to his policies. He tried on several occasions to limit that resistance by restructuring the foreign policy bureaucracy. The bureaucracy proved resilient, however, and each restructuring was soon followed by a resurgence in resistance. When the conflict with his career Foreign Service officers and military personnel threatened the outcome of his policies, Roosevelt abandoned his tactic of restructuring and instead resorted to bypassing the traditional organizations. Through the tool of lend-lease and the person of Harry Hopkins, Roosevelt created an alternative foreign policy organization—one committed to Roosevelt's goals.

Bypassing the bureaucracy was not, however, a long-term solution. The creation of competing U.S. organizations in the Soviet Union led to the development of a strident and public conflict over U.S. policy. When the crisis that was the struggle for Soviet survival safely passed, Roosevelt returned to his tactic of restructuring. He shook up both the State Department and lend-lease organizations in Washington and the agencies representing U.S. interests in the Soviet Union. In so doing, the president hoped to create a new bureaucracy, supportive of his aims and capable of carrying them out. His effort was only a temporary success. By early 1945, the old conflict between Roosevelt's policy and that of the U.S. representatives in Moscow had reemerged. Roosevelt's policy beliefs could not compete with the attitudes institutionalized in the foreign policy bureaucracy.

In April 1945 Roosevelt died almost the sole governmental supporter of his policy toward the Soviet Union. Those that shared his views operated in the extragovernmental world of his kitchen cabinet. Their role in and influence over U.S. foreign policy was predicated on their close personal relationship with Roosevelt. Although President Truman turned to Harry Hopkins and Joseph Davies at a moment of crisis and confusion in U.S.-Soviet relations, their influence in the new administration was fleeting. They were sick, old, and tired, and their relationship with Truman was not as close and comfortable as it had been with Roosevelt. For guidance in foreign policy, Truman would turn toward the institutional memory from the Roosevelt administration—the institutions and individuals Roosevelt had never succeeded in dominating. The result was a policy toward the Soviet Union Roosevelt neither predicted nor desired.

NOTES

Introduction

1. Outstanding examples of this scholarship are Robert Dallek, *Franklin D. Roosevelt and American Foreign Policy;* and Warren F. Kimball, *Juggler* and *Forged in War.*

2. William C. Bullitt, "How We Won the War and Lost the Peace"; and John R. Deane, *Strange Alliance.*

3. Herbert Feis, *Churchill, Roosevelt, Stalin;* and Gaddis Smith, *American Diplomacy During the Second World War, 1941–1945,* originally published in 1965. Smith's second edition, published in 1985, although still critical, is less so than his first edition.

4. William Appleman Williams, *Tragedy of American Diplomacy* (1962 ed.); Lloyd C. Gardner, *Architects of Illusion* and *Spheres of Influence;* and Gabriel Kolko, *Politics of War.*

5. John L. Snell, *Illusion and Necessity;* and Robert Divine, *Roosevelt and World War II.*

6. Gar Alperovitz, *Atomic Diplomacy;* and Diane Shaver Clemens, *Yalta.*

7. For a discussion of the level-of-analysis problem, see J. David Singer, "Level-of-Analysis Problem."

8. For works on lend-lease and the Soviet Union, see George C. Herring, *Aid to Russia;* Robert Huhn Jones, *Roads to Russia;* John Daniel Langer, "Harriman-Beaverbrook Mission"; Leon Martel, *Lend-Lease, Loans;* and Roger Munting, "Soviet Food Supply." On the second front, see Mark A. Stoler, *Politics of the Second Front.*

9. The best example of this type of study encompassing all of Roosevelt's ambassadors is David Mayers, *Ambassadors and America's Soviet Policy.* A more recent contribution is Dennis J. Dunn, *Caught Between Roosevelt and Stalin.* Dunn also makes use of limited Soviet archival sources. Unfortunately, his work is so polemical as to restrict its usefulness. Several other historians have written biographies of individual ambassadors. See Keith David Eagles, *Ambassador Joseph E. Davies;* Beatrice Farnsworth, *William C. Bullitt and the Soviet Union;* Elizabeth Kimball MacLean, *Joseph E. Davies;* Joseph Edward O'Connor, "Laurence A. Steinhardt."

10. Martin Weil, *Pretty Good Club;* Hugh DeSantis, *Diplomacy of Silence;* Natalie Grant, "Russian Section"; Thomas R. Maddux, "American Diplomats"; Thomas R. Maddux, "Watching Stalin Maneuver"; Thomas R. Maddux, *Years of Estrangement;* Frederic Lewis Propas, "State Department"; and Frederic L. Propas, "Creating a Hard Line."

11. Rudy Abramson, *Spanning the Century.* Fortunately, Standley and Harriman published memoir accounts of their experiences.

12. Alfred Vagts, *Military Attaché.*

13. David M. Glantz, "Observing the Soviets."

14. Dennis J. Dunn takes an extremely critical view of Faymonville. See Dunn, *Caught Between Roosevelt and Stalin.* Historians who have more carefully examined Faymonville and his role in Soviet-American relations include Kelly William Biggs, "Role of Philip Ries Faymonville"; James S. Herndon and Joseph O. Baylen, "Col. Philip R. Faymonville," 483–505; John Daniel Langer, "Red General"; and Thomas A. Julian, "Philip Ries Faymonville and the Soviet Union."

15. Warren F. Kimball, "Incredible Shrinking War," 357.

16. Mark A. Stoler, *Allies and Adversaries* and *Politics of the Second Front.*

17. Vojtech Mastny addresses the development of Soviet foreign policy during World War II in two of his books, *Russia's Road to the Cold War* and *Cold War and Soviet Insecurity.* Diane Shaver Clemens' study of the Yalta Conference makes extensive use of Soviet sources and provides a useful corrective to the many studies of the conference. Diane Shaver Clemens, *Yalta.*

18. A recent and useful contribution to this field is Gabriel Gorodetsky, *Soviet Foreign Policy.*

19. This tendency is noted by Mark A. Stoler and Warren F. Kimball. See Mark A. Stoler, "Half-Century of Conflict," 167; and Warren F. Kimball, "Incredible Shrinking War."

CHAPTER 1: The United States and the Bolshevik State, 1917–1932: Revolution and Intervention

1. For a useful survey of this period in Russian-American relations, see Norman E. Saul, *War and Revolution.*

2. For the reaction of key diplomatic figures in Russia during the tumultuous years of revolution and civil war, see William Allison, *American Diplomats.* Hugh DeSantis, in *Diplomacy of Silence,* explains the hostility of American diplomats to the Bolshevik program as stemming from their socioeconomic background. Other studies examining the background of the Foreign Service officers and the development of their beliefs include Robert D. Schulzinger, *Making of the Diplomatic Mind;* Martin Weil, *Pretty Good Club;* and William Barnes, John Heath Morgan, and United States Department of State Historical Office, *Foreign Service.*

3. Robert Freeman Smith, "Businessmen, Bureaucrats," 579.

4. Weil, *Pretty Good Club.* For the persistence of the importance of the Bolshevik espousal of world revolution, see also George F. Kennan, Memorandum for the Minister, 20 July 1932, 861.00/11496, Record Group (hereafter RG) 59, National Archives and Records Administration (hereafter NARA).

5. An interesting sampling of Foreign Service officers' retrospective views of the Soviet Union is found in Foy D. Kohler and Harvey L. Mose, *Soviet Union.*

6. William A. Williams argues that the decision to intervene in the Russian Civil

War was an antirevolutionary action in line with Woodrow Wilson's economic and moralistic open-door foreign policy. See William A. Williams, "American Intervention in Russia, 1917–1920," 32, 36, 41. See also N. Gordon Levin Jr., *Woodrow Wilson and World Politics;* and William A. Williams, *American Russian Relations, 1781–1947.* David S. Foglesong contends that the American intervention began with a combination of anti-German and anti-Bolshevik motives, but the anti-Bolshevik ones became predominant even before the end of World War II. See David S. Foglesong, *America's Secret War.* This interpretation is in contrast to the earlier contention of George F. Kennan that the United States intervened in order to reestablish the Russian front against Germany. George F. Kennan, *Russia and the West* and *Soviet-American Relations.* Betty Miller Unterberger argues in *United States, Revolutionary Russia* that the American intervention, at least in Siberia, was motivated by a desire to save the Czech legion rather than by a desire to interfere in Russian internal affairs.

7. For Soviet interpretations of the intervention, see A. Girshfel'd, "O roli SShA v organizatsii antisovetskoi"; and V. P. Naumov, *Letopis' geroicheskoi bor'by.*

8. The Secretary of State to the Italian Ambassador (Avezzana), 10 August 1920, in United States, Department of State, *Foreign Relations of the United States* (hereafter *FRUS*), 1920, 3:468.

9. Joan Hoff Wilson does a masterful job of outlining the often contradictory economic and political aspects of the nonrecognition policy in *Ideology and Economics.* For an examination of the origins of that policy from both the United States and Bolshevik perspectives, see David W. McFadden, *Alternative Paths.* For more information on Soviet-American-British economic relations in the 1920s, see Christine A. White, *British and American Commercial Relations.*

10. For an early example of the State Department's attitude toward Bolshevism, see Department of State, *Memorandum.* See also Wilson, *Ideology and Economics;* Daniel Yergin, *Shattered Peace;* Weil, *Pretty Good Club;* Thomas Maddux, *Years of Estrangement;* and Douglas Little, "Antibolshevism and American Foreign Policy."

11. For example, see Press Release Issued by the Department of State, March 21, 1923, *FRUS,* 1923, 2:755–58; the Secretary of State to the Chairman of the Republican National Committee (Butler), 23 February 1928, in *FRUS,* 1928, 3:822, 824; F. W. B. Coleman (Latvia) to the Secretary of State, 31 July 1930, 761.00/186, RG 59, NARA; Coleman (Latvia) to the Secretary of State, 4 September 1931, 761.00/213, RG 59, NARA; and Success or Failure of the Russian Experiment, from Skinner (Latvia) to the Secretary of State, 19 August 1932, 861.00/11496, RG 59, NARA.

12. George Kennan addresses this attitude among army officers in *Soviet-American Relations,* 1:43. The attitude is most evident in Graves' memoirs of the intervention: William S. Graves, *America's Siberian Adventure.*

13. Margot Light, *Soviet Theory,* 30; and Carole Fink, "NEP in Foreign Policy," 11–12.

14. Dmitri Volkogonov, *Trotsky,* 199.

15. Gabriel Gorodetsky, "Formulation of Soviet Foreign Policy," 30–31.

16. Ibid., 32.

17. David R. Stone, *Hammer and Rifle.*

18. Barnes, Morgan, and the State Department Historical Office, *Foreign Service,* 205. The Rogers Act of 15 May 1924 amalgamated the diplomatic and consular services into the unified Foreign Service. It also provided for increased salaries and a more meritocratic appointment and promotion system.

19. Frederic L. Propas, "Creating a Hard Line," 213.

20. Ibid. For more on the nature of the program and its effect on the specialists, see also Thomas R. Maddux, "American Diplomats," 471; and Maddux, "Watching Stalin Maneuver," 143–44.

21. No one had told Henderson or the others in his mission that Lithuania had declared its independence from the Russian Empire. Loy W. Henderson, *Question of Trust.* See also H. W. Brands, *Inside the Cold War.*

22. Henderson, *Question of Trust,* 45–46.

23. Henderson, *Question of Trust,* 11, 15, 27–32, 38, 45–46, 60, 62, 119.

24. Ibid., 165.

25. Ibid.

26. Ibid., 181.

27. See *FRUS,* 1921, 2:768.

28. Henry Lewis Stimson Diaries, X, 179 (microfilm edition, reel 2), Manuscripts and Archives, Yale University Library, New Haven, Conn.

29. The memoirs of Henderson and the first generation of Kelley's Soviet scholars are replete with examples of frustration at what they considered to be the unwillingness of politicians in Washington to take their views of the Soviet menace seriously. See Henderson, *Question of Trust;* George F. Kennan, *Memoirs;* and Charles E. Bohlen, *Witness to History.*

30. Katherine Sibley points out that the increasing commercial and economic ties between the United States and the Soviet Union throughout the 1920s legitimized the Kremlin regime and made possible Roosevelt's recognition of the Soviet Union in 1933. Katherine A. S. Sibley, *Loans and Legitimacy,* 5.

31. Memorandum by the Chief of the Division of Eastern European Affairs (Kelley), 27 July 1933, *FRUS,* 1933, 2:783.

32. Ibid., 782–87; the Chief of the Division of Eastern European Affairs (Kelley) to the Undersecretary of State (Phillips), 25 September 1933, *FRUS,* 1933, 2:790–91. Roosevelt's secretary of state, Cordell Hull, shared this opinion: the Secretary of State to President Roosevelt, 21 September 1933, ibid., 789–90.

CHAPTER 2: Roosevelt's Détente, 1932–1938

1. David M. Kennedy, *Freedom from Fear,* 87–88.

2. Ibid., 90–91.

3. George McJimsey, *Presidency of Franklin Delano Roosevelt,* 19, 26.

4. William E. Kinsella Jr., *Leadership in Isolation,* 1.

5. Robert Dallek, *Franklin D. Roosevelt and American Foreign Policy*, 68.

6. See Edward M. Bennett, *Franklin D. Roosevelt and the Search for Security*, 1–24. John Richman identifies the emergence of this duality with the election of Roosevelt and his decision to recognize the Soviet Union. See John Richman, *The United States and the Soviet Union*.

7. Peter G. Filene, *Americans and the Soviet Experiment*, 205–9, 260–64.

8. Ibid., 236–39.

9. Henry Lewis Stimson Diaries, XXV, 103 (microfilm edition, reel 5), Manuscripts and Archives, Yale University Library, New Haven, Conn.

10. Walter Duranty, *I Write as I Please*, 320–21.

11. John Morton Blum, *From the Morgenthau Diaries*, 59. See also Joan Hoff Wilson, *Ideology and Economics*, 120; Bennett, *Franklin D. Roosevelt and the Search for Security*, 22–23; and Martin Weil, *Pretty Good Club*, 67–71.

12. Richman, *The United States and the Soviet Union*, 7–9.

13. Loy W. Henderson, *Question of Trust*, 216.

14. Ibid., 218.

15. Ibid., 226. On one of Morgenthau's meetings with the Soviet Union's unofficial representative in the United States, B. Skvirskii, see "Telegramma neofitsial'nogo Predstavitelia SSSR v SshA v Narodnyi Komissariat Inostrannykh Del SSSR," 26 September 1933, in Ministerstvo Inostrannykh Del SSSR, *Dokumenty vneshnei politiki SSSR*, 544–45. For Roosevelt's opinion of the State Department, see Richman, *The United States and the Soviet Union*, 10–11.

16. Robert E. Bowers details the State Department's efforts to block recognition by linking the Soviet Union with upheaval in Latin America. See Robert E. Bowers, "Hull, Russian Subversion in Cuba, and Recognition of the USSR."

17. Blum, *From the Morgenthau Diaries*, 59.

18. Lloyd Gardner, *Architects of Illusion*, 7–8, 10, 24. See also Beatrice Farnsworth, *William C. Bullitt and the Soviet Union*, 36–46; David J. Mayers, *Ambassadors and America's Soviet Policy;* and Dennis J. Dunn, *Caught Between Roosevelt and Stalin*.

19. The Secretary of State to President Roosevelt, 5 October 1933, Enclosure 2: Memorandum by the Special Assistant to the Secretary of State (Bullitt), *FRUS*, 1933, 2:791–94.

20. Ibid.

21. The Soviet Commissar for Foreign Affairs (Litvinov) to President Roosevelt, 16 November 1933, *FRUS*, 1933, 2:805–6. The agreement is probably referred to as a "gentlemen's agreement" because the State Department's legal adviser had already written a memorandum advising that any agreement Litvinov might reach with Roosevelt would probably not be binding until "ratified by the Central Executive Committee of the USSR, or at least by the Presidium, if the Committee was not in session." See "Authority of M. Litvinov," memorandum by the Department of State, Legal Adviser, 1 November 1933, 711.61/344.7/8, RG 59, NARA.

22. Memorandum by President Roosevelt and the Soviet Commissar for Foreign Affairs (Litvinov), 15 November 1933, *FRUS*, 1933, 2:804.

23. Jonathan Haslam, *Soviet Foreign Policy,* 93–94.

24. Teddy J. Uldricks, "Soviet Security Policy in the 1930s," 67.

25. Geoffrey Roberts, *The Soviet Union and the Origins of the Second World War,* 26.

26. Jonathan Haslam, *The Soviet Union and the Struggle for Collective Security in Europe,* 1–2.

27. Sidney Aster, "Ivan Maisky," 317.

28. Mayers, *Ambassadors and America's Soviet Policy,* 110.

29. Farnsworth, *William C. Bullitt and the Soviet Union,* 31.

30. Ibid., 46, 58–63.

31. The Chargé in France (Marriner) to the Acting Secretary of State, 24 December 1933, *FRUS,* 1933, 2:830–32.

32. Bullitt to Roosevelt, 13 April 1934, as quoted in Orville H. Bullitt, *For the President,* 83.

33. George F. Kennan, *Memoirs,* 80; Charles E. Bohlen, *Witness to History,* 33.

34. Bullitt to Hull, "The Foreign Policy of the Soviet Union," 19 July 1935, 761.00/260, RG 59, NARA. Robert Kelley attached this letter to a memorandum from the Division of Eastern European Affairs that he sent to Hull, Phillips, and Moore. In that memorandum, dated 10 August 1935, Kelley wrote: "It is worthy of special note that the conclusions which Ambassador Bullitt has reached with regard to the fundamentals of the foreign policy of the Soviet Union, as a result of personal observation and contact with the rulers of that country, are in full agreement with those arrived at by competent observers from study of the avowed aims and ideas of the communist leaders and of the acts and policies of the instrumentalities under their control." See Kelley to Hull, Phillips, and Moore, 761.00/260, RG 59, NARA.

35. From Bullitt to Hull, "Comintern Activities and the VII Congress," 14 August 1935, 800B, Vol. 433 (1935 800B), RG 84, NARA.

36. Ibid.

37. The Ambassador in the Soviet Union (Bullitt) to the Secretary of State, 21 August 1935, *FRUS: The Soviet Union,* 244–48.

38. Louis Fischer, *Men and Politics,* 308; and Farnsworth, *William C. Bullitt and the Soviet Union,* 153.

39. James MacGregor Burns, *Roosevelt: The Lion and the Fox,* 263, 281.

40. Joseph E. Davies, *Mission to Moscow,* 1–3.

41. Kennan, *Memoirs,* 82; and Bohlen, *Witness to History,* 44.

42. Thomas R. Maddux, *Years of Estrangement,* 55–66.

43. Rumor and speculation surrounded the murder of Kirov and the ensuing purges and show trials. See Sarah Davies, *Popular Opinion,* 114–18. Contemporary historians have not entirely resolved the causes and results of the murder and its relationship to the ensuing "terror." See Amy W. Knight, *Who Killed Kirov?;* Robert Conquest, *Great Terror;* Robert C. Tucker, *Stalin in Power;* Dmitri Volkogonov, *Stalin;* J. Arch Getty and Oleg V. Naumov, *Road to Terror;* and Sheila Fitzpatrick, "Stalin and the Making of a New Elite."

44. Wiley was serving as the chargé between the departure of Bullitt and the arrival

of Davies. Wiley to the Secretary of State, 14 December 1934, 861.00/11579, RG 59, NARA.

45. Mayers, *Ambassadors and America's Soviet Policy,* 121–22.

46. The Ambassador in the Soviet Union (Davies) to the Secretary of State, 1 April 1938, *FRUS: The Soviet Union,* 542–51.

47. The Ambassador in the Soviet Union (Davies) to the Secretary of State, 6 June 1938, ibid., 552–59. See also the Ambassador in the Soviet Union (Davies) to the Secretary of State, 1 April 1938, ibid., 542–51; the Ambassador in the Soviet Union (Davies) to the Secretary of State, 6 June 1938, ibid., 559–66.

48. Dennis J. Dunn is particularly critical of Davies. Dunn, *Caught Between Roosevelt and Stalin.* A more balanced and persuasive interpretation is offered in Keith D. Eagles, *Ambassador Joseph E. Davies;* and Elizabeth Kimball MacLean, *Joseph E. Davies.* See also Elizabeth Kimball MacLean, "Joseph E. Davies and Soviet-American Relations"; Thomas R. Maddux, "Watching Stalin Maneuver"; Maddux, "American Diplomats"; and Richard H. Ullman, "Davies Mission."

49. The Ambassador in the Soviet Union (Davies) to the Secretary of State, 13 March 1938, ibid., 532–33. The "Trotskyist Bloc" was a group of twenty-one defendants charged with organized terrorism, sabotage, conspiracy to murder for the purpose of overthrowing the government, systematic organization of defeatist programs, and plots to murder Stalin, Voroshilov, Maksim Gorki, V. R. Menzhinski, and V. V. Kuibyshev.

50. The Ambassador in the Soviet Union (Davies) to the Secretary of State, 1 April 1938, *FRUS: The Soviet Union,* 542–51.

51. The Ambassador in the Soviet Union (Davies) to the Secretary of State, 2 March 1938, ibid., 527–28; the Ambassador in the Soviet Union (Davies) to the Secretary of State, 13 March 1938, ibid., 532–33; and the Ambassador in the Soviet Union (Davies) to the Secretary of State, 1 April 1938, ibid., 542–51.

52. Joseph E. Davies, *Mission to Moscow,* 180.

53. The Chargé in the Soviet Union (Henderson) to the Secretary of State, 13 June 1937, *FRUS: The Soviet Union,* 380–82.

54. "The First Three Years of American-Soviet Diplomatic Relations," the Chargé in the Soviet Union (Henderson) to the Secretary of State, 16 November 1936, 711.61/611, RG 59, NARA.

55. The Chargé in the Soviet Union (Henderson) to the Secretary of State, 18 February 1938, *FRUS: The Soviet Union,* 514–18.

56. "Transmitting two editorials on Soviet-American relations," the Chargé in the Soviet Union (Kirk) to the Secretary of State, 25 November 1938, 711.61/666, RG 59, NARA.

57. The Chargé in the Soviet Union (Henderson) to the Secretary of State, 18 February 1938, *FRUS: The Soviet Union,* 519–20.

58. Davies to Secretary of State, 1 April 1938, ibid., 542–51.

59. The Ambassador in the Soviet Union (Davies) to the Secretary of State, 6 June 1938, ibid., 552–59.

60. James S. Herndon and Joseph O. Baylen, "Col. Philip R. Faymonville"; John Daniel Langer, "Red General"; and Kelly William Biggs, "Role of Philip Ries Faymonville."

61. Demaree Bess, "The General Called the Turn," 101.

62. Anatole G. Mazour, "Philip R. Faymonville," 83–84.

63. Bess, "The General Called the Turn," 101.

64. Philip R. Faymonville, "The Outlook for Russia," n.d., box 1, Philip R. Faymonville Papers, United States Army Military History Institute, Carlisle Barracks, Pa.

65. Biggs, "Role of Philip Ries Faymonville," 42; Ralph Izard, "A General Looks at the Soviet Union," 12.

66. Biggs, "Role of Philip Ries Faymonville," 49; Izard, "A General Looks at the Soviet Union," 12; and Bess, "The General Called the Turn," 101.

67. "FDR: Day by Day—The Pare Lorentz Chronology," 16 November 1933 and 1 February 1934, Franklin Delano Roosevelt Library (hereafter FDRL), Hyde Park, N.Y.

68. Bullitt to Roosevelt, 1 January 1934, Diplomatic Correspondence, box 49, President's Secretary's Files, FDRL.

69. Bess, "The General Called the Turn," 12.

70. Henderson, *Question of Trust*, 315.

71. Bohlen, *Witness to History*, 44–45.

72. In a study of United States military attachés' reporting on the Soviet Union in the 1930s, David Glantz argues that Faymonville's reports were particularly accurate and perceptive: David Glantz, "Observing the Soviets," 182. Although arguing that Faymonville's reporting became less accurate, the further he ventured from his military expertise, Herndon and Baylen also point out the importance of Faymonville's attaché reports: Herndon and Baylen, "Col. Philip R. Faymonville," 485–99. Alfred Vagts also commended Faymonville's performance as attaché: Alfred Vagts, *Military Attaché*, xiii, 82.

73. The Chargé in the Soviet Union (Henderson) to the Secretary of State, 8 June 1937, *FRUS: The Soviet Union*, 378. Henderson affirms this interpretation of the Red Army in a later dispatch. The Chargé in the Soviet Union (Henderson) to the Secretary of State, 18 February 1938, ibid., 519–20.

74. Kennan, *Memoirs*, 83–85; Bohlen, *Witness to History*, 39–41; Daniel Yergin, *Shattered Peace*, 34–35; Frederic L. Propas, "State Department," 215–18, 220.

75. Yergin, *Shattered Peace*, 26–35.

76. MacLean, *Joseph E. Davies*, 63.

77. The "Kerensky debt" was the debt incurred by the provisional government in the months between the March 1917 and the November 1917 revolutions in Russia. Upon assuming power, the Bolshevik government renounced any obligation to pay back that debt and others incurred by previous Russian regimes. Repayment of this debt was one of the issues Litvinov and Roosevelt discussed in 1933. MacLean, *Joseph E. Davies*, 54–55.

78. Pierrepont Moffat to Sumner Welles, 2 November 1938, 121.5461/79, RG 59,

NARA; GSM to Sumner Welles, 8 February 1939, 121.5461/81, RG 59, NARA; Sumner Welles to Pierrepont Moffat 28 October 1938, folder 09, "State Department: European Affairs, 1938," box 48, Sumner Welles Papers, FDRL; and Chief of Staff to the President, "Subject: Military Attaché in Russia," 1 February 1939, President's Official File, 3601, FDRL.

79. Joseph E. Davies to Franklin D. Roosevelt, 18 January 1939, President's Official File, 3601, FDRL, and Franklin D. Roosevelt to Joseph E. Davies, 10 February 1939, President's Official File, 3601, FDRL.

CHAPTER 3: From Munich to Barbarossa

1. Geoffrey Roberts, *The Soviet Union and the Origins of the Second World War*, 47, 56.

2. G. Jukes, "The Red Army and the Munich Crisis," 200. Igor Lukes dismisses Jukes' argument and his reliance on the memoirs of Marshal M. V. Zakharov (1938 assistant to the chief of the General Staff B. M. Shaposhnikov), which does not contain any archival citations. Igor Lukes, "Stalin and Benes." Using an impressive array of published and archival Soviet/Russian and eastern European sources, Hugh Ragsdale convincingly defends Jukes' arguments and contends that the Soviet military did mobilize, and Romania was willing to provide Soviet forces access to Czechoslovakia. Hugh Ragsdale, "Soviet Military Preparations."

3. Roberts, *The Soviet Union and the Origins of the Second World War*, 54.

4. Ibid., 60–61.

5. James MacGregor Burns, *Roosevelt: The Lion and the Fox*, 318.

6. David M. Kennedy, *Freedom from Fear*, 406.

7. Robert Dallek, *Franklin D. Roosevelt and American Foreign Policy*, 144–53.

8. Ibid., 319–20, 327.

9. Wayne S. Cole, *Roosevelt and the Isolationists*, 140, 211, 295.

10. Robert A. Divine, *Illusion of Neutrality*.

11. John Erickson, *Soviet High Command*, 517–22; Alvin D. Coox, *Anatomy of a Small War*, 357; Vilnis Sipols, *Tainy diplomaticheskie*, 98; and Jonathan Haslam, *The Soviet Union and the Threat from the East*, 132–34.

12. The most authoritative work on the purges in the Red Army, based on Soviet archival sources, is O. F. Suvenirov, *Tragediia RKKA*.

13. Alfred Vagts, *Military Attaché*, 66. On anticommunist prejudices and their impact on events of 1939, see Michael Jabara Carley, *1939*.

14. Roberts, *The Soviet Union and the Origins of the Second World War*, 86.

15. Sidney Aster, "Ivan Maisky," 352.

16. The history of the events leading up to the signing of the German-Soviet non-aggression pact in August 1939 is still controversial. The main item of contention is the nature of the Soviet-German relationship, particularly the Soviet attitude toward its relations with Germany. On the one side, historians such as Gerhard L. Weinberg, Robert C. Tucker, R. C. Raack, and Aleksandr M. Nekrich argue that an agreement

with Germany was a long-held goal of the Kremlin. Stalin thus conducted negotiations with Britain and France primarily to obtain greater concessions from Hitler. In contrast, another group of historians argues that the German-Soviet pact was not the result of well-planned Soviet policy but rather the consequence of an inept and opportunistic Soviet foreign policy apparatus. These historians, including Gabriel Gorodetsky, Geoffrey Roberts, Teddy J. Uldricks, and Michael Jabara Carley, contend that while earnestly conducting negotiations with Britain and France, the Kremlin responded tentatively to German overtures beginning in late July 1939. As long as much of the evidence necessary to resolve this dispute with anything approaching certainty remains either undiscovered or nonexistent, it is impossible to state definitively which group's arguments are most accurate. Gorodetsky, Roberts, Uldricks, and Carley make use of the archival documents slowly being released from Moscow, whereas Weinberg and Tucker rely primarily on German interpretations of this period. Raack and Nekrich do use Soviet sources, but not the most recently available material. Given this, and the fact that historians continue to document the precarious state of the post-purge Soviet military and economy, the argument that Stalin sought to avoid war by seizing on German advances is the most convincing at present. See Gabriel Gorodetsky, *Grand Delusion* and *Stafford Cripps' Mission to Moscow;* Gerhard L. Weinberg, *Foreign Policy of Hitler's Germany;* Robert C. Tucker, *Stalin in Power;* R. C. Raack, *Stalin's Drive to the West;* Aleksandr M. Nekrich, *Pariahs, Partners, Predators;* Geoffrey Roberts, *The Soviet Union and the Origins of the Second World War;* Roberts, *Unholy Alliance;* Teddy J. Uldricks, "Evolving Soviet Views"; Carley, *1939.*

17. Lev Izrailevich Gintsberg, "Sovetsko-Germanskii Pakt," 35.

18. Ibid., 13.

19. Bezymenskii, "Sovetsko-Germanskie dogovory 1939," 5.

20. See Robert C. Tucker, *Stalin in Power,* 593–95; Isaac Deutscher, *Stalin,* 432; R. J. Overy and Andrew Wheatcroft, *Road to War,* 210; Gerhard L. Weinberg, *Germany and the Soviet Union,* 24; and Henry L. Roberts, "Maxim Litvinov," 363–64.

21. See Dmitri Volkogonov, *Stalin,* 346–49; and Z. Sheinis, *Maksim Maksimovich Litvinov,* 360–70.

22. Jonathan Haslam, *The Soviet Union and the Struggle for Collective Security in Europe,* 213; and Geoffrey Roberts, "Fall of Litvinov."

23. Weinberg, *Germany and the Soviet Union,* 24.

24. See Roberts, *The Soviet Union and the Origins of the Second World War,* 89, 108, 149.

25. Joseph Edward O'Connor, "Laurence A. Steinhardt," 16–17.

26. Ibid., 21–22.

27. Ibid., 22.

28. Ibid., 22–23.

29. Henry Cassidy, *Moscow Dateline,* 76.

30. O'Connor, "Laurence A. Steinhardt," 27–31, 33. See also Laurence Steinhardt to Loy Henderson, 20 October 1939, "Letterbook Aug. 9, 1939 to Feb. 3, 1940," box 78, Laurence A. Steinhardt Papers (hereafter LSP), LOC.

31. The Ambassador in the Soviet Union (Steinhardt) to the Secretary of State, 28 August 1939, *FRUS: The Soviet Union,* 1939, 845–46.

32. Memorandum by the Assistant Chief of the Division of European Affairs (Henderson), 29 August 1939, *FRUS: The Soviet Union,* 1939, 847–50.

33. The Ambassador in the Soviet Union (Steinhardt) to the Secretary of State), 2 September 1939, *FRUS: The Soviet Union,* 1939, 854.

34. Laurence Steinhardt to Loy Henderson, 20 October 1939, "Letterbook Aug. 9, 1939 to Feb. 3, 1940," box 78, LSP, LOC.

35. Steinhardt to Wiley, 21 September 1939, "Letterbook Aug. 9, 1939 to Feb. 3, 1940," box 78, LSP, LOC.

36. FDR memorandum to Hull, 10 January 1940, *FDR Personal Letters,* part 2, 4:986–87.

37. Steinhardt to Rudolf E. Schoenfeld, 9 December 1939, "Letterbook Aug. 9, 1939 to Feb. 3, 1940," box 78, LSP, LOC.

38. See Charles E. Bohlen, *Witness to History,* 64–66; Loy W. Henderson, *Question of Trust,* 541–55. These memoirs sum up the general attitudes of United States diplomatic personnel in Moscow and Washington, D.C. For concrete examples of these attitudes, see the Chargé in the Soviet Union (Grummon) to the Secretary of State, 24 May 1939, *FRUS,* 1939, 1:258–59; the Ambassador in the Soviet Union (Steinhardt) to the Undersecretary of State (Welles), 16 August 1939, *FRUS,* 1939, 1:296–99; the Ambassador in the Soviet Union (Steinhardt) to the Secretary of State, 1 September 1939, *FRUS,* 1939, 1:347–48, Memorandum by the Assistant Chief of the Division of European Affairs (Henderson), 2 September 1939, *FRUS,* 1939, 1:349–50; the Ambassador in the Soviet Union (Steinhardt) to the Secretary of State, 27 September 1939, *FRUS,* 1939, 1:455–56; the Ambassador in the Soviet Union (Steinhardt) to the Secretary of State, 30 October 1939, *FRUS,* 1939, 1:492–93; the Ambassador in the Soviet Union (Steinhardt) to the Secretary of State, 4 October 1939, *FRUS,* 1939, 1:958–59; Memorandum by Loy W. Henderson, 22 July 1939,, 761.00/324, RG 59, NARA; William C. Bullitt to Loy Henderson, 1 November 1939, "William C. Bullitt, 1936–1974," box 2, Loy W. Henderson Papers (hereafter LHP), LOC; and "Chip" Bohlen to Loy Henderson, 1 November 1939, "USSR-US Personnel in USSR, 1939–43," box 16, LHP, LOC.

39. Stuart Grummon, Chargé d' Affaires in Moscow to Loy Henderson, 7 July 1939, "USSR–U.S. Personnel in USSR, 1939–1943," box 16, LHP, LOC.

40. Loy Henderson to Samuel Harper, 24 August 1939, "Harper, Samuel, 1939–1943," box 1, LHP, LOC.

41. John Wiley to Loy Henderson, 7 September 1939, "Wiley, John C., 1938–1961," box 2, LHP, LOC.

42. Carley, *1939.*

43. Ivan D. Yeaton, "Memoirs," 25, n.d., box 3, Faymonville Papers, USA MHI, Carlisle Barracks, Pa.

44. The manager of the United Press Bureau in Moscow made this observation in March 1944. Report of the Military Intelligence Division of the War Department

General Staff, "Russian Policy-Domestic and Foreign," 2 March 1944, MID 092, Policy, USSR, Army Intelligence Project Decimal File, 1039, RG 319, NARA.

45. Chip Bohlen to Henderson, 1 November 1939, "USSR-U.S. Personnel in USSR, 1939–43," box 16, LHP, LOC.

46. Wiley to Henderson, 1 November 1939, "Wiley, John C., 1938–1961," box 2, LHP, LOC.

47. William C. Bullitt to Henderson, 1 November 1939, "William C. Bullitt, 1936–1974," box 2, LHP, LOC.

48. Henderson to Wiley, 19 December 1939, "Baltic states, 1928–1976," box 6, LHP, LOC.

49. Henderson to Bohlen, "USSR-U.S. Personnel," box 16, LHP, LOC.

50. O'Connor, "Laurence A. Steinhardt," 76.

51. Steinhardt to Henderson, 23 December 1939, "Letterbook Aug. 9, 1939 to Feb. 3, 1940," box 78, LSP, LOC.

52. Ibid.

53. Steinhardt to Henderson, 29 January 1940, "Letterbook Aug. 9, 1939 to Feb. 3, 1940," box 78, LSP, LOC.

54. On Bullitt and Henderson's pleasure with Steinhardt's reports, see Henderson to Steinhardt, 5 April 1940, "G-I 1940," box 29, LSP, LOC. On Steinhardt's assessment of Soviet-German relations, see Steinhardt to Henderson, 2 March 1940, "Letterbook Feb. 5, 1940–Apr. 26, 1940," box 79, LSP, LOC; and Henderson to Steinhardt, 31 March 1941, "G-I, 1941," box 33, LSP, LOC.

55. Steinhardt to Henderson, 6 January 1940, "Letterbook Aug. 9, 1939 to Feb. 3, 1940," box 78, LSP, LOC.

56. Division of European Affairs Memorandum, "Certain Aspects of Soviet Ethics in Its Foreign Relations," 3 October 1940, 711.61/782, RG59, NARA.

57. Division of European Affairs, Summary of Dispatch 1382, 4 June 1941 from Moscow, 861.00/11891, RG 59, NARA.

58. Scott A. Koch, "Role of U.S. Army Military Attachés."

59. Bruce W. Bidwell, *History of the Military Intelligence Division*, 381, 390.

60. Ibid., 384.

61. Yeaton, "Memoirs," 4–5.

62. Ibid., 9–10.

63. Ibid., 11–12.

64. Military Attaché, Moscow, Report number 1734, 18 June 1940, "Campaign to Increase Discipline in the Red Army," 861.20 MID Reports/30, RG 59, NARA.

65. Ibid.

66. Military Attaché, Moscow, Report number 1735, "New Campaign to Increase Discipline in the Red Fleet," 861.20 MID Reports/29, RG 59, NARA.

67. Yeaton to Assistant Chief of Staff, G-2, telegram 207, 21 April 1941, folder From: Russia-Moscow. Incoming (2-8-40) through (8-1-41), box 579, RG 319, NARA.

68. Military Attaché, Moscow, Report Number 1952, 2 June 1941, "Characteristics of the Population," 861.00/11903, RG 59, NARA.

69. Ibid.

70. Military Attaché, Moscow, Report Number 1965, 16 June 1941, "Army (General)," 861.20 MID Reports/38, RG 59, NARA.

71. Ibid.

72. David M. Glantz, *Stumbling Colossus*, 119.

73. Military Attaché, Moscow, Report Number 1965, 16 June 1941, "Army (General)," 861.20 MID Reports/38, RG 59, NARA.

74. Glantz, *Stumbling Colossus*, 160.

75. Yeaton wrote to his incoming assistant military attaché, "I never read anything Russian because it's not worth reading and I haven't made a translation since I came." Yeaton to Captain Joseph A. Michela, 15 June 1940, "Russia. Correspondence File of I. D. Yeaton as Military Attaché, Moscow, 1939–1941," box 1, Ivan D. Yeaton Papers, Hoover Institution Archives, Stanford, California.

76. The German military attaché in Moscow, Lieutenant-General Köstring, was more concerned about Soviet military capabilities than were the U.S. attachés. In late 1940 he warned Hitler not to underestimate the Red Army. See Walter Goerlitz, *History of the German General Staff*, 385.

77. Ibid., 107, 146, 205, 260; and Lennart Samuelson, *Plans for Stalin's War Machine*, 195–96. Samuelson argues that the Red Army on the eve of Barbarossa was more balanced and better equipped than earlier thought and that, with regard to industrial mobilization, the Soviet Union was ahead of Germany.

78. The briefings the War Department and General Staff provided to Roosevelt in summer 1941 were based on the reports Yeaton sent from Moscow. Consequently, they were extremely pessimistic. Concerned about the contrast between these predictions and those emanating from the British and former Ambassador Davies, Roosevelt sent Hopkins to Moscow in August 1941 to ascertain the situation in the Soviet Union. Henry Stimson to Franklin Roosevelt, 23 June 1941, "Book 4: Russia Attack, Early Political Decisions," box 306, Sherwood Collection, Hopkins Papers, FDRL; Forrest C. Pogue, *George C. Marshall*, 2:72; Robert E. Sherwood, *Roosevelt and Hopkins*, 327. This topic will be covered in more detail in the next chapter.

79. Yeaton to MID, telegram 222, 7 June 1941, folder From: Russia-Moscow. Incoming (2-8-40) through (8-1-41), box 579, RG 319, NARA.

80. "(lunch) Daniel Callaghan and Col. Philip R. Faymonville and Edwin M. (Pa) Watson," 27 July 1939, times: 1300–; location: office; source: Stenographer's Diary, White House Usher's Diary, "FDR: Day by Day—The Pare Lorentz Chronology," FDR Library.

81. Keith David Eagles, *Ambassador Joseph E. Davies*, 317.

82. Roberts, *The Soviet Union and the Origins of the Second World War*, 104–13.

83. Ibid., 135–36.

84. The Secretary of State to the Ambassador in the Soviet Union (Steinhardt), 1 March 1941, *FRUS*, 1941, 1:712–13.

85. The Ambassador in the Soviet Union (Steinhardt) to the Secretary of State, 3 March 1941, *FRUS*, 1941, 1:713–14.

86. The Secretary of State to the Ambassador in the Soviet Union (Steinhardt), 4 March 1941, *FRUS,* 1941, 1:714.

87. The Ambassador in the Soviet Union (Steinhardt) to the Secretary of State, 7 June 1941, *FRUS,* 1941, 1:620–21; Military Attaché Report USSR, "Army (General)," 861.20 MID Reports/38, RG 59, NARA; Military Attaché Report USSR, "Characteristics of the Population," 861.00/11903, RG 59, NARA;

88. I.B. 85, 19 June 1941, IBE, box 1, RG 319, NARA.

89. The Ambassador in the Soviet Union (Steinhardt) to the Secretary of State, 17 June 1941, *FRUS,* 1941, 1:764–66.

90. The Secretary of State to the Ambassador in the Soviet Union (Steinhardt), 14 June 1941, *FRUS,* 1941, 1:757–58.

91. Memorandum Prepared in the Division of European Affairs, 21 June 1941, *FRUS,* 1941, 1:766–67.

CHAPTER 4: Roosevelt Feeds the Bear: The Decision to Aid the Soviets

1. John Erickson, *Road to Stalingrad,* 124.

2. David M. Glantz and Jonathan M. House, *When Titans Clashed,* 49.

3. Ibid., 51–53.

4. Ibid., 53.

5. A. Eremenko, *Arduous Beginning,* 71; and Glantz and House, *When Titans Clashed,* 58.

6. Glantz and House, *When Titans Clashed,* 56.

7. Erickson, *Road to Stalingrad,* 138.

8. Glantz and House, *When Titans Clashed,* 53.

9. Ibid., 58–61.

10. Ibid., 67–71.

11. Erickson, *Road to Stalingrad,* 138.

12. Glantz and House, *When Titans Clashed,* 72.

13. Ibid.

14. Ibid., 75–76.

15. Yeaton to MID, no. 222, 7 June 1941, folder From: Russia-Moscow. Incoming (2-8-40) through (8-1-41), box 579, RG 319, NARA. See also Bradley F. Smith, *Sharing Secrets,* 73.

16. Yeaton to MID, no. 234, 27 June 1941, folder From: Russia-Moscow. Incoming (2-8-40) through (8-1-41), box 579, RG 319, NARA.

17. Yeaton to MID, no. 237, 30 June 1941, folder From: Russia-Moscow. Incoming (2-8-40) through (8-1-41), box 579, RG 319, NARA.

18. Yeaton to MID, no. 244, 15 July 1941, folder From: Russia-Moscow. Incoming (2-8-40) through (8-1-41), box 579, RG 319, NARA.

19. Letter from Lieutenant General Mason-MacFarlane to the Chief of the Impe-

rial General Staff (CIGS), 14 July 1941, WO 216/124, Public Record Office (PRO), Kew, United Kingdom.

20. Yeaton to MID, no. 2, 6 August 1941, folder From: Russia-Moscow. Incoming (8-5-41) through (11-8-41), box 579, RG 319, NARA.

21. MID to Yeaton, no. 12, 9 August 1941, folder 1, box 585, RG 319, NARA.

22. Yeaton to MID, no. 4, 11 August 1941, folder From: Russia-Moscow. Incoming (8-5-41) through (11-8-41), box 579, RG 319, NARA.

23. Yeaton to Asst. Chief of Staff, G2, no. 207, 21 April 1941, folder From: Russia-Moscow. Incoming (2-8-40) through (8-1-41), box 579, RG 319, NARA.

24. Yeaton to MID, no. 9, 19 August 1941, folder From: Russia-Moscow. Incoming (8-5-41) through (11-8-41), box 579, RG 319, NARA.

25. Yeaton to G2, no. 40, 26 September 1941, folder From: Russia-Moscow. Incoming (8-5-41) through (11-8-41), box 579, RG 319, NARA.

26. Yeaton to MID, no. 8, 18 August 1941, folder From: Russia-Moscow. Incoming (8-5-41) through (11-8-41), box 579, RG 319, NARA.

27. MID to Yeaton, no. 17, 19 August 1941, folder 1, box 585, RG 319, NARA.

28. Yeaton to MID, no. 13, 22 August 1941, folder From: Russia-Moscow. Incoming (8-5-41) through (11-8-41), box 579, RG 319.

29. Letter from L. G. Mason-MacFarlane to CIGS, 14 July 1941, WO 216/124, PRO.

30. Alexander Werth, *Russia at War,* 280.

31. Cyrus L. Sulzberger, *Long Row of Candles,* 159.

32. Frederick D. Sharp to General Sherman Miles, Assistant Chief of Staff, G-2, 1 November 1941, MID 041.221 M/A Russia, box 151, Army Intelligence Project Decimal File, RG 319, NARA.

33. Harry L. Hopkins to Henry Stimson, 14 October 1941, folder "Book 4: Russia Attacked," box 305, Harry L. Hopkins Papers, FDRL.

34. Ibid.

35. I.B. 85, "Estimate of the Russo-German Situation," 19 June 1941, box 1, Intelligence Branch Estimates, RG 319, NARA.

36. Glantz and House, *When Titans Clashed,* 300; David M. Glantz, *Stumbling Colossus,* 10–11.

37. I.B. 85, "Estimate of the Russo-German Situation," 19 June 1941, box 1, Intelligence Branch Estimates, RG 319, NARA.

38. The Acting Secretary of State to the Ambassador in the Soviet Union (Steinhardt), 14 July 1941, *FRUS, 1941,* 1:892–93.

39. Col. Percy G. Black to General Miles, "Subject: Military Mission to Siberia," 17 July 1941, MID 210.684 Russia, box 1040, Army Intelligence Project Decimal File, RG 319, NARA. See also Bradley F. Smith, *Sharing Secrets,* 73.

40. I.B. 108, "Soviet Guerrilla Warfare," 2 August 1941, box 2, Intelligence Branch Estimates, RG 319, NARA.

41. George C. Marshall, *Papers,* 2:565, n. 2.

42. The Ambassador in the Soviet Union (Steinhardt) to the Secretary of State, 23 June 1941, *FRUS,* 1941, 1:885.

43. The Ambassador in the Soviet Union (Steinhardt) to the Secretary of State, 29 June 1941, *FRUS,* 1941, 1:886–87.

44. The Ambassador in the Soviet Union (Steinhardt) to the Secretary of State, 1 July 1941, *FRUS,* 1941, 1:890.

45. The Ambassador in the Soviet Union (Steinhardt) to the Secretary of State, 28 June 1941, *FRUS,* 1941, 1:176–77.

46. The Ambassador in the Soviet Union (Steinhardt) to the Secretary of State, 9 July 1941, *FRUS,* 1941, 1:179–81.

47. The Ambassador in the Soviet Union (Steinhardt) to the Secretary of State, 29 June 1941, *FRUS,* 1941, 1:774–75.

48. The Ambassador in the Soviet Union (Steinhardt) to the Secretary of State, 7 July 1941, *FRUS,* 1941, 1:895–96.

49. The Ambassador in the Soviet Union (Steinhardt) to the Secretary of State, 17 July 1941, *FRUS,* 1941, 1:630–31.

50. The Ambassador in the Soviet Union (Steinhardt) to the Secretary of State, 5 August 1941, *FRUS,* 1941, 1:634–35.

51. The Ambassador in the Soviet Union (Steinhardt) to the Secretary of State, 23 August 1941, *FRUS,* 1941, 1:642–45.

52. The Ambassador in the Soviet Union (Steinhardt) to the Secretary of State, 7 August 1941, *FRUS,* 1941, 1:636–37.

53. The Ambassador in the Soviet Union (Steinhardt) to the Secretary of State, 17 August 1941, *FRUS,* 1941, 1:640–41.

54. The Ambassador in the Soviet Union (Steinhardt) to the Secretary of State, 26 October 1941, *FRUS,* 1941, 1:651–52; the Ambassador in the Soviet Union (Steinhardt) to the Secretary of State, 9 November 1941, *FRUS,* 1941, 1:656–57.

55. Elizabeth Kimball MacLean, *Joseph E. Davies,* 71–72.

56. Ibid., 72.

57. Elizabeth Kimball MacLean, "Joseph E. Davies and Soviet-American Relations," 75.

58. Memorandum, Joseph E. Davies to Harry L. Hopkins, 8 July 1941, folder "Book 4: Russia Attacked," box 305, Hopkins Papers.

59. Ibid., 258. Warren F. Kimball, *Most Unsordid Act.*

60. Winston S. Churchill, *Grand Alliance,* 369.

61. As quoted in ibid., 369.

62. Ibid., 372.

63. As quoted in T. H. Vail Motter, *Persian Corridor,* 21.

64. Ibid.

65. Henry L. Stimson to Franklin D. Roosevelt, 23 June 1941, "Book 4: Russia Attacked, Early Political Decisions," box 305, Hopkins Papers; see also Dawson, *Decision to Aid Russia,* 114; and George C. Herring, *Aid to Russia,* 8.

66. Stimson's views were not exclusively shaped by the Military Intelligence Divi-

sion. On 30 July 1941 he met with Colonel Faymonville to discuss the Soviet-German war. In his diary Stimson described the meeting: "I found that he was optimistic on the subject of Russia's ability to hold out in her fight against Germany. He said that there would be of course a loss of territory and great losses of material and of men—bloody fighting—but that he expected that organized governmental groups of the Russians would be able to hold out indefinitely. I asked him about the organization of the Russian industries in the Urals and he said that was in the definite view that they had planned to do and that the plan had been pretty well carried out but not altogether." Henry Lewis Stimson Diaries, XXXIV, 216–17 (microfilm edition, reel 6), Manuscripts and Archives, Yale University Library, New Haven, Conn. The next day, 31 July, Stimson met with the Soviet Military Mission in the United States. With the Soviet military men, Stimson discussed the progress of the war, Soviet guerrilla warfare, and the Soviet-German war in the air. Ibid., 220–21.

67. Ibid., 26; Maurice Matloff and Edwin M. Snell, *Strategic Planning for Coalition Warfare, 1941–1942*, 14–15.

68. Mark A. Stoler, *Allies and Adversaries*, 31; Matloff and Snell, *Strategic Planning for Coalition Warfare*, 15, 19–20; and Herring, *Aid to Russia*, 8, 13–15.

69. Matloff and Snell, *Strategic Planning for Coalition Warfare*, 19–20; and Forrest C. Pogue, *George C. Marshall*, 2:49, 2:65.

70. Cordell Hull, *Memoirs*, 2:973.

71. Dawson, *Decision to Aid Russia*, 64.

72. Memorandum, Adolf A. Berle to Harry Hopkins, 30 July 1941, "Book 4: Russia Is Attacked: Early Political Decisions," box 305, Hopkins Papers.

73. Robert Huhn Jones, *Roads to Russia*, 38–39.

74. Memorandum by the Assistant Secretary of State (Berle) to the Acting Secretary of State, 30 July 1941, *FRUS*, 1941, 1:798–99.

75. Memorandum of Conversation, by the Acting Chief of the Division of European Affairs (Atherton), 30 June 1941, *FRUS*, 1941, 1:778–79.

76. Memorandum, A. A. Berle to Sumner Welles, 7 July 1941, 711.61/823, RG 59, NARA.

77. Ibid.

78. Steinhardt remained committed to this policy as well. See Herring, *Aid to Russia*, 280.

79. Dawson, *Decision to Aid Russia*, 98–100.

80. Ibid., 69–82.

81. Ibid., 119–22; Herring, *Aid to Russia*, 7–9. For a reflection of the administration's internal discussions of the matter, see Memorandum from Oscar Cox to Harry L. Hopkins, 23 June 1941, folder "Book 4: Russia Attacked, Early Political Decisions," box 305, Sherwood Collection, Hopkins Papers. In this memorandum Cox explains: "Our practical choice is clear. Whether or not we like Russia's internal and other policies, we will aid Russia, in our national interest, to eliminate the far more immediate danger to our security from Hitler's already partially executed plans to rule the world."

82. Ibid., 126–29.

83. Ibid., 130.

84. Ibid., 134.

85. Ibid., 139; and MacLean, *Joseph E. Davies*, 71–75.

86. Dawson, *Decision to Aid Russia*, 138, 143; MacLean, *Joseph E. Davies*, 73; and Herring, *Aid to Russia*, 8–9.

87. Dawson, *Decision to Aid Russia*, 138.

88. Ibid., 151.

89. Ibid.

90. Ibid., 153–54.

91. Robert E. Sherwood, *Roosevelt and Hopkins*, 317.

92. Ibid., 317–19. See also Kimball, *Juggler*, 30–35.

93. Robert E. Sherwood, *Roosevelt and Hopkins*, 321.

94. Ibid., 327.

95. Hopkins visited the British embassy during his stay in Moscow. Mason-MacFarlane recorded his impressions of his meeting with Hopkins: "Furthermore he soon discovered the rottenness and defeatism of the local American Ambassador and Embassy and I hope we'll see some change soon." Letter from Mason-MacFarlane to Major General F. H. N. Davidson, 31 July 1941, WO 32/15548, PRO.

96. Letter, Ivan D. Yeaton to Thomas A. Julian, 8 August 1968, folder "Faymonville, Philip Ries, 1888–1962 BG," box 3, Ivan D. Yeaton Papers, Hoover Institution Archives, Stanford, CA.

97. Memorandum by Harry L. Hopkins, 30 July 1941, *FRUS*, 1941, 1:802–5.

98. Ibid.; and memorandum by Harry L. Hopkins, 31 July 1941, *FRUS*, 1941, 1:805–14.

99. Sherwood, *Roosevelt and Hopkins*, 328, 344.

100. Ibid., 339, 341, 343–44; Dwight William Tuttle, *Harry L. Hopkins and Anglo-American-Soviet Relations*, 106.

101. Kimball, *Juggler*, 33.

102. Sherwood, *Roosevelt and Hopkins*, 343, 359; the Secretary of State to the Ambassador in the United Kingdom (Winant), 5 September 1941, *FRUS*, 1941, 1:828–29; Motter, *Persian Corridor*, 21; Dawson, *Decision to Aid Russia*, 178–79; and MacLean, *Joseph E. Davies*, 75.

103. Memorandum from FDR to Wayne Coy, 2 August 1941, folder "Lend-Lease to Russia (1)," box 10, Wayne Coy Papers, FDRL.

104. Memorandum by President Roosevelt to the Secretary of War (Stimson), 30 August 1941, *FRUS*, 1941, 1:826–27.

105. Dawson, *Decision to Aid Russia*, 255.

106. Ibid., 255.

107. Dawson, *Decision to Aid Russia*, 207–10; Herring, *Aid to Russia*, 14–15.

108. Dawson, *Decision to Aid Russia*, 157; Pogue, *George C. Marshall*, 2:49.

109. Dawson, *Decision to Aid Russia*, 211.

110. Stoler, *Allies and Adversaries*, 54–56.

111. Jones, *Roads to Russia*, 57–58.

112. Dawson, *Decision to Aid Russia*, 196.

113. Telegram from Hopkins to Harriman, 20 September 1941, folder "September 1–21, 1941," box 160, W. Averell Harriman Papers, LOC; see also Dawson, *Decision to Aid Russia*, 185–87.

114. Letter from Harry L. Hopkins to John G. Winant, 5 September 1941, folder "Book 4: Harriman-Beaverbrook Mission (folder 1)," box 306, Sherwood Collection, Hopkins Papers.

115. Telegram for the Ambassador from Mr. Hopkins to be communicated to the Prime Minister, 9 September 1941, folder "September 1–21, 1941," box 160, Harriman Papers.

116. Dawson, *Decision to Aid Russia*, 251.

117. Sherwood, *Roosevelt and Hopkins*, 387; Dawson, *Decision to Aid Russia*, 252.

118. Dawson, *Decision to Aid Russia*, 251.

119. W. Averell Harriman and Elie Abel, *Special Envoy*, 84–85.

120. Ibid.

121. Memorandum of Conversation with Mr. Stalin at Meeting with W. A. Harriman and Lord Beaverbrook Tuesday night, 30 September 1941, at the Kremlin, folder "September 28–30, 1941," box 160, Harriman Papers.

122. Ibid.

123. Lord Beaverbrook's notes on third meeting—Mr. Stalin, Mr. Harriman, and Lord Beaverbrook—Tuesday, 30 September 1941, at the Kremlin, folder "September 28–30, 1941," box 160, Harriman Papers; memorandum of comments regarding Ambassadors Steinhardt, Cripps, Oumansky, and Maisky during Third Meeting with Mr. Stalin at the Kremlin, 30 September 1941, folder "September 28–30, 1941," box 160, Harriman Papers.

124. Notes regarding the British and American Ambassadors to Moscow and Lt. General [Mason-] M[a]cFarlane, Chief of the British Military Mission—3 October 1941, folder "October 1–3, 1941," box 160, Harriman Papers.

125. Harriman and Abel, *Special Envoy*, 93.

126. Dawson, *Decision to Aid Russia*, 256.

127. Sherwood, *Roosevelt and Hopkins*, 395.

128. As cited in Sherwood, *Roosevelt and Hopkins*, 395.

129. Ibid., 396.

130. Memorandum of Conversation with Mr. Stalin at Meeting with W. A. Harriman and Lord Beaverbrook Tuesday night, 30 September 1941, at the Kremlin, folder "September 28–30, 1941," box 160, Harriman Papers.

CHAPTER 5: "All Aid to the Hilt": Developing a U.S. Policy Toward the Soviet Union, 1941–1943

1. Robert E. Sherwood, *Roosevelt and Hopkins*, 376–77.

2. Robert Sherwood points out that although Stettinius was officially in charge of

the OLLA, Hopkins still held most of the responsibility for Soviet aid. Sherwood, *Roosevelt and Hopkins,* 376–77.

3. Major-General J. H. Burns to the Adjutant General, United States Army, "Recommendation for Distinguished Service Medal to Colonel Philip R. Faymonville, Ordnance Department (03349)," 20 June 1946, folder "Faymonville," box 140, Harry L. Hopkins Papers, FDRL.

4. Ibid.

5. John Daniel Langer, "Formulation of American Aid Policy," 92.

6. When italicized, *front* refers to a Soviet unit; in roman type, "front" means the point at which opposing forces meet. David M. Glantz, *Barbarossa,* 132.

7. David M. Glantz, *Siege of Leningrad,* 42–57.

8. Glantz, *Barbarossa,* 137–58; David M. Glantz and Jonathan House, *When Titans Clashed,* 78; Alexander Werth, *Russia at War,* 231; and John Erickson, *Road to Stalingrad,* 214, 217.

9. Glantz, *Barbarossa,* 187–89; Erickson, *Road to Stalingrad,* 217; Alexander Werth, *Russia at War,* 231.

10. Glantz and House, *When Titans Clashed,* 80.

11. Glantz, *Barbarossa,* 148–53; Erickson, *Road to Stalingrad,* 218.

12. Erickson, *Road to Stalingrad,* 218; Werth, *Russia at War,* 235.

13. Werth, *Russia at War,* 232, 235.

14. Ibid., 240–41.

15. Ibid., 241.

16. Glantz, *Barbarossa,* 175–77; and Glantz and House, *When Titans Clashed,* 83–85.

17. Erickson, *Road to Stalingrad,* 266.

18. Glantz and House, *When Titans Clashed,* 85; Erickson, *Road to Stalingrad,* 266.

19. Malcolm Mackintosh, *Juggernaut,* 98–101.

20. Ibid., 106–8.

21. Ibid., 108; H. P. Willmott, *Great Crusade,* 163.

22. Waldo Heinrichs, *Threshold of War,* 49.

23. Gerhard L. Weinberg, *World at Arms,* 252–53.

24. Ibid., 254; Heinrichs, *Threshold of War,* 123–25.

25. See Weinberg, *World at Arms,* 254.

26. Ibid., 253.

27. Heinrichs, *Threshold of War,* 134–35.

28. Ibid., 126.

29. Ibid., 139–42.

30. Ibid., 177.

31. Ibid., 180–83.

32. Ibid., 199.

33. Ibid., 201.

34. Ibid., 205–6.

35. Ibid., 213–14.

36. Ibid., 217. Throughout this period, Secretary of State Cordell Hull advocated a firmer policy toward Japan; see James MacGregor Burns, *Roosevelt: The Soldier of Freedom,* 13, 144–45, and 150.

37. Weinberg, *World at Arms,* 260.

38. The idea of United States involvement in World War II assuming elements of a "crusade" is discussed in greater detail in Robert Dallek, *American Style of Foreign Policy,* 125; and Warren F. Kimball, *Juggler,* 17. See also Robert A. Divine's study of the rise of an internationalist movement in the United States during World War II and its crusade to "banish war from the world." Robert A. Divine, *Second Chance,* 5.

39. Lloyd C. Gardner, *Spheres of Influence.*

40. Mark A. Stoler, *Allies and Adversaries,* 102, 123.

41. Willmott, *Great Crusade,* 170–79, 193–96.

42. Stalin's chief aim in his offensive was to destroy or severely damage German Army Group Center and to force German forces to conduct a strategic withdrawal to a "safe" distance from Moscow.

43. "Telegram USSR Ambassador to USA (M. Litvinov) to NKID USSR," 12 March 1942, Union of Soviet Socialist Republics, *Sovetsko-amerikanskie otnosheniia,* 1:155–57.

44. Ibid. See similar accounts in Llewellyn Woodward, *British Foreign Policy,* 5:32, 2:237, 2:239.

45. "Record of Talks with Roosevelt (29 May 1942: Before Dinner)," document 68, Oleg A. Rzheshevsky, *War and Diplomacy,* 2:173–75.

46. Stoler, *Allies and Adversaries,* 74–77; David Carlton, *Churchill and the Soviet Union,* 98–99; Warren F. Kimball, *Forged in War,* 142–45; Russell F. Weigley, *Eisenhower's Lieutenants,* 32–33; and Russell F. Weigley, *American Way of War,* 318–22.

47. Memorandum from FDR to Cordell Hull, 17 January 1942, Franklin D. Roosevelt, *FDR: His Personal Letters,* 2:1273.

48. David Mayers, *Ambassadors and America's Soviet Policy,* 140.

49. Ibid., 139–40.

50. On Roosevelt's perception of the ambassador's role, see John Daniel Langer, "Formulation of American Aid Policy," 133; and Mayers, *Ambassadors and America's Soviet Policy,* 140. On Standley's view of his role in the Soviet Union, see George C. Herring, *Aid to Russia,* 82–84. For Standley's belief that he should "talk turkey," see William H. Standley and Arthur A. Ageton, *Admiral Ambassador to Russia,* 111.

51. See, for example, Hopkins' remark to Stettinius that Standley's "principal job will be handling with Faymonville the supply end in Moscow." Memorandum from Harry L. Hopkins to Stettinius, 13 March 1942, folder 4, "Book 5: Aid to Russia #23," box 309, Hopkins Papers.

52. Standley and Ageton, *Admiral Ambassador to Russia,* 94.

53. Memorandum of Conversation, 5 March 1942, folder 12, box 166, Sumner Welles Papers, FDRL.

54. Ibid.

55. Ibid.

56. Ibid.

57. Ibid., 94–97.

58. Ibid., 117.

59. Ibid., 94–95.

60. Ibid., 117.

61. Ibid., 152–58, 160–63.

62. "The Ambassador to the Soviet Union (Standley) to the Secretary of State," 24 April 1942, *FRUS,* 1942, 3:545–48; and the Ambassador in the Soviet Union (Standley) to the Secretary of State, 26 April 1942, *FRUS,* 1942, 3:548–49.

63. The Ambassador in the Soviet Union (Standley) to the Secretary of State, 5 July 1942, *FRUS,* 1942, 3:606.

64. Ibid.

65. Ibid., 195.

66. The Chargé in the Soviet Union (Thurston) to the Secretary of State, 3 February 1942, *FRUS,* 1942, 3:688–89.

67. The Chargé in the Soviet Union (Thurston) to the Secretary of State, 20 March 1942, *FRUS,* 1942, 3:421–31.

68. Memorandum by the Assistant Chief of the Division of European Affairs (Henderson), 15 July 1942, *FRUS,* 1942, 3:449–50.

69. Memorandum by the Assistant Chief of the Division of European Affairs (Henderson), 18 May 1943, *FRUS,* 1943, 3:528.

70. Memorandum by the Assistant Chief of the Division of European Affairs (Henderson) to the Undersecretary of State (Welles), 9 April 1942, *FRUS,* 1942, 3:435–37.

71. Memorandum by the Assistant Chief of the Division of European Affairs (Henderson), 25 October 1941, *FRUS,* 1941, 1:80.

72. Memorandum by the Assistant Chief of the Division of European Affairs (Henderson) to the Acting Chief of the Division (Atherton), 11 June 1943, *FRUS,* 1943, 3:543–44.

73. The Secretary of State to President Roosevelt, 4 February 1942, *FRUS,* 1942, 3:504–5.

74. "Memorandum: British-Soviet Negotiations Looking Forward to the Conclusion of a Treaty of a Political Character with Particular Reference to Soviet Suggestions that Certain Territories Taken Over by the Soviet Union During the Period September 1, 1939–June 22, 1941, be Recognized as Soviet Territory," 4 February 1942, *FRUS,* 1942, 3:505–12.

75. On Welles' relationship with Roosevelt, see Benjamin Welles, *Sumner Welles;* and Irwin F. Gellman, *Secret Affairs.* On Harry Hopkins' relationship with Roosevelt, see Sherwood, *Roosevelt and Hopkins;* George McJimsey, *Harry Hopkins;* and Dwight William Tuttle, *Harry L. Hopkins and Anglo-American-Soviet Relations.* On Welles' friendship with Berle, see Welles, *Sumner Welles,* 143.

76. Memorandum of Conversation by the Undersecretary of State (Welles), 18 February 1942, *FRUS,* 1942, 3:512–21.

77. Welles' son and biographer is slightly confusing on this issue. On the one hand, Benjamin Welles establishes that Sumner Welles was firmly committed to the Atlantic Charter, even arguing that it was Sumner Welles' "baby." On the other hand, Benjamin Welles argues that his father considered Roosevelt's policy regarding the Anglo-Soviet treaty and postwar frontiers to be dangerous because it postponed the resolution of territorial issues. Benjamin Welles does not establish whether Sumner Welles was against postponement because he thought territorial adjustments wrong, or because it was a delay of the inevitable that would exacerbate Allied relations. Sumner Welles' record of his conversations with Halifax indicate that Welles was against territorial settlements of any kind because they would violate the principles of the Atlantic Charter. In that regard, and as Roosevelt's subsequent conversations with Stalin at Teheran and Yalta indicate, Welles' views were closer to those in the State Department than those in the Oval Office. See Welles, *Sumner Welles*, 308, 330–31.

78. Memorandum by the Assistant Secretary of State (Berle) to the Acting Secretary of State, 3 April 1942, *FRUS*, 1942, 3:539–41.

79. The Undersecretary of State (Welles) to the Assistant Secretary of State (Berle), 4 April 1942, *FRUS*, 1942, 3:541–42.

80. Memorandum of Conversation, by Mr. Elbridge Durbrow of the Division of European Affairs, 22 August 1942, *FRUS*, 1942, 3:628–29.

81. The Ambassador to the Soviet Union (Standley) to the Secretary of State, 3 May 1942. *FRUS*, 1942, 3:551.

82. Standley and Ageton, *Admiral Ambassador to Russia*, 202–3.

83. The Ambassador to the Soviet Union (Standley) to the Secretary of State, 22 July 1942. *FRUS*, 1942, 3:613.

84. Standley and Ageton, *Admiral Ambassador to Russia*, 204–18.

85. Ibid., 203.

86. Ibid., 237.

87. The Chargé in the Soviet Union (Thurston) to the Secretary of State, 5 March 1942, 861.20/535, RG 59, NARA.

88. Memorandum by the Division of European Affairs, 26 March 1942, 861.20/552, RG 59, NARA.

89. The American Ambassador in the Soviet Union (Standley) to the Secretary of State, 861.20/542, RG 59, NARA.

90. Memorandum from Thomas B. McCabe to Harry L. Hopkins, 21 March 1942, folder 4, "Book 5: Aid to Russia #26," box 309, Hopkins Papers.

91. Memorandum from Harry L. Hopkins to Thomas B. McCabe, 24 March 1942, folder 4, "Book 5: Aid to Russia #26," box 309, Hopkins Papers.

92. Ibid., 239.

93. The Ambassador in the Soviet Union (Standley) to the Secretary of State, 7 May 1942. *FRUS*, 1942, 3:555.

94. Standley and Ageton, *Admiral Ambassador to Russia*, 247.

95. Ibid., 246.

96. Ibid., 243.

97. Memorandum by Charles E. Bohlen, 22 October 1942, folder "Memo (CEB), 1942–44," box 4, Lot 34D379, RG 59, NARA.

98. Memorandum from J. H. Burns to Harry L. Hopkins, 30 November 1942, folder 1, box 309, Hopkins Papers.

99. Ibid.

100. Memorandum by J. H. Burns, 9 December 1942, folder 4, box 309, Hopkins Papers; Standley and Ageton, *Admiral Ambassador to Russia*, 314.

101. Standley and Ageton, *Admiral Ambassador to Russia*, 314–15.

102. "Letter from W. H. Standley to Sumner Welles," 2 September 1942, folder 14, "Sta.–Ste., 1942," box 83, Welles Papers.

103. Footnote 5, *FRUS*, 1942, 3:615.

104. President Roosevelt to Mr. Wendell L. Willkie, 2 August 1942, *FRUS*, 1942, 3:615.

105. Standley and Ageton, *Admiral Ambassador to Moscow*, 268.

106. Ibid.

107. Sherwood, *Roosevelt and Hopkins*, 635.

108. Memo by Standley, 24 October 1942, *FRUS*, 1942, 3:647.

109. Standley and Ageton, *Admiral Ambassador to Russia*, 283–84. There is no other written account of this incident.

110. Ibid., 286.

111. Ibid., 293.

112. Ibid., 295.

113. Sherwood, *Roosevelt and Hopkins*, 640.

114. Joseph E. Davies, Diary, 16 October 1942, Joseph E. Davies Papers, the Manuscript Division, Library of Congress.

115. "Conversation with Admiral Standley," 24 October 1942, Davies Papers. These are the rough draft notes for the diary entry of 16 October 1942. Interestingly, in the final draft of the diary entry this line is abridged to, "I replied frankly and did my best to cool him off." In this final entry, Davies continues, "I urged him not to retire and not to press the matter. If he took up the matter at all, he should do so not that it reflected on his 'position' or his personal dignity—that to do so might cause some people to think he was 'little.' . . . I urged him to go back and 'to forget the Willkie incident.'"

116. Memo for Sumner Welles from W. H. Standley, 17 March 1942, box 49, "Russia," President's Secretary's File, FDRL.

117. Joseph E. Davies, Diary, 26 October 1942, Davies Papers.

118. Ibid., Diary, 29 October 1942, Davies Papers.

119. Ibid.

120. Memorandum of Conversation, 5 March 1942, folder 12, box 166, Welles Papers.

121. Ibid.

122. Standley and Ageton, *Admiral Ambassador to Russia*, 333.

123. Quentin Reynolds, *The Curtain Rises*, 86–87.

124. Davies, Diary, 9 March 1943, Davies Papers.

125. Davies, "Memorandum Prepared for the President of Chronological Development of Stalin's Attitude as I Analyzed It," March 1943, Davies Papers.

126. *Congressional Record—Senate,* 9 March 1943, 1701.

127. Ibid., 1702.

128. File 4770, President's Official File, FDRL. See also Ralph B. Levering, *American Opinion and the Russian Alliance,* 107–10.

129. Reynolds, *The Curtain Rises,* 85, 88.

130. *Congressional Record—Senate,* 9 March 1943, 1703.

131. Ibid.

132. Werth, *Russia at War,* 628.

133. Ibid.

134. Davies, Diary, 10 March 1943, Davies Papers.

135. The Ambassador in the Soviet Union (Standley) to the Secretary of State, 11 March 1943. *FRUS,* 1943, 3:636.

136. Ibid.

137. Ibid.

138. Telegram from NKID USSR to Soviet Ambassador in USA (Litvinov), 10 March 1943, Union of Soviet Socialist Republics, *Sovetsko-amerikanskie otnosheniia,* 1:292–93.

139. Memo for Harry Hopkins, 10 August 1943, file "Russia," box 217, Hopkins Papers.

140. In several telegrams to the foreign ministry in Moscow, the Soviet ambassador to the United States described hostility toward the Soviet Union and resistance to the president's policy of no-questions-asked aid among State Department and military officials. See Telegram from Ambassador of USSR in USA (Oumansky) to NKID USSR, 22 June 1941; Telegram from Ambassador of USSR in USA (Oumansky) to NKID USSR, 13 July 1941; and Telegram from Ambassador of USSR in USA (Oumansky) to NKID USSR, 29 July 1941, in Union of Soviet Socialist Republics, *Sovetsko-Amerikanskie otnosheniia,* 1:42–44, 64–66, 77–79.

141. Davies, Diary, 2 October 1943, Davies Papers.

142. Memorandum of Press Conference of March 9, 1943, by the Chief of the Division of Current Information (McDermott), *FRUS,* 1943, 3:628–29.

143. Davies, Diary, 12 March 1943, Davies Papers.

144. The Ambassador in the Soviet Union (Standley) to the Secretary of State, 10 March 1943, *FRUS,* 1943, 3:509–12.

145. The American Ambassador in the Soviet Union (Standley) to the Secretary of State, 18 March 1943, *FRUS,* 1943, 3:513–14.

146. Davies, Diary, 13 March 1943, Davies Papers.

147. Standley and Ageton, *Admiral Ambassador to Russia,* 350.

148. Ibid., 356–57.

149. The American Ambassador in the Soviet Union (Standley) to the Secretary of

State, (undated), folder 2, part 2, box 309, Hopkins Papers; and the American Ambassador in the Soviet Union (Standley) to the Secretary of State, 14 May 1943, folder 4, box 309, Hopkins Papers.

150. The Ambassador in the Soviet Union (Standley) to the Secretary of State, 1 June 1943, folder 4, box 309, Hopkins Papers.

151. Standley and Ageton, *Admiral Ambassador to Russia,* 360.

152. Ibid., 363.

153. Davies, Journal, 20 April 1943, Davies Papers.

154. "Mr. Joseph E. Davies in Moscow, 1943," 17 July 1943, "Subject: Philip R. Faymonville," file 64–HQ–4568, FBI.

155. "Telegram from Standley to the Secretary of State (Section 2)," 22 May 1943, 121.861/159, RG 59, NARA.

156. Ibid.

157. Reynolds, *The Curtain Rises,* 84.

158. Davies, Journal, 24 May 1943, Davies Papers.

159. Davies, "Moscow Atmosphere," Journal, 24 May 1943, Davies Papers. Davies edited his journal, apparently for future publication in memoir form. As a result, there are several drafts of each journal entry in his papers at the Library of Congress.

160. "Mr. Joseph E. Davies in Moscow, 1943," 17 July 1943, "Subject: Philip R. Faymonville," file 64–HQ–4568, FBI.

161. "Letter from Davies to Standley," 25 May 1943, Davies Papers.

162. Standley and Ageton, *Admiral Ambassador to Russia,* 377.

163. "Report of my Secretary on the Standley Letter," 25 May 1943, Davies Papers.

164. Telegram from Standley to Secretary of State, 25 May 1943. 121.861/162, RG 59, NARA.

165. Ibid., section 2.

166. Ibid. This opinion was shared by Quentin Reynolds, who wrote, "We were all frankly embarrassed by the picture." Reynolds, *The Curtain Rises,* 82.

167. Telegram from Standley to the Secretary of State and the President, 29 May 1943. 121.861/165, RG 59, NARA. An amusing and striking example of how the difference in perspective is reflected in documentary sources can be found in a letter from Davies to Roosevelt on the same date: "As to the particular situation I was engaged upon, I believe that the result there of has been completely successful." Davies to President Roosevelt, 29 May 1943, folder "Davies, Joseph E," box 137, Hopkins Papers.

168. Reynolds, *The Curtain Rises,* 80.

169. Letter from Standley to Roosevelt, 3 May 1943, "Russia," box 49, President's Secretary's File. Roosevelt's response accepting the resignation was drafted on 8 June 1943, but there is no date indicating when it was sent. Letter from Roosevelt to Standley, n.d., "Russia," box 49, President's Secretary's File. The time lapse between the date of Standley's resignation and Roosevelt's response is probably because Standley sent his resignation via mail rather than telegraph. It would have taken some time to get to Washington.

170. On Faymonville's earlier respect for the Red Army, see David M. Glantz, "Observing the Soviets." Many observers noted Faymonville's continued optimism. See Harrison Evans Salisbury, *Journey for Our Times*, 150; and "Russian Policy—Domestic and Foreign, Henry Shapiro, Military Intelligence Report," 2 March 1944, MID 072, Policy, USSR, folder 1039, Army Intelligence Project Decimal File, RG 319, NARA.

171. For the Soviet unwillingness to cooperate with Michela because of his anti-Soviet attitude, see Bradley F. Smith, *Sharing Secrets*, 33. Each of Michela's military attaché reports has a section on the front page in which he lists sources.

172. On Faymonville's sources, see David M. Glantz, "Observing the Soviets," 182–83. Glantz also points out that in the 1930s, Faymonville's conclusions were confirmed by the U.S. Army attaché in Riga.

173. Faymonville had long held the opinion that the Soviet Union would be a useful counterweight to Japan. See Chapter 2. Faymonville's effort to be "objective" and the soundness of his military observations were noted by the aircraft designer Alexander Yakovlev, and historians Alfred Vagts and Dimitri Fedotoff White. See James S. Herndon and Joseph O. Baylen, "Col. Philip R. Faymonville," 503–5. Quentin Reynolds was impressed by Faymonville, his relationship with Soviet authorities, and the accuracy of his observations. Reynolds notes, "I saw him as frequently as possible and took my line from him." See Quentin Reynolds, *Only the Stars*, 132–33.

174. Michela (Kuibychev) to Milid, no. 93, 3 November 1941, folder 2, From: Russia-Moscow. Incoming (8-15-41) through (11-8-41), RG 319, NARA.

175. Michela (Kuibychev) to Milid, no. 102, 10 November 1941, folder 3, From: Russia-Moscow. Incoming (11-10-41) through (12-30-41), RG 319, NARA.

176. Michela (Kuibychev) to Milid, no. 129, 21 December 1941, folder 3, From: Russia-Moscow. Incoming (11-10-41) through (12-30-41), RG 319, NARA.

177. Michela (Kuibychev) to Milid, no. 7, 16 January 1942, folder 1, From: Russia-Kouibychev [*sic*]. Incoming (1-1-42) through (7-9-42), RG 319, NARA; Memorandum from the Chief of Staff, I.B. 173, 17 February 1942, MID 319.1 Situation, USSR, folder 1040, Army Intelligence Project Decimal File, RG 319, NARA.

178. "Military Attaché (Moscow) Report no. 2036," 10 March 1942, MID 370.2 USSR, folder 1045, Army Intelligence Project Decimal File, RG 319, NARA.

179. Ibid.

180. Memorandum for the Assistant Chief of Staff, OPD, 20 July 1942, MID 319.1 Situation, USSR, Army Intelligence Project Decimal File, RG 319, NARA.

181. Glantz and House, *When Titans Clashed*, 98–129.

182. Memorandum for the Assistant Chief of Staff, OPD, 20 July 1942, MID 319.1 Situation, USSR, Army Intelligence Project Decimal File, RG 319, NARA.

183. Glantz and House, *When Titans Clashed*, 302–3.

184. Michela (Moscow) to Milid, no. 12, 18 January 1943, folder 6, From: Russia-Moscow. Incoming (1-2-43) through (3-3-43), RG 319, NARA.

185. See also Michela's "Military Attaché Report USSR, No. 2337," 3 May 1943, MID 350.05 USSR, Army Intelligence Project Decimal File, RG 319, NARA; "Michela (Moscow) to Milid," no. 207, 24 May 1943, folder 8, From: Russia-Moscow. Incoming

(4-13-43) through (6-1-43), RG 319, NARA. See David M. Glantz and Jonathan M. House, *Battle of Kursk.*

186. "Military Attaché Report USSR, no. 2016," 15 January 1942, MID 350.05 USSR, Army Intelligence Project Decimal File, RG 319, NARA.

187. Ibid.

188. "Military Attaché Report USSR, no. 2099," 21 May 1942, MID 350.05 USSR, Army Intelligence Project Decimal File, RG 319, NARA.

189. "Military Attaché Report USSR, no. 2303," 18 February 1943, MID 350.05 USSR, Army Intelligence Project Decimal File, RG 319, NARA.

190. Ibid.

191. Davies, Diary, 24 April 1943, Davies Papers.

192. "Dreyfus of Teheran," 12 May 1943, Davies Papers.

193. Memo for Harry Hopkins, 10 August 1943, "Russia," box 217, Hopkins Papers.

194. Davies, Journal, 24 May 1943, Davies Papers.

195. See Yeaton (Moscow) to Milid, no. 242, 11 July 1941; Yeaton (Moscow) to Milid, no. 248, 23 July 1941, folder 1, From: Russia-Moscow. Incoming (2-8-40) through (8-1-41); Yeaton (Moscow) to Milid, no. 17, 27 August 1941; Yeaton (Moscow) to Milid, no. 19, 27 August 1941; Yeaton (Moscow) to Milid, no. 66, 6 October 1941, folder 2, From: Russia-Moscow. Incoming (8-5-41) through (11-8-41); Michela (Kouibyshev) to Milid, no. 132, 25 December 1941, folder 3, From: Russia-Moscow. Incoming (11-10-41) through (12-30-41); Michela (Kouibychev) to Milid., no. 1-10, folder 1, From: Russia-Kouibychev. Incoming (1-1-42) through (7-9-42), RG 319, NARA.

196. Michela (Kouibychev) to G-2, no. 12, 28 January 1942, folder 1, From: Russia-Kouibychev. Incoming (1-1-42) through (7-9-42), RG 319, NARA.

197. Miles to Michela, folder 3, To: Russia-Moscow. Outgoing (11-26-41) through (3-30-42), RG 319, NARA; Lee to Michela, folder 3, To: Russia-Moscow. Outgoing (11-26-41) through (3-30-42), RG 319, NARA.

198. Michela (Kouibychev) to G-2, no. 29, 3 March 1942, folder 1, From: Russia-Kouibychev. Incoming (1-1-42) through (7-9-42), RG 319, NARA.

199. Lee to Michela, no. 153, folder 3, To: Russia-Moscow. Outgoing (11-26-41) through (3-30-42), RG 319, NARA.

200. Michela to Chief of Military Intelligence Service, 31 March 1942, MID 092. USSR, Army Intelligence Project Decimal File, RG 319, NARA.

201. Ibid.

202. Michela to Chief, Military Intelligence Service, 30 June 1942, MID 335.11 M/A USSR, Army Intelligence Project Decimal File, RG 319, NARA.

203. Michela to Chief, Military Intelligence Service, 30 September 1942, MID 092. USSR, Army Intelligence Project Decimal File, RG 319, NARA.

204. Memorandum from Michela to Major General Geo. V. Strong, 20 October 1942, MID 042.221 M/A USSR, Army Intelligence Project Decimal File, RG 319, NARA.

205. Michela (Moscow) to Milid, no. 100, 12 March 1943, folder 7, From: Russia-Moscow. Incoming (3-4-43) through (4-11-43), RG 319, NARA.

206. Michela (Moscow) to Milid, no. 118, 22 March 1943, folder 7, From: Russia-Moscow. Incoming (3-4-43) through (4-11-43), RG 319, NARA.

207. Michela (Moscow) to Milid, no. 168, 23 April 1942, folder 8, From: Russia-Moscow. Incoming (4-13-43) through (6-1-43), RG 319, NARA.

208. Michela (Moscow) to Milid, no. 192, 12 May 1943, folder 8, From: Russia-Moscow. Incoming (4-13-43) through (6-1-43), RG 319, NARA.

209. Ibid.

210. Military Intelligence Service to Michela (Moscow), no. 446, 18 March 1943, folder 7, To: Russia-Moscow. Outgoing (2-6-43) through (3-21-43), RG 319, NARA.

211. Michela (Moscow) to Milid, no. 198, 17 May 1943, folder 8, From: Russia-Moscow. Incoming (4-13-43) through (6-1-43), RG 319, NARA.

212. Standley and Ageton, *Admiral Ambassador to Russia,* 389.

213. Faymonville's FBI file contains several fragmentary documents. Most of the documents have large segments blacked out for reasons of national security. One document is a telegram from somebody in Moscow to somebody in Washington. The author of the message wrote: "Suggest check of Barcuse personnel file in both State and War Departments for possible leads. . . . I believe General Michela well satisfied. Every safe step taken to secure evidence which I personally doubt was ever there." Two pages further into the file, there is a telegram from Hoover in which he writes: "Reference your message March eighteen last concerning check of Barcuse personnel file at State and War Departments." "Philip R. Faymonville," file 64-HQ-4568, FBI.

214. Memorandum from D. M. Ladd to E. A. Tamm, 19 September 1942, "Philip R. Faymonville," file 64-HQ-4568, FBI.

215. "Philip R. Faymonville," SF file 62-2349, 8-23-43, "Philip R. Faymonville," file 64-HQ-4568, FBI.

216. "Mr. Joseph Davies in Moscow, 1943," 17 July 1943, "Philip R. Faymonville," file 64-HQ-4568, FBI.

217. Memorandum for Mr. Burton, 8 April 1943, "Philip R. Faymonville," file 64-HQ-4568, FBI.

218. Ibid.

219. "Hoover to [blacked out]," n.d., "Philip R. Faymonville," file 64-HQ-4568, FBI.

220. "The Influence of Brigadier General Philip R. Faymonville on Soviet-American Military Relations," 26 July 1943. The Sydney P. Spalding Papers, United States Army, Military History Institute.

221. Ibid.

222. Ibid.

223. Memorandum for the Chief of Staff, 26 July 1943, Spalding Papers.

224. Davies, Diary, 24 September 1943 and 25 September 1943, Davies Papers.

225. Memo for Hopkins, "Faymonville, Philip R." file, box 140, Hopkins Papers.

226. Davies, Diary, 2 October 1943, Davies Papers.

227. "U.S. to Coordinate Services in Russia," *New York Times,* 19 October 1943.

228. "General Is Reduced After Duty in Soviet," *New York Times,* 18 November 1943.

229. Willmott, *Great Crusade,* 180–82.

230. Glantz and House, *When Titans Clashed,* 108–25; and Erickson, *Road to Stalingrad,* 343–93.

231. Glantz and House, *When Titans Clashed,* 129–148; and John Erickson, *Road to Berlin,* 1–44.

232. See Glantz and House, *When Titans Clashed,* 160–76; Glantz and House, *Battle of Kursk;* and John Erickson, *Road to Berlin,* 87–135.

233. See Willmott, *Great Crusade,* 344–47.

234. Ibid., 317–23.

CHAPTER 6: Forging Peace: Relations Between the United States and the Soviet Union, 1943–1945

1. John Daniel Langer, "Formulation of American Aid Policy," 182–210; George McJimsey, *Harry Hopkins,* 292–93; H. W. Brands, *Inside the Cold War,* ix; George C. Herring, *Aid to Russia,* 123–25; and Robert Huhn Jones, *Roads to Russia,* 171.

2. The Acting Secretary of State to the Chargé in the Soviet Union (Hamilton), 1 October 1943, *FRUS,* 1943, 3:704–5.

3. For a discussion of the development of Harriman's attitude toward the Soviet Union, see Herring, *Aid to Russia,* 109–12, 128, 130–32.

4. Raymond H. Dawson, *Decision to Aid Russia,* 251.

5. "Remarks on Russia," 22 January 1942, 373H Harriman Mission, USSR Section, Division of European Affairs, RG 59, NARA.

6. Ibid.

7. See W. Averell Harriman and Elie Abel, *Special Envoy,* 253.

8. Personal and Secret for Hopkins from Harriman, 22 February 1943, folder 2, part 1, book 5: Aid to Russia, box 309, Harry L. Hopkins Papers, Franklin D. Roosevelt Library (hereafter FDRL).

9. Letter from W. A. Harriman to Edward R. Stettinius, 16 April 1943, folder 2, part 2, book 5: Aid to Russia, Hopkins Papers.

10. Harriman and Abel, *Special Envoy,* 3, 12–14.

11. See, for example, Harriman's letter to Hopkins in the wake of Standley's March 1943 press conference. Ibid., 198.

12. Ibid., 206.

13. Ibid., 226–27.

14. The President's Personal Representative (Harriman) to the President, 5 July 1943, *Foreign Relations of the United States: Diplomatic Papers. The Conferences at Cairo and Tehran, 1943* (hereafter *FRUS: Cairo and Tehran*), 13–15.

15. Adolf A. Berle, *Navigating the Rapids,* 446.

16. Harriman and Abel, *Special Envoy,* 219–220, 224.

17. Ibid., 279.

18. Ibid., 252.

19. Ibid., 252–53.

20. John R. Deane, *Strange Alliance*, 3.

21. Ibid., 90–91.

22. H. P. Willmott, *Great Crusade*, 314–40, 393–413, 422–26, 456–67.

23. Ibid., 353–63, 430–36, and 445–47; and Russell F. Weigley, *Eisenhower's Lieutenants*.

24. The Red Army's Iassy offensive of May 1944 is covered by David M. Glantz, *Forgotten Battles*, 45–46; F. M. von Senger und Etterlin, *Gegenschlag*, 110–40.

25. David M. Glantz and Jonathan M. House, *When Titans Clashed*, 192–94.

26. Stalin ordered the Red Army to launch the Belorussian offensive on 23 June, at least in part to support Allied operations in Normandy. Glantz and House, *When Titans Clashed*, 195–203.

27. Ibid., 179–276.

28. Soviet military literature records that Stalin halted his offensive on Berlin on 2 February. Recent archival releases, however, indicate that in late January, Stalin did indeed order an advance on Berlin only to order a halt in the operation on or about 8 February because the Big Three were meeting at Yalta. Although existing Soviet accounts claim that the halt was due to the necessity to defend the advancing force's open flanks, consolidate Red Army gains, and permit necessary refitting and replenishment of forces, subsequent Soviet military actions indicate the possibility that the halt was a deliberate measure designed to allow the Soviet Stavka to shift its offensive efforts southward toward Vienna. On 16 April 1945, three days after Vienna fell to the Red Army, the Red Army commenced its final assault on Berlin. Diane Shaver Clemens discusses this issue in her work on Yalta. See Diane Shaver Clemens, *Yalta*, 85–95. For the recent archival findings, see Vladimir Antonovich Zolotarev, *Velikaia Otechestvennaia: Bitva za Berlin*, 56–64.

29. For the orders and directives that pertained to this and other Red Army offensive operations in 1945, see Vladimir Antonovich Zolotarev, *Velikaia Otechestvennaia: Stavka VGK*.

30. Robert Service, *History of Twentieth-Century Russia*, 156–59, 177–78.

31. That the security of the Soviet state in the postwar world is a consistent theme in Soviet wartime foreign policy is evident in a series of documents published in 1995. See "Zaniat'sia podgotovkoi budushchego mira."

32. Vojtech Mastny, *Cold War and Soviet Insecurity*, 12.

33. Martin H. Folly, "Forging the Grand Alliance."

34. "Bohlen Minutes: Roosevelt-Stalin Meeting, 29 November 1943," *FRUS: Cairo and Tehran*, 529–33.

35. "Bohlen Minutes: Third Plenary Meeting, 6 February 1945, 4 p.m.," *Foreign Relations of the United States: The Conferences at Malta and Yalta, 1945* (hereafter *FRUS: Malta and Yalta*), 669.

36. Mastny, *Cold War and Soviet Insecurity*, 15, 20.

37. Ibid., 21. See also Vladislav Zubok and Constantine Pleshakov, *Inside the Kremlin's Cold War*, 6–7, 27.

38. "Maisky's memo," 11 January 1944, Archive of the Foreign Policy of the Russian Federation (hereafter AVPRF), f. 6, op. 6, d. 11.14, 1–40, as cited in Vladimir O. Pechatnov, "The Big Three After World War II," 2–6.

39. Ibid., 6.

40. Ibid., 5.

41. "On the Question of Soviet-American Relations," 14 July 1944, AVP RF, f. 6, op. 6, d. 703, p. 17, l. 47, as cited in Pechatnov, "The Big Three After World War II," 9.

42. "On the Relationship with the USA," 10 January 1945, AVP RF, f. 6, op. 7, d. 173, p. 17, ll. 49, 50 as cited in Pechatnov, "The Big Three After World War II," 11.

43. "F. Roosevelt to J. V. Stalin," 5 May 1943, document 83, Union of Soviet Socialist Republics, Ministry of Foreign Affairs, *Correspondence,* 2:63–64; "J. V. Stalin to F. Roosevelt," 26 May 1943, no. 88, ibid., 2:66; and Elizabeth Kimball MacLean, *Joseph E. Davies,* 104.

44. Richard M. Leighton and Robert W. Coakley, *Global Logistics and Strategy,* 557–60, 564–73, 583–86, 589–90; and T. H. Vail Motter, *Persian Corridor,* 177–80.

45. Although the decisions reached in January 1943 at the Casablanca Conference between the United States and Great Britain meant that the second front in northern France would be delayed until 1944, Churchill told Stalin that the United Kingdom and the United States were still "pushing preparation to the limit of our resources for a cross-Channel operation in August [1943]." See "Most Secret and Personal Message from the Prime Minister, Mr. Winston Churchill, to M. Stalin," received on 12 February 1943, no. 112, Union of Soviet Socialist Republics, Ministry of Foreign Affairs, *Correspondence,* 1:93–94. Roosevelt and Stalin also discussed the postponement of the second front in their correspondence. See "From President Roosevelt to Mr. Stalin (Personal and Most Secret)," received on 4 June 1943, no. 90, ibid., 2:67–69; and "Personal and Secret Message from Premier J. V. Stalin to the President, Mr. Roosevelt," 11 June 1943, no. 92, ibid., 2:70–71. For more discussion of the exchange over the second front, see McJimsey, *Harry Hopkins,* 294; MacLean, *Joseph E. Davies,* 113–16; Mark A. Stoler, *Politics of the Second Front,* 14, 104; Mark A. Stoler, *Allies and Adversaries,* 78–79, 86–87; Leighton and Coakley, *Global Logistics and Strategy,* 564; and Maurice Matloff, *Strategic Planning,* 13–14, 21–27.

46. "Personal and Secret Message from Premier J. V. Stalin to the Prime Minister, Mr. W. Churchill and the President, Mr. F. D. Roosevelt," 24 August 1943, no. 105, Ministry of Foreign Affairs of the USSR, *Correspondence,* 2:85–86.

47. "Secret and Personal from Marshal Stalin to the President," 8 November 1943, no. 134, ibid., 104–5.

48. "Bohlen Minutes: Roosevelt-Stalin Meeting," 28 November 1943, *FRUS: Cairo and Tehran,* 482–86. A complete discussion and analysis of the Teheran Conference can be found in Keith Eubank, *Summit at Teheran;* and Paul D. Mayle, *Eureka Summit.*

49. Bohlen Minutes: Roosevelt-Stalin Meeting, 28 November 1943, *FRUS: Cairo and Tehran,* 482–86; Bohlen Minutes: Roosevelt-Stalin Meeting, 29 November 1943, ibid., 529–33; Bohlen Minutes: Roosevelt-Stalin Meeting, 1 December 1943, ibid., 594–96; and Bohlen Minutes: 1st Plenary Meeting, 28 November 1943, ibid., 487–97.

50. Bohlen Minutes: Roosevelt-Stalin Meeting, 1 December 1943, ibid., 594–96; Union of Soviet Socialist Republics, *Sovetskii Soiuz na mezhdunarodnykh konferentsiiakh*, 2:168–70.

51. See Telegram from Soviet Ambassador in U.S. (Litvinov) to People's Commissariat for Foreign Affairs (NKID) of the Union of Soviet Socialist Republics (USSR), 5 May 1943, Ministerstvo Inostrannykh Del, SSSR., *Sovetsko-Amerikanskie Otnosheniia Vo Vremia Velikoi Otechestvennoi Voiny, 1941–1945: Dokumenty i materialy*, vol. 1, 1941–43, 314–15; Telegram from Chargé d'Affaires USSR in USA (Gromyko) to NKID USSR, 19 July 1943, ibid., 351–52.

52. See, for example, John Lewis Gaddis, *The United States and the Origins of the Cold War, 1941–1947*, 173. The entire "realist" school of U.S. diplomatic historians has made similar complaints about Roosevelt's foreign policy.

53. The phrase "got along fine" is taken from Roosevelt's 24 December 1943 fireside chat. See "Christmas Eve Fireside Chat on International Conference," 24 December 1943, Franklin D. Roosevelt, *Public Papers and Addresses*, 12:558. Roosevelt discussed his shared goal with Stalin at a press conference on 17 December 1943. See "Press Conference," 17 December 1943, ibid., 550.

54. For a discussion of Soviet actions and policy in eastern Europe, see Vojtech Mastny, *Russia's Road to the Cold War*, 195–212.

55. The literature on the development of Polish-Soviet relations during the war is extensive and polemical. For the analyses of some of the London Poles, see Stanislaw Mikolajczyk, *Rape of Poland;* and Jan M. Ciechanowski, *Warsaw Rising*. Gabriel Kolko offers a very different interpretation of Soviet actions in Poland, even accepting Soviet claims that the Germans murdered the Poles at Katyn. See Gabriel Kolko, *Politics of War*. For a more balanced interpretation, see Vojtech Mastny, *Russia's Road to the Cold War*.

56. Stalin ordered the First Belorussian *Front's* Second Tank Army to advance north-ward from the Magnushev bridgehead. The army was commanded by its deputy commander, Major General A. I. Radzievsky, since its commander, Lieutenant General S. I. Bogdanov, had been wounded in the fighting for Lublin. Between 1 and 5 August, German counterattacks decimated two of the tank army's three mobile corps. See Glantz and House, *When Titans Clashed*, 211–13.

57. Ibid., 213–14.

58. Ciechanowski, *Warsaw Rising;* Glantz and House, *When Titans Clashed*, 210–15; and John Erickson, *Road to Berlin*, 230–90.

59. Erickson, *Road to Berlin*, 282–90.

60. Glantz and House, *When Titans Clashed*, 213–14; and Erickson, *Road to Berlin*, 230–90.

61. Clemens summarizes these discussions in her work on Yalta. See Clemens, *Yalta*, 44–58.

62. This conference is analyzed in detail in Clemens, *Yalta*.

63. "Agreement Regarding Entry of the Soviet Union into the War Against Japan," 11 February 1945, *FRUS: Malta and Yalta*, 984.

64. "Protocol of Proceedings," 11 February 1945, ibid., 975–82.

65. "Communiqué Issued at the End of the Conference," 11 February 1945, ibid., 968–75.

66. At the crossroads between the end of World War II and the beginning of the cold war, Yalta is a subject of continued virulent controversy. Some historians consider that at Yalta, Roosevelt was duped by Stalin. Others believe that Yalta was a crime— a conference at which Roosevelt deliberately sold out eastern Europe to the Soviet Union. Revisionist historians argue that, in fact, Roosevelt took advantage of Soviet goodwill and, indeed, compromised far less than Stalin at this conference. The common denominator in these studies is that Yalta is viewed as an opening gambit in the subsequent deterioration in Soviet–United States relations. In contrast, Warren Kimball argues that the Yalta Conference has become mythical because most consider it outside its wartime context. Kimball points out that "in most ways Yalta was a fulfillment of what had already been worked out. . . . But the Yalta 'myth' became, like the Versailles Treaty and World War I, a misleading symbol of what might have been or rather, what critics wish had been." Kimball, *Forged in War,* 317.

67. "Protocol of Proceedings," 11 February 1945, *FRUS: Malta and Yalta,* 975–82.

68. William D. Leahy, *I Was There,* 315–16.

69. "Personal and Top Secret for Marshal Stalin from President Roosevelt," received 24 March 1945, document no. 281, Ministry of Foreign Affairs of the USSR, *Correspondence,* 2:198–99; "Personal and Secret from Premier J. V. Stalin to the President, Mr. F. Roosevelt," sent 29 March 1945, document no. 283, ibid., 200–201; "Personal and Secret for Marshal Stalin from President Roosevelt," received on 1 April 1945, document no. 285, ibid., 204–5; "Personal, Most Secret, from Marshal J. V. Stalin to the President, Mr. Roosevelt," sent 3 April 1945, document no. 286, ibid., 205–6; "Personal and Top Secret for Marshal Stalin from President Roosevelt," received on 5 April 1945, document no. 287, ibid., 207–8; "Personal and Secret from Premier J. V. Stalin to the President, Mr. F. Roosevelt," sent 7 April 1945, document no. 288, ibid., 208–10.

70. "Personal and Top Secret for Marshal Stalin from President Roosevelt," received on 13 April 1945, document no. 290, ibid., 214.

71. "Personal and Secret for Marshal Stalin from President Roosevelt," received 4 March 1945, document no. 276, ibid., 194; "Personal and Secret from Premier J. V. Stalin to the President, Mr. F. Roosevelt," sent 5 March 1945, document no. 277, ibid., 194–95; "Personal and Secret for Marshal Stalin from President Roosevelt," received 18 March 1945, document no. 278, ibid., 195–96; "Personal and Secret from Premier J. V. Stalin to the President, Mr. F. Roosevelt," sent 22 March 1945, document no. 279, ibid., 196–97.

72. "Top Secret and Personal from the President for the Prime Minister," 11 March 1945, document R-714, Warren F. Kimball, *Churchill and Roosevelt,* 3:561–62.

73. See, for example, the Ambassador in the Soviet Union (Harriman) to the Secretary of State, 25 March 1945, *FRUS,* 1945, 5:180–82.

74. "Personal and Top Secret for Marshal Stalin from President Roosevelt,"

received on 1 April 1945, document no. 284, Ministry of Foreign Affairs of the USSR, *Correspondence,* 2:201–4.

75. Kimball, *Churchill and Roosevelt,* 3:564, 567–68.

76. "Top Secret and Personal from the President to the Prime Minister," 6 April 1945, document R-736, ibid., 617.

77. "Top Secret and Personal from the President to the Prime Minister," 11 April 1945, document R-742, ibid., 630.

78. Memorandum on Embassy Staff, Moscow, 1 December 1943, box 139, Hopkins Papers.

79. Harriman and Abel, *Special Envoy,* 229.

80. Frederic L. Propas, "Creating a Hard Line," 216–17, 222.

81. Thomas R. Maddux, "American Diplomats," 477–83, 485. In a later article, Maddux discusses the negative impact the Soviet experts' perspective had on their analyses of Soviet diplomacy. See Thomas R. Maddux, "Watching Stalin Maneuver."

82. David Mayers explicitly links Kennan's experience in Moscow in the 1930s with his wartime argument that the United States could not form a partnership with the Soviet Union. See David Mayers, "George Kennan and the Soviet Union," 547.

83. Langer, "Formulation of American Aid Policy," 183; and Charles E. Bohlen, *Witness to History,* 125.

84. Bohlen, *Witness to History,* 125.

85. Ibid., 153.

86. Ibid., 177.

87. Ibid., 207.

88. George F. Kennan, *Memoirs,* 180.

89. For an outstanding study of the development of Kennan's attitude and his influence on Harriman, see David Mayers, *George Kennan and the Dilemmas of U.S. Foreign Policy.* See also Walter L. Hixson, *George F. Kennan.*

90. Kennan, *Memoirs,* 224–25.

91. Ibid., 521.

92. Ibid., 528.

93. Letter from Kennan to Bohlen, 26 January 1945, folder "Personal Correspondence, 1944–46," box 1, Lot 74D379 (Bohlen), RG 59, NARA.

94. Kennan, *Memoirs,* 532–46. In his memoirs, Kennan acknowledged that this memorandum contained the "basic elements" of his containment doctrine, and he pointed out that his views were shaped by his wartime experiences (247, 251).

95. Harriman makes this observation in his memoirs. Harriman and Abel, *Special Envoy,* 278.

96. "Christmas Eve Fireside Chat on International Conference," 24 December 1943, Franklin D. Roosevelt, *Public Papers and Addresses,* 12:558.

97. Bohlen, *Witness to History,* 153.

98. Harriman and Abel, *Special Envoy,* 291.

99. Ibid., 309.

100. Ibid., 317.

101. The Ambassador in the Soviet Union (Harriman) to the Secretary of State, 11 January 1944, *FRUS,* 1944, 3:1223–24; the Ambassador in the Soviet Union (Harriman) to the Secretary of State,t 18 January 1944, ibid., 1230–32; the Ambassador in the Soviet Union (Harriman) to the Secretary of State, 21 January 1944, ibid., 1232–33; the Ambassador in the Soviet Union (Harriman) to the Secretary of State, 12 June 1944, ibid., 1282–83; and the Ambassador in the Soviet Union (Harriman) to the Secretary of State, 11 August 1944, ibid., 1311–13.

102. The Ambassador in the Soviet Union (Harriman) to the Secretary of State, 15 August 1944, ibid., 1376, 1377. Andrei Vyshinski was the First Assistant People's Commissar for Foreign Affairs of the Soviet Union. Harriman had met with him in Molotov's absence.

103. The Ambassador in the Soviet Union (Harriman) to the Secretary of State, 9 January 1944, *FRUS,* 1944, 4:1036–37; the Ambassador in the Soviet Union (Harriman) to the Chairman of the President's Soviet Protocol Committee (Hopkins), 13 February 1944, ibid., 1052–53; the Ambassador in the Soviet Union (Harriman) to the Secretary of State, 14 February 1944, ibid., 1054–55; the Ambassador in the Soviet Union (Harriman) to the Secretary of State, 13 March 1944, ibid., 951.

104. The Ambassador in the Soviet Union (Harriman) to the Secretary of State, 21 January 1944, *FRUS,* 1944, 3:1232–33.

105. The Ambassador in the Soviet Union (Harriman) to Mr. Harry L. Hopkins, Special Assistant to President Roosevelt, 10 September 1944, *FRUS,* 1944, 4:988–90.

106. The Ambassador in the Soviet Union (Harriman) to the Secretary of State, 3 September 1944, ibid., 1129–30. The matter Harriman specifically referred to in this cable was Soviet unwillingness to allow U.S. trucks to pass through to China.

107. Letter from A. Clark-Kerr to Sir R. Stafford Cripps, 3 June 1943, F.O. 800/301, Public Record Office (hereafter PRO), Kew, United Kingdom.

108. Deane, *Strange Alliance,* 50–62. A more detailed account of United States–Soviet collaboration in the intelligence field is in Bradley F. Smith, *Sharing Secrets.*

109. Deane, *Strange Alliance,* 107; Thomas A. Julian, "Operations at the Margin," 631–32; Mark Joseph Conversino, "Operation Frantic," v.

110. R. L. Walsh, "Final Report: Russian Shuttle Bombing Project of 1944, (?)" typewritten report (carbon copy), p. 2, R. L. Walsh Papers, United States Army Military History Institute, Carlisle Barracks, Pa. (hereafter USA MHI).

111. Ibid., 4. See also Wellington Alexander Samouce, "I *Do* Understand the Russians," Wellington Alexander Samouce Papers, USA MHI, 15; Deane, *Strange Alliance,* 114.

112. Samouce, "I *Do* Understand the Russians," 90. Deane assumes this tone of blame (tempered by forgiveness) as well; Deane, *Strange Alliance,* 122.

113. A. S. Orlov, "Na aerodromakh Ukrainy," 220–23.

114. Mark J. Conversino, *Fighting with the Soviets,* 91–92.

115. Ibid., 92–93.

116. See Conversino, "Operation Frantic," vi; and Deane, *Strange Alliance,* 123–24.

This behavior ranged from affairs with local women to smuggling defectors out on U.S. Army Air Forces flights.

117. R. L. Walsh, "Personal Report of Russian Assignment—June 1944 to October 15, 1944," 19 October 1944, typewritten report (carbon copy), p. 3, Walsh Papers.

118. Walsh, "Final Report. Russian Shuttle Bombing Project of 1944," 4–7.

119. *FRUS: Malta and Yalta 1945*, 758, 836.

120. G. Patrick March, "Yanks in Siberia," 336.

121. Deane, *Strange Alliance*, 195–96.

122. Ministry of Foreign Affairs of the USSR, *Correspondence*, 2:194.

123. Ibid., 195.

124. Ibid., 196.

125. Ibid., 196–97.

126. For details about this incident, which involved the killing of Soviet Lieutenant General G. P. Kotov, the commander of the Red Army's Sixth Guards Rifle Corps, and the subsequent Soviet shooting down of at least one U.S. aircraft, see David M. Glantz and Aleksandr A. Maslov, "How and Why Did the Americans Kill Soviet General Kotov," 142–71.

127. Deane, *Strange Alliance*, 96–97.

128. "For Joint Chiefs of Staff from Deane," 17 January 1944, folder 4, box 176, Hopkins Papers.

129. Deane, *Strange Alliance*, 255.

130. Deane to Marshall, 2 December 1944, "Russia, 1942–1945," box 5, President's Secretary's File, FDRL.

131. Stoler, *Allies and Adversaries*, 182, 184.

132. Ibid., 213.

133. Ibid., 219. A summary of the Joint Intelligence Committee report can be found at "Joint Chiefs of Staff, Memorandum for Information No. 374," 2 February 1945, United States, Joint Chiefs of Staff, *Records of the Joint Chiefs of Staff*.

134. Edward R. Stettinius Jr., *Roosevelt and the Russians*, 85–87.

135. Harriman describes his efforts to implement the Yalta agreements in his memoirs. See Harriman and Abel, *Special Envoy*, 418–31. Bohlen also discusses his interpretation of efforts to implement Yalta agreements in his memoirs. See Bohlen, *Witness to History*, 201–2, 207.

136. *FRUS*, 1945, vol. 5, contains many telegrams from Harriman outlining these difficulties. A useful summary of all of this material is in Harriman's memoirs. See Harriman and Abel, *Special Envoy*, 426–31.

137. John Lewis Gaddis, *Russia, the Soviet Union and the United States*, 168–69.

138. Memorandum of Conversation, by Mr. Charles E. Bohlen, Assistant to the Secretary of State, 20 April 1945, *FRUS*, 1945, 5:231–34. See also Diane S. Clemens, "Averell Harriman, John Deane"; Deborah Welch Larson, *Origins of Containment*, 121–25; Walter Isaacson and Evan Thomas, *Wise Men*, 255–68.

139. Memorandum by Mr. Charles E. Bohlen, Assistant to the Secretary of State, of

a Meeting at the White House, 23 April 1945, 2 PM, *FRUS,* 1945, 5:252–55. See also Herring, *Aid to Russia,* 194–215, 287–90; Mayers, *Ambassadors and America's Soviet Policy,* 159; and Gaddis, *The United States and the Origins of the Cold War,* 200–204. Soviet historians have noted this as well. See Gleb Tsvetkov, *Politika SShA v otnoshenii SSSR nakanune Vtoroi Mirovoi Voiny,* 187; and V. L. Israelian, *Diplomaticheskaia istoriia Velikoi Otechestvennoi Voiny,* 320.

140. McJimsey, *Harry Hopkins,* 374, 377–80; and MacLean, *Joseph E. Davies,* 134–73.

CHAPTER 7: Conclusions

1. Clemens summarizes the transformation in U.S. policy from cooperation to confrontation. See Diane S. Clemens, "Averell Harriman, John Deane." More recently, Mark A. Stoler has examined the evolution of U.S. Joint Chiefs of Staff attitudes toward the Soviet Union. Stoler argues that the Joint Chiefs did not abandon cooperation as quickly as the U.S. embassy in Moscow or the State Department did, but by early 1946 the Joint Chiefs were fully converted to the view of the Soviet Union as an adversary. See Mark A. Stoler, "Allies or Adversaries?" 145–65.

2. For a useful discussion of the historiography of the origins of the cold war, see Howard Jones and Randall B. Woods, "Origins of the Cold War," 234–69. On public opinion, see Ralph B. Levering, *American Opinion and the Russian Alliance.* The classic statement of the global open-door element in U.S. foreign policy is William Appleman Williams, *Tragedy of American Diplomacy,* new ed. (1988). See also Walter LaFeber, *America, Russia, and the Cold War.* On Soviet actions, see Vojtech Mastny, *Russia's Road to the Cold War.*

3. W. Averell Harriman and Elie Abel, *Special Envoy,* 553.

4. Charles E. Bohlen, *Witness to History,* 334, and 244–73.

5. George F. Kennan, *Memoirs,* 325–26.

6. Ibid., 313–15.

7. Bradley F. Smith, *Sharing Secrets,* 166; John Daniel Langer, "Red General," 220; and Westbrook Pegler, "Fair Enough," *Washington Times-Herald,* n.d., in "Philip R. Faymonville," file 64-HQ-4568, FBI.

8. Robert Huhn Jones, *Roads to Russia,* 187.

9. MacLean, *Joseph E. Davies,* 173.

10. John Daniel Langer, "Formulation of American Aid Policy," 197.

11. Anatole G. Mazour, "Philip R. Faymonville," 84.

12. For the best overall summary of current theoretical approaches to the study of U.S. diplomatic history, see Michael J. Hogan and Thomas G. Paterson, *Explaining the History of American Foreign Relations.*

13. Graham T. Allison, *Essence of Decision.* See also Graham T. Allison and Morton H. Halperin, "Bureaucratic Politics." For a useful introduction to bureaucratic politics theory and diplomatic history, see J. Garry Clifford, "Bureaucratic Politics."

14. See Mark A. Stoler, *Allies and Adversaries.*

15. For a discussion of the role of psychology in U.S. diplomatic history, see Richard H. Immerman, "Psychology." For a compelling study of the psychology of the early cold war, see Deborah Welch Larson, *Origins of Containment.*

16. See Robert C. Tucker, *Stalin in Power;* and Dmitri Volkogonov, *Stalin.*

17. Frank Costigliola, "Unceasing Pressure for Penetration."

18. Michael H. Hunt, "Ideology," 194. See also Michael H. Hunt, *Ideology and U.S. Foreign Policy.*

19. Hugh DeSantis argues that the men who made up the Foreign Service in the early twentieth century were a relatively homogeneous group. Nonetheless, he points out that "they did not share the same social experiences." As a result, they developed somewhat different perceptions of the Soviet Union. See Hugh DeSantis, *Diplomacy of Silence*, 4. On Henderson's background, see Loy W. Henderson, *Question of Trust*, 3–11. See also Martin Weil, *Pretty Good Club.*

20. Robert A. Divine, *Roosevelt and World War II*, 9–10.

21. Daniel Yergin, *Shattered Peace*, 11.

22. Williams, *Tragedy of American Diplomacy* (1988 new ed.); Lloyd C. Gardner, *Architects of Illusion;* LaFeber, *America, Russia, and the Cold War, 1945–1966.*

23. Vojtech Mastny, *Cold War and Soviet Insecurity*, 12–13, 21; and Warren F. Kimball, *Juggler*, 17–19, 195–200.

BIBLIOGRAPHY

Archival Sources

FEDERAL BUREAU OF INVESTIGATION
"Faymonville, Philip R.," File.

FRANKLIN DELANO ROOSEVELT LIBRARY
(Albert) Wayne Coy Papers
Stephen T. Early Papers
Harry L. Hopkins Papers
R. Walton Moore Papers
Sumner Welles Papers
John Cooper Wiley Papers
President's Official File
President's Personal File
President's Secretary's File
President's Soviet Protocol Committee Papers

HOOVER INSTITUTION ON WAR, REVOLUTION AND PEACE ARCHIVES
Philip R. Faymonville Papers
Ivan D. Yeaton Papers

LIBRARY OF CONGRESS MANUSCRIPT COLLECTIONS
Joseph E. Davies Papers
W. Averell Harriman Papers
Loy W. Henderson Papers
Laurence A. Steinhardt Papers

NATIONAL ARCHIVES AND RECORDS ADMINISTRATION
RG 38, Records of the Office of the Chief of Naval Operations
RG 59, General Records of the Department of State
RG 84, Foreign Service Post Files
RG 165, Records of the War Department General and Special Staffs. *Correspondence of the Military Intelligence Division Relating to General, Political, Economic, and Military Conditions in Russia and the Soviet Union, 1918–1941* (National Archives Microfilm Publication M1443).
RG 319, Records of the Army Staff, Assistant Chief of Staff, G-2 (Intelligence).

United Kingdom Public Record Office
FO 371, Foreign Office: General Correspondence: Political
FO 418, Confidential Print Russia and Soviet Union
FO 800, Private Collections: Ministers and Officials: Various
FO 954, Avon Papers
WO 32, Registered Files: General Series
WO 178, War of 1939–1945: War Diaries: Military Missions
WO 193, Directorate of Military Operations: Collation Files
WO 208, Directorate of Military Intelligence
WO 216, Chief of the (Imperial) General Staff Papers

UNITED STATES ARMY MILITARY HISTORY INSTITUTE
Philip R. Faymonville Papers
Wellington Alexander Samouce Papers
Sidney P. Spalding Papers
R. L. Walsh Papers
Ivan D. Yeaton Papers

Non-Archival Sources

Abramson, Rudy. *Spanning the Century: The Life of W. Averell Harriman, 1891–1986.* New York: Morrow, 1992.

Allison, Graham T. *Essence of Decision: Explaining the Cuban Missile Crisis.* Boston: Little, Brown, 1971.

Allison, Graham T., and Morton H. Halperin, "Bureaucratic Politics: A Paradigm and Some Policy Implications." *World Politics* 24, issue supplement: Theory and Policy in International Relations (Spring 1972): 40–79.

Allison, William. *American Diplomats in Russia: Case Studies in Orphan Diplomacy, 1916–1919.* Westport, CT: Praeger, 1997.

Alperovitz, Gar. *Atomic Diplomacy: Hiroshima and Potsdam.* New York: Random House, 1965.

Aster, Sidney. "Ivan Maisky and Parliamentary Anti-Appeasement, 1938–1939." In *Lloyd George: Twelve Essays,* edited by A. J. P. Taylor, 317–57. London: Hamish Hamilton, 1971.

Barnes, William, John Heath Morgan, and United States Department of State. Historical Office. *The Foreign Service of the United States: Origins, Development, and Functions.* Washington, DC: Historical Office Bureau of Public Affairs, Department of State, 1961.

Beitzell, Robert. *The Uneasy Alliance: America, Britain, and Russia, 1941–1943.* New York: Knopf, 1972.

Beitzell, Robert, ed. *Tehran, Yalta, Potsdam: The Soviet Protocols.* Hattiesburg, MS: Academic International, 1970.

Bennett, Edward M. *Franklin D. Roosevelt and the Search for Security: American-Soviet Relations, 1933–1939.* Wilmington, DE: Scholarly Resources, 1985.

———. *Franklin D. Roosevelt and the Search for Victory: American-Soviet Relations, 1939–1945.* Wilmington, DE: Scholarly Resources, 1990.

Berezhkov, Valentin. *History in the Making.* Translated by Dudley Hagen and Barry Jones. Moscow: Progress, 1983.

———. *Tegeran, 1943: Na konferentsii Bol'shoi Troiki i v Kuluarakh.* Moscow: Izd. agentstva pechati novosti, 1963.

Berle, Adolf A. *The Adolf A. Berle Diary.* Hyde Park, NY: Franklin D. Roosevelt Library, 1978. Microfilm.

———. *Navigating the Rapids, 1918–1971: From the Papers of Adolf A. Berle.* Edited by Beatrice Bishop Berle and Travis Beal Jacobs. New York: Harcourt Brace Jovanovich, 1973.

Bernstein, Marvin D., and Francis L. Loewenheim. "Aid to Russia: The First Year." In *American Civil-Military Decisions: A Book of Case Studies,* edited by Harold Stein, 97–152. University: University of Alabama Press, 1963.

Bess, Demaree. "The General Called the Turn." *Saturday Evening Post,* 29 August 1942, 12, 101–2.

Bezymenskii, L. A. "Sovetsko-Germanskie dogovory 1939 G.: Novye dokumenty i starye problemy." *Novaia i noveishaia istoriia,* no. 3 (1998): 3–26.

Bidwell, Bruce W. *History of the Military Intelligence Division, Department of the Army General Staff: 1775–1941.* Frederick, MD: University Publications of America, 1986.

Biggs, Kelly William. "The Role of Philip Ries Faymonville in Soviet-American Relations." Master's thesis, Georgetown University, 1992.

Birse, A. H. *Memoirs of an Interpreter.* New York: Coward-McCann, 1967.

Bishop, Donald G. *The Roosevelt-Litvinov Agreements: The American View.* Syracuse, NY: Syracuse University Press, 1965.

Blum, John Morton. *The Progressive Presidents: Roosevelt, Wilson, Roosevelt, Johnson.* New York: Norton, 1980.

Blum, John Morton, ed. *From the Morgenthau Diaries. Years of Crisis, 1928–1938.* Boston: Houghton Mifflin, 1959.

———. *From the Morgenthau Diaries. Years of Urgency, 1938–1941.* Boston: Houghton Mifflin, 1965.

Bohlen, Charles E. *Witness to History, 1929–1969.* New York: Norton, 1973.

Bonwetsch, Bernd. "Stalin, the Red Army, and the 'Great Patriotic War.'" In *Stalinism and Nazism: Dictatorships in Comparison,* edited by Ian Kershaw and Moshe Lewin, 185–207. Cambridge: Cambridge University Press, 1997.

Bowers, Robert E. "Hull, Russian Supervision in Cuba, and Recognition of the USSR." *Journal of American History* 52, no. 3 (December 1966): 542–54.

Brands, H. W. *Inside the Cold War: Loy Henderson and the Rise of the American Empire, 1918–1961.* New York: Oxford University Press, 1991.

Browder, Robert Paul. *The Origins of Soviet-American Diplomacy.* Princeton, NJ: Princeton University Press, 1953.

Bullitt, Orville H., ed. *For the President: Personal and Secret Correspondence Between Franklin D. Roosevelt and William C. Bullitt.* Boston: Houghton Mifflin, 1972.

Bullitt, William C. "How We Won the War and Lost the Peace." *Life,* 30 August 1948, 82–97.

Burke, John P., and Fred I. Greenstein. *How Presidents Test Reality: Decisions on Vietnam, 1954 and 1965.* New York: Russell Sage Foundation, 1989.

Burns, James MacGregor. *Roosevelt: The Lion and the Fox.* New York: Harcourt, Brace & World, 1956.

———. *Roosevelt: The Soldier of Freedom.* New York: Harcourt Brace Jovanovich, 1970.

Carley, Michael Jabara. *1939: The Alliance that Never Was and the Coming of World War II.* Chicago: Ivan R. Dee, 1999.

Carlton, David. *Churchill and the Soviet Union.* Manchester: Manchester University Press, 2000.

Cassidy, Henry. *Moscow Dateline, 1941–1943.* Boston: Houghton Mifflin, 1943.

Chubar'ian, A. O., ed. *Voina i politika, 1939–1941.* Moscow: Nauka, 1999.

Churchill, Winston S. *The Grand Alliance.* Vol. 3 of *The Second World War.* Boston: Houghton Mifflin, 1950.

Ciechanowski, Jan M. *The Warsaw Rising of 1944.* London: Cambridge University Press, 1974.

Clemens, Diane S. "Averell Harriman, John Deane, the Joint Chiefs of Staff, and the 'Reversal of Co-operation' with the Soviet Union in April 1945." *International History Review* 14, no. 2 (May 1992): 277–306.

———. *Yalta.* New York: Oxford University Press, 1970.

Clifford, J. Garry. "Bureaucratic Politics." In *Explaining the History of American Foreign Relations,* edited by Michael J. Hogan and Thomas G. Paterson, 141–50. Cambridge: Cambridge University Press, 1991.

Cole, Wayne S. *Roosevelt and the Isolationists, 1932–1945.* Lincoln: University of Nebraska Press, 1983.

Congressional Record. 1933–45. Washington, DC.

Conquest, Robert. *The Great Terror: A Reassessment.* New York: Oxford University Press, 1990.

Conversino, Mark J. *Fighting with the Soviets: The Failure of Operation Frantic, 1944–1945.* Lawrence: University Press of Kansas, 1997.

———. "Operation Frantic: The American Experience in the Soviet Ukraine, 1944–1945." PhD diss., Indiana University, 1992.

Coox, Alvin D. *The Anatomy of a Small War: The Soviet-Japanese Struggle for Changfukeng/Khasan, 1938.* Westport, CT: Greenwood Press, 1977.

Costigliola, Frank. "'Unceasing Pressure for Penetration': Gender, Pathology, and Emotion in George Kennan's Formulation of the Cold War." *Journal of American History* 83, no. 4 (March 1997): 1309–39.

Craig, Gordon A., and Felix Gilbert. *The Diplomats: 1919–1939.* Princeton, NJ: Princeton University Press, 1953.

Dallek, Robert. *The American Style of Foreign Policy: Cultural Politics and Foreign Affairs.* New York: Knopf, 1983.

———. *Franklin D. Roosevelt and American Foreign Policy, 1932–1945.* Oxford: Oxford University Press, 1979.

Dallin, Alexander. "Stalin and the German Invasion." *Soviet Union/Union Soviétique* 18, no. 1–3 (1991): 19–37.

Davies, Joseph E. *Mission to Moscow.* Garden City, NY: Garden City Publishing, 1943.

Davies, Sarah. *Popular Opinion in Stalin's Russia: Terror, Propaganda and Dissent, 1934–1941.* Cambridge: Cambridge University Press, 1997.

Dawson, Raymond H. *The Decision to Aid Russia, 1941: Foreign Policy and Domestic Politics.* Chapel Hill: University of North Carolina Press, 1959.

Deane, John R. *The Strange Alliance. The Story of Our Efforts at Wartime Co-operation with Russia.* New York: Viking, 1946, 1947.

Department of State. *Memorandum on Certain Aspects of the Bolshevik Movement in Russia.* Washington, DC: Department of State, 1919.

DeSantis, Hugh. *The Diplomacy of Silence: The American Foreign Service, the Soviet Union, and the Cold War, 1933–1947.* Chicago: University of Chicago Press, 1979, 1980.

Deutscher, Isaac. *Stalin: A Political Biography.* 2nd ed. New York: Oxford University Press, 1966.

Dilks, David, ed. *The Diaries of Sir Alexander Cadogan, O.M., 1938–1945.* New York: G. P. Putnam's Sons, 1972.

Divine, Robert A. *The Illusion of Neutrality.* Chicago: University of Chicago Press, 1962.

———. *Roosevelt and World War II.* Baltimore: Johns Hopkins University Press, 1969.

———. *Second Chance: The Triumph of Internationalism in America During World War II.* New York: Atheneum, 1967.

Dodd, William E., and Martha Dodd. *Ambassador Dodd's Diary, 1933–1938.* New York: Harcourt, Brace, 1941.

Dulles, Foster Rhea. *The Road to Teheran. The Story of Russia and America, 1781–1943.* Princeton, NJ: Princeton University Press, 1944.

Dunn, Dennis J. *Caught Between Roosevelt and Stalin: America's Ambassadors to Moscow.* Lexington: University Press of Kentucky, 1998.

Duranty, Walter. *I Write as I Please.* New York: Simon and Schuster, 1935.

Eagles, Keith David. *Ambassador Joseph E. Davies and American-Soviet Relations, 1937–1941.* New York: Garland, 1985.

Eremenko, A. *The Arduous Beginning.* Translated by Vic Shneierson. Moscow: Progress, 1966.

Erickson, John. *The Road to Berlin: Continuing the History of Stalin's War with Germany.* Boulder, CO: Westview Press, 1983.

———. *The Road to Stalingrad: Stalin's War with Germany.* New Haven, CT: Yale University Press, 1999.

———. *The Soviet High Command: A Military-Political History, 1918–1941.* New York: St. Martin's Press, 1962.

Eubank, Keith. *Summit at Teheran*. New York: Morrow, 1985.

Farnsworth, Beatrice. *William C. Bullitt and the Soviet Union*. Bloomington: Indiana University Press, 1967.

Feis, Herbert. *Churchill, Roosevelt, Stalin: The War They Waged and the Peace They Sought*. Princeton, NJ: Princeton University Press, 1957.

Filene, Peter G. *Americans and the Soviet Experiment, 1917–1933*. Cambridge, MA: Harvard University Press, 1967.

Fink, Carole. "The NEP in Foreign Policy: The Genoa Conference and the Treaty of Rapallo." In *Soviet Foreign Policy, 1917–1991: A Retrospective*, edited by Gabriel Gorodetsky, 11–20. London: Frank Cass, 1994.

Fischer, George. "Genesis of U.S.-Soviet Relations in World War II." *The Review of Politics* 12, no. 3 (July 1950): 363–78.

Fischer, Louis. *Men and Politics: An Autobiography*. New York: Duell, Sloan and Pearce, 1941.

Fitzpatrick, Sheila. "Stalin and the Making of a New Elite, 1928–1939." *Slavic Review* 38, no. 3 (September 1979): 377–402.

Fleischhauer, Ingeborg. *Der Pakt: Hitler, Stalin und Die Initiative Der Deutschen Diplomatie, 1938–1939*. Berlin: Ullstein, 1990.

———. "Soviet Foreign Policy and the Origins of the Hitler-Stalin Pact." In *From Peace to War: Germany, Soviet Russia and the World, 1939–1941*, edited by Bernd Wegner, 27–45. Providence, RI: Berghahn Books, 1997.

Foglesong, David S. *America's Secret War Against Bolshevism: U.S. Intervention in the Russian Civil War, 1917–1920*. Chapel Hill: University of North Carolina Press, 1995.

Folly, Martin H. *Churchill, Whitehall and the Soviet Union, 1940–45*. New York: St. Martin's Press, 2000.

———. "Forging the Grand Alliance: The United States and the Anglo-Soviet Treaty, May 1942." Paper presented at the annual meeting of the Society for Historians of American Foreign Relations, Toronto, Canada, June 2000.

Gaddis, John Lewis. *Russia, the Soviet Union, and the United States: An Interpretive History*. New York: Wiley, 1978.

———. *The United States and the Origins of the Cold War, 1941–1947*. 2nd ed. New York: Columbia University Press, 2000.

Gardner, Lloyd C. *Architects of Illusion: Men and Ideas in American Foreign Policy, 1941–1949*. Chicago: Quadrangle Books, 1970.

———. *Spheres of Influence: The Great Powers Partition Europe, from Munich to Yalta*. Chicago: I. R. Dee, 1993.

Gellman, Irwin F. *Secret Affairs: Franklin Roosevelt, Cordell Hull, and Sumner Welles*. Baltimore: Johns Hopkins University Press, 1995.

George, Alexander L. *Presidential Decisionmaking in Foreign Policy: The Effective Use of Information and Advice*. Boulder, CO: Westview Press, 1980.

Getty, J. Arch, and Oleg V. Naumov. *The Road to Terror: Stalin and the Self-Destruction of the Bolsheviks, 1932–1939*. New Haven, CT: Yale University Press, 1999.

Gintsberg, Lev Izrailevich. "Sovetsko-Germanskii Pakt: Zamysel i ego realizatsiia." *Otechestvennaia istoriia*, no. 3 (1996): 29–40.

Girshfel'd, A. "O roli SShA v organizatsii antisovetskoi interventsii v Sibiri i na dal'nem vostoke." *Voprosy Istorii* 8 (August 1948): 3–22.

Glantz, David M. *Barbarossa: Hitler's Invasion of Russia 1941.* Charleston, SC: Tempus, 2001.

———. *Forgotten Battles of the Soviet-German War 1941–1945.* Carlisle, PA: Self-published, 1998.

———. "Observing the Soviets: U.S. Army Attachés in Eastern Europe During the 1930s." *Journal of Military History* 55, no. 2 (April 1991): 153–83.

———. *The Siege of Leningrad 1941–1944: 900 Days of Terror.* London: Brown Part-works, 2001.

———. "Soviet Mobilization in Peace and War, 1924–1942: A Survey." *Journal of Soviet Military Studies* 5, no. 3 (September 1992): 323–62.

———. *Stumbling Colossus: The Red Army on the Eve of World War.* Lawrence: University Press of Kansas, 1998.

Glantz, David M., and Aleksandr A. Maslov. "How and Why Did the Americans Kill Soviet General Kotov?" *Journal of Slavic Military Studies* 1, no. 2 (June 1998): 142–71.

Glantz, David M., and Jonathan M. House. *The Battle of Kursk.* Lawrence: University Press of Kansas, 1999.

———. *When Titans Clashed: How the Red Army Stopped Hitler.* Lawrence: University Press of Kansas, 1995.

Goerlitz, Walter. *History of the German General Staff, 1657–1945.* Translated by Brian Battershaw. New York: Praeger, 1953.

Golikov, F. I. *On a Military Mission to Great Britain and the USA.* Translated by Nadezhda Burova. Moscow: Progress, 1987.

Gorodetsky, Gabriel. "The Formulation of Soviet Foreign Policy: Ideology and *Realpolitik.*" In *Soviet Foreign Policy, 1917–1991: A Retrospective,* edited by Gabriel Gorodetsky, 30–44. London: Frank Cass, 1994.

———. *Grand Delusion: Stalin and the German Invasion of Russia.* New Haven, CT: Yale University Press, 1999.

———. "The Origins of the Cold War: Stalin, Churchill and the Formation of the Grand Alliance." *Russian Review* 47, no. 2 (April 1988): 145–70.

———. *Stafford Cripps' Mission to Moscow, 1940–42.* Cambridge: Cambridge University Press, 1984.

Gorodetsky, Gabriel, ed. *Soviet Foreign Policy, 1917–1991: A Retrospective.* London: Frank Cass, 1994.

Grant, Natalie. "The Russian Section, a Window on the Soviet Union." *Diplomatic History* 2, no. 1 (Winter 1978): 107–15.

Graves, William S. *America's Siberian Adventure, 1918–1920.* New York: Jonathan Cape & Harrison Smith, 1931.

Great Britain. Foreign Office. *Documents on British Foreign Policy, 1919–1939.* Edited by E. L. Woodward and Rohan d'Olier Butler. London: H. M. Stationery Office, 1949.

Gromyko, Andrei. *Memoirs.* Translated by Harold Shukman. New York: Doubleday, 1989.

Harper, Paul V., ed. *The Russia I Believe In: The Memoirs of Samuel N. Harper, 1902–1941.* Chicago: University of Chicago Press, 1945.

Harriman, W. Averell. *America and Russia in a Changing World: A Half Century of Personal Observation.* Garden City, NY: Doubleday, 1971.

Harriman, W. Averell, and Elie Abel. *Special Envoy to Churchill and Stalin, 1941–1946.* New York: Random House, 1975.

Harrington, Daniel F. "Kennan, Bohlen, and the Riga Axioms." *Diplomatic History* 2, no. 4 (Fall 1978): 423–37.

Harvey, Oliver, and John Harvey. *The Diplomatic Diaries of Oliver Harvey, 1937–1940.* London,: Collins, 1970.

Haslam, Jonathan. "Litvinov, Stalin and the Road Not Taken." In *Soviet Foreign Policy, 1917–1991: A Retrospective,* edited by Gabriel Gorodetsky, 55–62. London: Frank Cass, 1994.

———. *Soviet Foreign Policy, 1930–1933: The Impact of the Depression.* New York: St. Martin's Press, 1983.

———. "Soviet Foreign Policy 1939–1941: Isolation and Expansion." *Soviet Union/ Union Soviétique* 18, no. 1–3 (1991): 103–21.

———. *The Soviet Union and the Struggle for Collective Security in Europe, 1933–39.* New York: St. Martin's Press, 1984.

———. *The Soviet Union and the Threat from the East, 1933–41: Moscow, Tokyo and the Prelude to the Pacific War.* London: Macmillan, in association with the Centre for Russian and East European Studies, University of Birmingham, 1992.

Haynes, John Earl, and Harvey Klehr. *Venona: Decoding Soviet Espionage in America.* New Haven, CT: Yale University Press, 1999.

Heinrichs, Waldo. *Threshold of War: Franklin D. Roosevelt and American Entry into World War II.* New York: Oxford University Press, 1988.

Henderson, Loy W. *A Question of Trust: The Origins of U.S.-Soviet Diplomatic Relations: The Memoirs of Loy W. Henderson.* Edited by George W. Baer. Stanford: Hoover Institution Press, 1986

Herndon, James S., and Joseph O. Baylen. "Col. Philip R. Faymonville and the Red Army, 1934–43." *Slavic Review* 34, no. 3 (September 1975): 483–505.

Herring, George C. *Aid to Russia, 1941–1946: Strategy, Diplomacy, the Origins of the Cold War.* New York: Columbia University Press, 1973.

Hixson, Walter L. *George F. Kennan: Cold War Iconoclast.* New York: Columbia University Press, 1989.

Hogan, Michael J., and Thomas G. Paterson, eds. *Explaining the History of American Foreign Relations.* Cambridge: Cambridge University Press, 1991.

Hopkins, Harry. "The Inside Story of My Meeting with Stalin." *American Magazine,* July 1941, 14–15, 114–17.

Hull, Cordell. *The Memoirs of Cordell Hull*. 2 vols. New York: Macmillan, 1948.

Hunt, Michael H. "Ideology." In *Explaining the History of American Foreign Relations*, edited by Michael J. Hogan and Thomas G. Paterson, 193–201. Cambridge: Cambridge University Press, 1991.

———. *Ideology and U.S. Foreign Policy*. New Haven, CT: Yale University Press, 1987.

Iakovlev, N. N. "Franklin D. Ruzvel't i Amerikano-Sovetskoe sotrudnichestvo 1941–1945 gg." In *Vtoraia Mirovaia Voina: Materialy nauchnoi konferentsii, posviashchennoi 20-i godovshchine pobedy nad fashistkoi Germaniei*, 372–82. Moscow: Nauka, 1966.

Ickes, Harold L. *The Secret Diary of Harold L. Ickes*. 3 vols. New York: Simon and Schuster, 1953–54.

Immerman, Richard H. "Psychology." In *Explaining the History of American Foreign Relations*, edited by Michael J. Hogan and Thomas G. Paterson, 151–64. Cambridge: Cambridge University Press, 1991.

Isaacson, Walter, and Evan Thomas. *The Wise Men: Six Friends and the World They Made*. New York: Touchstone, 1988.

Israelian, V. "Bol'shaia Troika: SSSR, SShA, Angliia 1941–1942 gody." *Soviet Union/Union Soviétique* 18, no. 1–3 (1991): 123–37.

———. *Diplomaticheskaia istoriia Velikoi Otechestvennoi Voiny, 1941–1945 gg.* Moscow: Izdatel'stvo Instituta Mezhdunarodnykh otnoshenii, 1959.

Izard, Ralph. "A General Looks at the Soviet Union." *Worker Magazine*, 13 March 1949, 12.

"Iz dnevnika i pisem posla Velikobritanii v SSSR v 1941–1942 gg. S. Krippsa." *Novaia i noveishaia istoriia*, no. 3 (May–June 1991): 118–44.

Johnson, Richard Tanner. *Managing the White House: An Intimate Study of the Presidency*. New York: Harper & Row, 1974.

Jones, Howard, and Randall B. Woods. "Origins of the Cold War in Europe and the Near East: Recent Historiography and the National Security Imperative." In *America in the World: The Historiography of American Foreign Relations Since 1941*, edited by Michael J. Hogan, 234–69. Cambridge: Cambridge University Press, 1995.

Jones, Robert Huhn. *The Roads to Russia: United States Lend-Lease to the Soviet Union*. Norman: University of Oklahoma Press, 1969.

Jukes, G. "The Red Army and the Munich Crisis." *Journal of Contemporary History* 26, no. 2 (April 1991): 195–214.

Julian, Thomas A. "Operations at the Margin: Soviet Bases and Shuttle Bombing." *Journal of Military History* 57, no. 4 (October 1993): 627–52.

———. "Philip Ries Faymonville and the Soviet Union." Paper presented at the annual meeting of the Society for Historians of American Foreign Relations, Washington, DC, 1988.

Kennan, George F. *American Diplomacy, 1900–1950*. Chicago: University of Chicago Press, 1951.

———. *Memoirs, 1925–1950*. Boston: Little, Brown, 1967.

————. *Russia and the West Under Lenin and Stalin.* Boston: Little, Brown, 1960.

————. *Soviet-American Relations.* 2 vols. Princeton, NJ: Princeton University Press, 1956–58.

Kennedy, David M. *Freedom from Fear: The American People in Depression and War, 1929–1945.* New York: Oxford University Press, 1999.

Khrushchev, Nikita. *Khrushchev Remembers.* Translated and edited by Strobe Talbott. New York: Bantam Books, 1971.

Kimball, Warren F. "Franklin Ruzvel't—glavnokomanduiushchii. 1941–1945 gg." *Novaia i noveishaia istoriia,* no. 1 (January–February 1993): 114–30.

————. "Stalingrad: A Chance for Choices." *Journal of Military History* 60, no. 1 (January 1996): 89–114.

————. *Forged in War: Roosevelt, Churchill, and the Second World War.* New York: Morrow, 1997.

————. "The Incredible Shrinking War: The Second World War, Not (Just) the Origins of the Cold War. So What the Hell Were We Fighting for Such a Long, Long Time Ago?" *Diplomatic History* 25, no. 3 (Summer 2001): 347–65.

————. *The Juggler: Franklin Roosevelt as Wartime Statesman.* Princeton, NJ: Princeton University Press, 1991.

————. *The Most Unsordid Act: Lend-Lease, 1939–1941.* Baltimore: Johns Hopkins University Press, 1969.

Kimball, Warren F., ed. *Churchill and Roosevelt: The Complete Correspondence.* 3 vols. Princeton, NJ: Princeton University Press, 1984.

Kinsella, William E., Jr. *Leadership in Isolation: FDR and the Origins of the Second World War.* Cambridge, MA: Schenkman, 1978.

Kirshin, Yuri Y. "The Soviet Armed Forces on the Eve of the Great Patriotic War." In *From Peace to War: Germany, Soviet Russia and the World, 1939–1941,* edited by Bernd Wegner, 381–94. Providence, RI: Berghahn Books, 1997.

Knight, Amy W. *Who Killed Kirov? The Kremlin's Greatest Mystery.* New York: Hill and Wang, 1999.

Koch, Scott A. "The Role of U.S. Army Military Attachés Between the World Wars." *Studies in Intelligence* 38, no. 5 (1995). Available at: http://www.cia.gov/csi/studies/95unclass/index.html.

Kohler, Foy D., and Mose L. Harvey. *The Soviet Union: Yesterday, Today, Tomorrow. A Colloquy of American Long Timers in Moscow.* Miami: Center for Advanced International Studies, University of Miami, 1975.

Kolko, Gabriel. *The Politics of War: The World and United States Foreign Policy, 1943–1945.* New York: Pantheon Books, 1990.

Koval,' Viktor Savyeh. *Oni khoteli ukrast' u nas pobedu. Ocherki vneshnei politiki SShA vo vtoroi mirovoi voine (1939 Vi 1943).* Kiev: Naukova dumka, 1964.

Krasilshchik, S., ed. *World War II: Dispatches from the Soviet Front.* New York: Sphinx Press, 1985.

LaFeber, Walter. *America, Russia, and the Cold War, 1945–1992.* New York: McGraw-Hill, 1993.

Langer, John Daniel. "The Formulation of American Aid Policy Toward the Soviet Union, 1940–1943: The Hopkins Shop and the Department of State." PhD diss., Yale University, 1975.

————. "The Harriman-Beaverbrook Mission and the Debate over Unconditional Aid for the Soviet Union, 1941." *Journal of Contemporary History* 14, no. 3 (July 1979): 463–82.

————. "The 'Red General': Philip R. Faymonville and the Soviet Union, 1917–1952." *Prologue* 8, no. 4 (Winter 1976): 208–21.

Langer, William L., and S. Everett Gleason. *The Challenge to Isolation, 1937–1940.* New York: Published for the Council on Foreign Relations by Harper & Brothers, 1952.

————. *The Undeclared War, 1940–1941.* New York: Published for the Council on Foreign Relations by Harper & Brothers, 1953.

Larionov, Valentin. "Pochemu vermakht ne pobedil v 1941 godu." *Soviet Union / Union Soviétique* 18, no. 1–3 (1991): 197–204.

Larson, Deborah Welch. *Origins of Containment: A Psychological Explanation.* Princeton, NJ: Princeton University Press, 1985.

Lash, Joseph P. *Eleanor and Franklin: The Story of the Relationship, Based on Eleanor Roosevelt's Private Papers.* New York: Norton, 1971.

Leahy, William D. *I Was There: The Personal Story of the Chief of Staff to Presidents Roosevelt and Truman Based on His Notes and Diaries Made at the Time.* New York: Whittlesey House, 1950.

Leighton, Richard M., and Robert W. Coakley. *Global Logistics and Strategy, 1940–1943.* Washington, DC: Office of the Chief of Military History, Department of the Army, 1955.

Levering, Ralph B. *American Opinion and the Russian Alliance, 1939–1945.* Chapel Hill: University of North Carolina Press, 1976.

Levin, N. Gordon, Jr. *Woodrow Wilson and World Politics: America's Response to War and Revolution.* New York: Oxford University Press, 1968.

Light, Margot. *The Soviet Theory of International Relations.* New York: St. Martin's Press, 1988.

Linn, Brian McAllister. *Guardians of Empire: The U.S. Army and the Pacific, 1902–1940.* Chapel Hill: University of North Carolina Press, 1997.

Little, Douglas. "Antibolshevism and American Foreign Policy, 1919–1939: The Diplomacy of Self-Delusion." *American Quarterly* 35, no. 4 (Autumn 1983): 376–90.

Litvinov, Maxim. *Notes for a Journal.* New York: Morrow, 1955.

Lukes, Igor. "Stalin and Benes at the End of September 1939: New Evidence from the Prague Archives." *Slavic Review* 52, no. 1 (Spring 1993): 28–48.

Lundestad, Geir. *The American Non-Policy Towards Eastern Europe, 1943–1947: Universalism in an Area Not of Essential Interest to the United States.* Tromso, Norway: Universitetsforlaget, 1978.

Mackintosh, Malcolm. *Juggernaut: A History of the Soviet Armed Forces.* New York: Macmillan, 1967.

MacLean, Elizabeth Kimball. "Joseph E. Davies and Soviet-American Relations, 1941–1943." *Diplomatic History* 4, no. 4 (Fall 1980): 73–93.

———. *Joseph E. Davies: Envoy to the Soviets.* Westport, CT: Praeger, 1992.

Maddux, Thomas R. "American Diplomats and the Soviet Experiment: The View from the Moscow Embassy, 1934–1939." *South Atlantic Quarterly* 74, no. 4 (Autumn 1975): 468–87.

———. "Watching Stalin Maneuver Between Hitler and the West: American Diplomats and Soviet Diplomacy, 1934–1939." *Diplomatic History* 1, no. 2 (Spring 1977): 140–54.

———. *Years of Estrangement: American Relations with the Soviet Union, 1933–1941.* Tallahassee: University Presses of Florida, 1980.

March, G. Patrick. "Yanks in Siberia: U.S. Navy Weather Stations in Soviet East Asia, 1945." *Pacific Historical Review* 57, no. 3 (August 1988): 327–42.

Mark, Eduard. "American Policy Toward Eastern Europe and the Origins of the Cold War, 1941–1946: An Alternative Interpretation." *Journal of American History* 68, no. 2 (September 1981): 313–36.

Marshall, George C. *The Papers of George Catlett Marshall.* Edited by Larry I. Bland, Sharon R. Ritenour, and Clarence E. Wunderlin. 4 vols. Baltimore: Johns Hopkins University Press, 1981–2004.

Martel, Leon. *Lend-Lease, Loans, and the Coming of the Cold War: A Study of the Implementation of Foreign Policy.* Boulder, CO: Westview Press, 1979.

Mastny, Vojtech. *The Cold War and Soviet Insecurity: The Stalin Years.* New York: Oxford University Press, 1996.

———. *Russia's Road to the Cold War: Diplomacy, Warfare, and the Politics of Communism, 1941–1945.* New York: Columbia University Press, 1979.

———. "Soviet War Aims at the Moscow and Teheran Conferences of 1943." *Journal of Modern History* 47, no. 3 (September 1975): 481–504.

Matloff, Maurice. *Strategic Planning for Coalition Warfare, 1943–1944.* Washington, DC: Office of the Chief of Military History, Department of the Army, 1959.

Matloff, Maurice, and Edwin M. Snell. *Strategic Planning for Coalition Warfare, 1941–1942.* Washington, DC: Office of the Chief of Military History, Department of the Army, 1953.

Mayers, David. *The Ambassadors and America's Soviet Policy.* New York: Oxford University Press, 1995.

———. *George Kennan and the Dilemmas of U.S. Foreign Policy.* New York: Oxford University Press, 1988.

———. "George Kennan and the Soviet Union, 1933–1938: Perceptions of a Young Diplomat." *International History Review* 4 (November 1983): 525–49.

Mayle, Paul D. *Eureka Summit: Agreement in Principle and the Big Three at Tehran, 1943.* Newark: University of Delaware Press, Associated University Presses, 1987.

Mazour, Anatole G. "Philip R. Faymonville." *California Historical Society Quarterly* 42, no. 1 (March 1963): 82–84.

McFadden, David W. *Alternative Paths: Soviets and Americans, 1917–1920.* New York: Oxford University Press, 1993.

McJimsey, George. *Harry Hopkins: Ally of the Poor and Defender of Democracy.* Cambridge, MA: Harvard University Press, 1987.

———. *The Presidency of Franklin Delano Roosevelt.* Lawrence: University Press of Kansas, 2000.

McNeill, William Hardy. *America, Britain, and Russia: Their Cooperation and Conflict, 1941–1946.* London: Oxford University Press, 1953.

Mikolajczyk, Stanislaw. *The Rape of Poland: Pattern of Soviet Aggression.* Westport, CT: Greenwood Press, 1972.

Miller, Edward S. *War Plan Orange: The U.S. Strategy to Defeat Japan, 1897–1945.* Annapolis, MD: Naval Institute Press, 1991.

Ministerstvo Inostrannykh Del SSSR. *Dokumenty vneshnei politiki SSSR.* Moscow: Izdatel'stvo Politicheskoi Literatury, 1970.

Moffat, Jay Pierrepont. *The Moffat Papers: Selections from the Diplomatic Journals of Jay Pierrepont Moffat, 1919–1943.* Edited by Nancy Harrison Hooker. Cambridge, MA: Harvard University Press, 1956.

Motter, T. H. Vail. *The Persian Corridor and Aid to Russia.* Washington, DC: Center of Military History, United States Army, 1989.

Munting, Roger. "Soviet Food Supply and Allied Aid in the War, 1941–1945." *Soviet Studies* 36, no. 4 (October 1984): 582–93.

Naumov, V. P. *Letopis' geroicheskoi bor'by: Sovetskaia istoriografiia Grazhdanskoi Voiny i imperialisticheskoi interventsii v SSSR.* Moscow: Izdatel'stvo "Mysl," 1972.

Nekrich, Aleksandr M. *Pariahs, Partners, Predators: German-Soviet Relations, 1922–1941.* New York: Columbia University Press, 1997.

Nixon, Edgar B., ed. *Franklin D. Roosevelt and Foreign Affairs.* 17 vols. Cambridge, MA: Belknap, 1969.

O'Connor, Joseph Edward. "Laurence A. Steinhardt and American Policy Toward the Soviet Union, 1939–1941." PhD diss., University of Virginia, 1968.

Ocherki istorii Rossiskoi vneshnei razvedki. Vol. 4, *1941–1945 gg.* Moscow: Mezhdunarodnye otnosheniia, 1999.

Offner, Arnold A. "Uncommon Ground: Anglo-American-Soviet Diplomacy, 1941–1942." *Soviet Union/Union Soviétique* 18, no. 1–3 (1991): 237–57.

Orlov, A. S. "Na aerodromakh Ukrainy." In *Vtoraia Mirovaia Voina: Aktual'nye problemy (k 50-letiiu pobedy),* edited by O. A. Rzheshevsky, 214–30. Moscow: Nauka, 1995.

Orlov, A. S., and V. P. Kozhanov. "Lend-Liz: Vzgliad cherez polveka." *Novaia i noveishaia istoriia,* no. 3 (May–June 1994): 176–94.

Overy, R. J., and Andrew Wheatcroft. *The Road to War.* Rev. and updated 2nd ed. London: Penguin, 1999.

Papachristou, Judith. "Soviet-American Relations and the East-Asian Imbroglio, 1933–1941." In *Essays in Twentieth Century American Diplomatic History Dedicated to Professor Daniel M. Smith*, edited by Clifford L. Egan and Alexander W. Knott, 111–36. Washington, DC: University Press of America, 1982.

Parrish, Michael. "Soviet Historiography of the Great Patriotic War 1970–1985: A Review." *Soviet Studies in History* 23, no. 3 (1984–85).

———. *Soviet Security and Intelligence Organizations, 1917–1990: A Biographical Dictionary and Review of Literature in English*. Westport, CT: Greenwood Press, 1992.

Pechatnov, Vladimir O. "The Big Three After World War II: New Documents on Soviet Thinking About Post War Relations with the United States and Great Britain." Working Paper No. 13. Washington, DC: Cold War International History Project, Woodrow Wilson International Center for Scholars, 1995.

Phillips, Hugh D. "Rapprochement and Estrangement: The United States in Soviet Foreign Policy in the 1930s." In *Soviet-U.S. Relations 1933–1942*, 9–17. Moscow: Progress, 1989.

Phillips, William. *Ventures in Diplomacy*. Boston: Beacon Press, 1952.

Pogue, Forrest C. *George C. Marshall*. 4 vols. New York: Viking, 1963–1987.

"Pozitsiia Iaponii v otnoshenii SSSR v 1941 g. po materialam arkhiva sluzhby vneshnai razvedki RF." *Novaia i noveishaia istoriia*, no. 1 (January–February 1996): 92–103.

Propas, Frederic L. "Creating a Hard Line Toward Russia: The Training of State Department Soviet Experts, 1927–1937." *Diplomatic History* 8, no. 3 (Summer 1984): 209–26.

———. "The State Department, Bureaucratic Politics and Soviet-American Relations, 1918–1938." PhD diss., University of California–Los Angeles, 1982.

Raack, R. C. *Stalin's Drive to the West, 1938–1945: The Origins of the Cold War*. Stanford: Stanford University Press, 1995.

Ragsdale, Hugh. "Soviet Military Preparations and Policy in the Munich Crisis: New Evidence." *Jahrbücher für Geschichte Osteuropas* 47, no. 2 (1999): 210–26.

Resis, Albert. "Spheres of Influence in Soviet Wartime Diplomacy." *Journal of Modern History* 53, no. 3 (September 1981): 417–39.

Resis, Albert, ed. *Molotov Remembers: Inside Kremlin Politics. Conversations with Felix Chuev*. Chicago: Ivan R. Dee, 1993.

Reynolds, David, Warren F. Kimball, and A. O. Chubarian, eds. *Allies at War: The Soviet, American, and British Experience, 1939–1945*. New York: St. Martin's Press, 1994.

Reynolds, Quentin James. *The Curtain Rises*. New York: Random House, 1944.

———. *Only the Stars Are Neutral*. New York: Random House, 1942.

Richman, John. *The United States and the Soviet Union: The Decision to Recognize*. Raleigh, NC: Camberleigh & Hall, 1980.

Roberts, Geoffrey. "The Fall of Litvinov: A Revisionist View." *Journal of Contemporary History* 27, no. 4 (October 1992): 639–57.

———. *The Soviet Union and the Origins of the Second World War: Russo-German Relations and the Road to War, 1933–1941*. New York: St. Martin's Press, 1995.

————. *The Unholy Alliance: Stalin's Pact with Hitler.* Bloomington: Indiana University Press, 1989.

Roberts, Henry L. "Maxim Litvinov." In *The Diplomats, 1919–1939,* edited by Gordon A. Craig and Felix Gilbert, 344–77. Princeton, NJ: Princeton University Press, 1953.

Rokossovsky, K. K. *A Soldier's Duty.* Translated by Robert Daglish. Moscow: Progress, 1985.

Romerstein, Herbert, and Eric Breindel. *The Venona Secrets: Exposing Soviet Espionage and America's Traitors.* Washington, DC: Regnery Publishing, 2000.

Roosevelt, Franklin D. *FDR: His Personal Letters.* Edited by Elliot Roosevelt. 4 vols. New York: Duell, Sloan and Pearce, 1947–50.

————. *The Public Papers and Addresses of Franklin D. Roosevelt.* Edited by Samuel I. Rosenman. 13 vols. New York: Harper and Brothers, 1938–1950.

Rosenman, Samuel I. *Working with Roosevelt.* New York: Harper & Brothers, 1952.

Rostow, Walt W. *The Dynamics of Soviet Society.* 3rd ed. New York: Norton, 1967.

Russian Federation. Ministry of Foreign Affairs. [Ministerstvo Inostrannykh Del, Rossiiskoi Federatsii.] *Dokumenty vneshnei politiki, 22 iiunia 1941–1 ianvaria 1942.* Vol. 24. Moscow: Mezhdunarodnye otnosheniia, 2000.

Rzheshevsky, Oleg A. *Voina i diplomatiia: Dokumenty, kommentarii (1941–1942).* Moscow: Nauka, 1997.

————. *War and Diplomacy, the Making of the Grand Alliance: Documents from Stalin's Archives Edited with a Commentary.* Translated by T. Sorokina. Edited by Harold Shukman. Vol. 2, *New History of Russia.* Amsterdam: Harwood Academic, 1996.

Sainsbury, Keith. *The Turning Point: Roosevelt, Stalin, Churchill, and Chiang-Kai-Shek, 1943: The Moscow, Cairo, and Teheran Conferences.* Oxford: Oxford University Press, 1985.

Salisbury, Harrison Evans. *A Journey for Our Times: A Memoir.* New York: Harper & Row, 1983.

Samuelson, Lennart. *Plans for Stalin's War Machine: Tukhachevskii and Military-Economic Planning, 1925–1941.* New York: St. Martin's Press, 2000.

Saul, Norman E. *War and Revolution: The United States and Russia, 1914–1921.* Lawrence: University Press of Kansas, 2001.

Schulzinger, Robert D. *The Making of the Diplomatic Mind: The Training, Outlook, and Style of United States Foreign Service Officers, 1908–1931.* Middletown, CT: Wesleyan University Press, 1975.

Service, Robert. *A History of Twentieth-Century Russia.* Cambridge, MA: Harvard University Press, 1997.

Sevostianov, Grigory. "The USSR and the USA: Two Courses in World Politics, 1933–1938." In *Soviet-U.S. Relations, 1933–1942,* 160–95. Moscow: Progress, 1989.

Sheinis, Z. *Maksim Maksimovich Litvinov: Revoliutsioner, diplomat, chelovek.* Moscow: Izd-vo polit. lit-ry, 1989.

Sherwood, Robert E. *Roosevelt and Hopkins: An Intimate History.* New York: Harper & Brothers, 1948.

Sibley, Katherine A. S. *Loans and Legitimacy: The Evolution of Soviet-American Relations, 1919–1933.* Lexington: University Press of Kentucky, 1996.

Singer, J. David. "The Level-of-Analysis Problem in International Relations." In *International Politics and Foreign Policy: A Reader in Research and Theory,* edited by James N. Rosenau, 20–29. New York: The Free Press, 1969.

Sipols, Vilnis. *Tainy diplomaticheskie: Kanun Velikoi Otechestvennoi, 1939–1941.* Moscow: TOO "Novina," 1997.

Sipols, V. Ia. *Velikaia pobeda i diplomatiia, 1941–1945.* Moscow: Novina, 2000.

Smith, Bradley F. *Sharing Secrets with Stalin: How the Allies Traded Intelligence, 1941–1945.* Lawrence: University Press of Kansas, 1996.

Smith, Gaddis. *American Diplomacy During the Second World War, 1941–1945.* New York: Wiley, 1965.

———. *American Diplomacy During the Second World War, 1941–1945.* 2nd ed. New York: Knopf, 1985.

Smith, Robert Freeman. "Businessmen, Bureaucrats, Historians, and the Shaping of United States Foreign Policy." *Reviews in American History* 2, no. 4 (December 1974): 575–81.

Snell, John L. *Illusion and Necessity: The Diplomacy of Global War, 1939–1945.* Boston: Houghton Mifflin, 1965.

Solov'ev, B. G. "O politicheskom kharaktere Vtoroi Mirovoi Voiny." *Novaia i noveishaia istoriia,* no. 3 (May–June 1991): 93–99.

Sontag, Raymond James, and James Stuart Beddie, eds. *Nazi-Soviet Relations, 1939–1941: Documents from the Archives of the German Foreign Office.* Washington, DC: Department of State, 1948.

Stalin, Joseph. *Sochineniia.* Moscow: Ogiz Gos. izd-vo polit. lit-y, 1946.

———. *Works.* Moscow: Foreign Languages Publishing House, 1952.

Standley, William H., and Arthur A. Ageton. *Admiral Ambassador to Russia.* Chicago: Henry Regnery, 1955.

Stettinius, Edward R., Jr. *Roosevelt and the Russians: The Yalta Conference.* Garden City, NY: Doubleday, 1949.

Stimson, Henry L., and McGeorge Bundy. *On Active Service in Peace and War.* New York: Harper & Brothers, 1947, 1948.

Stoler, Mark A. "Allies or Adversaries? The Joint Chiefs of Staff and Soviet-American Relations, Spring 1945." In *Victory in Europe 1945: From World War to Cold War,* edited by Arnold A. Offner and Theodore A. Wilson, 145–65. Lawrence: University Press of Kansas, 2000.

———. *Allies and Adversaries: The Joint Chiefs of Staff, the Grand Alliance, and U.S. Strategy in World War II.* Chapel Hill: University of North Carolina Press, 2000.

———. "A Half-Century of Conflict: Interpretations of U.S. World War II Diplomacy." In *America in the World: The Historiography of American Foreign Relations Since*

1941, edited by Michael J. Hogan, 166–205. Cambridge: Cambridge University Press, 1995.

———. *The Politics of the Second Front: American Military Planning and Diplomacy in Coalition Warfare, 1941–1943.* Westport, CT: Greenwood Press, 1977.

Stone, David R. *Hammer and Rifle: The Militarization of the Soviet Union, 1926–1933.* Lawrence: University Press of Kansas, 2000.

Stuart, Graham H. *The Department of State: A History of Its Organization, Procedure, and Personnel.* New York: Macmillan, 1949.

Sulzberger, Cyrus L. *A Long Row of Candles: Memoirs and Diaries (1934–1954).* Toronto: Macmillan, 1969.

Suvenirov, O. F. *Tragediia RKKA 1937–1938.* Moscow: Terra, 1998.

Taubman, William. *Stalin's American Policy: From Entente to Détente to Cold War.* New York: Norton, 1982.

Tegeran, Ialta, Potsdam: Sbornik dokumentov. Moscow: Izd. "Mezhdunarodnye otnosheniia," 1970.

Tsvetkov, Gleb. *Politika SShA v otnoshenii SSSR nakanune Vtoroi Mirovoi Voiny.* Kiev: Izdatel'stvo politicheskoi literatury ukrainy, 1973.

Tucker, Robert C. *Stalin in Power: The Revolution from Above, 1928–1941.* New York: Norton, 1990.

Tully, Grace. *FDR: My Boss.* New York: Charles Scribner's Sons, 1949.

Tuttle, Dwight William. *Harry L. Hopkins and Anglo-American-Soviet Relations, 1941–1945.* New York: Garland, 1983.

Uldricks, Teddy J. "A. J. P. Taylor and the Russians." In *The Origins of the Second World War Reconsidered: The A. J. P. Taylor Debate After Twenty-Five Years,* edited by Gordon Martel, 162–86. Boston: Allen & Unwin, 1986.

———. "Evolving Soviet Views of the Nazi-Soviet Pact." In *Labyrinth of Nationalism, Complexities of Diplomacy: Essays in Honor of Charles and Barbara Jelavich,* edited by Richard Frucht, 331–60. Columbus, OH: Slavica, 1992.

———. "The Icebreaker Controversy: Did Stalin Plan to Attack Hitler?" *Slavic Review* 58, no. 3 (Fall 1999): 626–43.

———. "Soviet Security Policy in the 1930s." In *Soviet Foreign Policy, 1917–1991: A Retrospective,* edited by Gabriel Gorodetsky, 65–74. London: Frank Cass, 1994.

Ullman, Richard H. "The Davies Mission and United States–Soviet Relations, 1937–1941." *World Politics* 9, no. 2 (January 1957): 220–39.

Union of Soviet Socialist Republics. [Ministerstvo Inostrannykh Del, SSSR.] *Perepiska Predsedatelia Soveta Ministrov SSSR s Prezidentami Ssha i Prem'er-Ministrami Velikobritanii vo vremia Velikoi Otechestvennoi Voiny, 1941–1945 gg.* 2nd ed. 2 vols. Moscow: Izdatel'stvo politicheskoi literatury, 1989.

———. Ministry of Foreign Affairs. *Correspondence Between the Chairman of the Council of Ministers of the USSR and the Presidents of the USA and the Prime Ministers of Great Britain During the Great Patriotic War of 1941–1945.* 2 vols. Moscow: Foreign Languages Publishing House, 1957.

————. *Sovetskii Soiuz na mezhdunarodnykh konferentsiiakh perioda Velikoi Otechest-vennoi Voiny 1941–1945 gg.* Vol. 2, *Tegeranskaia konferentsiia rukovoditelei trekh soiuznykh derzhav—SSSR, SShA i Velikobritanii (28 noiabria–1 dekabria 1943 g.) Sbornik dokumentov.* Moscow: Izdatel'stvo politicheskoi literatury, 1978.

————. *Sovetskii Soiuz na mezhdunarodnykh konferentsiiakh perioda Velikoi Otechest-vennoi Voiny 1941–1945 gg.* Vol. 4, *Krymskaia konferentsiia rukovoditelei trekh soiuznykh derzhav—SSSR, SShA i Velikobritanii (4–11 fevralia 1945 g.) Sbornik dokumentov.* Moscow: Izdatel'stvo politicheskoi literatury, 1979.

————. *Sovetsko-Amerikanskie otnosheniia vo vremia Velikoi Otechestvennoi Voiny, 1941–1945: Dokumenty i materialy.* 2 vols. Moscow: Politizdat, 1984.

United States. Department of State. *Foreign Relations of the United States: Diplomatic Papers.* Washington, CD: U.S. GPO, 1948–69.

————. *Foreign Relations of the United States: Diplomatic Papers. The Soviet Union, 1933–1939.* Washington, CD: U.S. GPO, 1952.

————. Historical Division. *Foreign Relations of the United States: Diplomatic Papers. The Conferences at Malta and Yalta, 1945.* Washington, CD: U.S. GPO, 1955.

————. Historical Office. *Foreign Relations of the United States: Diplomatic Papers. The Conferences at Cairo and Tehran, 1943.* Washington, CD: U.S. GPO, 1961.

————. Historical Office. *Foreign Relations of the United States: Diplomatic Papers. The Conferences at Washington, 1941–1942 and Casablanca, 1943.* Washington, CD: U.S. GPO, 1968.

United States. Joint Chiefs of Staff. *Records of the Joint Chiefs of Staff. Part I, 1942–1945, the Soviet Union.* Frederick, MD: University Publications of America, 1981. Microfilm.

Unterberger, Betty Miller. *The United States, Revolutionary Russia, and the Rise of Czechoslovakia.* Chapel Hill: University of North Carolina Press, 1989.

Vagts, Alfred. *The Military Attaché.* Princeton, NJ: Princeton University Press, 1967.

Volkogonov, Dmitri. *Stalin: Triumph and Tragedy.* Translated by Harold Shukman. London: Weidenfeld and Nicolson, 1991.

Volkogonov, Dmitri. *Trotsky: The Eternal Revolutionary.* Translated by Harold Shukman. New York: The Free Press, 1996.

Volokitina, T. V. "Stalin i smena strategicheskogo kurs kremlia v kontse 40-kh godov: Ot kompromissov k konfrontatsii." In *Stalinskoe desiatiletie kholodnoi voiny: Fakty i gipotezy,* edited by I. V. Gaiduk, N. I. Egorova, and A. O. Chubar'ian, 10–22. Moscow: Nauka, 1999.

Volokitina, T. V., ed. *Sovetskii faktor v vostochnoi Evrope, 1944–1953: Dokumenty.* Vol. 1, *1944–1948.* Moscow: Rosspen, 1999.

von Senger und Etterlin, F. M. *Der Gegenschlag: Kampfbeispiele Und Führungsgrund-sätze Der Beweglichen Abwehr.* Neckargemünd: Kurt Vowinckel, 1959.

Wehle, Louis B. *Hidden Threads of History: Wilson Through Roosevelt.* New York: Macmillan, 1953.

Weigley, Russell F. *The American Way of War: A History of United States Military Strat-egy and Policy.* New York: Macmillan, 1973.

————. *Eisenhower's Lieutenants: The Campaign of France and Germany, 1944–1945.* Bloomington: Indiana University Press, 1981.

Weil, Martin. *A Pretty Good Club: The Founding Fathers of the U.S. Foreign Service.* New York: Norton, 1978.

Weinberg, Gerhard L. *The Foreign Policy of Hitler's Germany: Starting World War II, 1937–1939.* Chicago: University of Chicago Press, 1980.

————. *Germany and the Soviet Union, 1939–1941.* Leiden: E. J. Brill, 1954.

————. *A World at Arms: A Global History of World War II.* Cambridge: Cambridge University Press, 1994.

Weinstein, Allen, and Alexander Vassiliev. *The Haunted Wood: Soviet Espionage in America—The Stalin Era.* New York: Random House, 1999.

Welles, Benjamin. *Sumner Welles: FDR's Global Strategist.* New York: St. Martin's Press, 1997.

Welles, Sumner. *The Time for Decision.* New York: Harper & Brothers, 1944.

Werth, Alexander. *Russia at War, 1941–1945.* New York: Carroll & Graf, 1964.

————. *Moscow War Diary.* New York: Knopf, 1942.

White, Christine A. *British and American Commercial Relations with Soviet Russia, 1918–1924.* Chapel Hill: University of North Carolina Press, 1992.

Williams, William A. "American Intervention in Russia, 1917–1920." *Studies on the Left* 3, no. 4 (Fall 1963): 24–48.

————. *American Russian Relations, 1781–1947.* New York: Rinehart, 1952.

————. *The Tragedy of American Diplomacy.* Enlarged rev. ed. New York: Delta, 1962.

————. *The Tragedy of American Diplomacy.* New ed. New York: Norton, 1988.

Willmott, H. P. *The Great Crusade: A New Complete History of the Second World War.* New York: The Free Press, 1989.

Wilson, Joan Hoff. *Ideology and Economics: U.S. Relations with the Soviet Union, 1918–1933.* Columbia: University of Missouri Press, 1974.

Wilson, Theodore A. "In Aid of America's Interests: The Provision of Lend-Lease to the Soviet Union, 1941–1942." In *Soviet-U.S. Relations, 1933–1942,* 121–39. Moscow: Progress, 1989.

Woodward, Llewellyn. *British Foreign Policy in the Second World War.* 5 vols. London: Her Majesty's Stationery Office, 1970–1976.

Yergin, Daniel. *Shattered Peace: The Origins of the Cold War and the National Security State.* Boston: Houghton Mifflin, 1977.

"Zaniat'sia podgotovkoi budushchego mira." *Istochnik* 4 (1995): 114–58.

Zeidler, Manfred. "German-Soviet Economic Relations During the Hitler-Stalin Pact." In *From Peace to War: Germany, Soviet Russia and the World, 1939–1941,* edited by Bernd Wegner, 95–111. Providence, RI: Berghahn Books, 1997.

Ziemke, Earl F. "Stalin as a Strategist, 1940–1941." *Military Affairs* 47, no. 4 (December 1983): 173–80.

Zolotarev, Vladimir Antonovich. *Velikaia Otechestvennaia.* Vol. 5 (4), *Stavka VGK: Dokumenty i materialy 1944–1945.* Russkii Arkhiv. Moscow: Terra, 1999.

Zolotarev, Vladimir Antonovich, ed. *Velikaia Otechestvennaia.* Vol. 4 (5), *Bitva za*

Berlin (Krasnaia Armiia v poverzhennoi Germanii). Russkii Arkhiv. Moscow: Terra, 1995.

Zubok, Vladislav, and Constantine Pleshakov. *Inside the Kremlin's Cold War: From Stalin to Khrushchev.* Cambridge, MA: Harvard University Press, 1996.

INDEX